*f*P

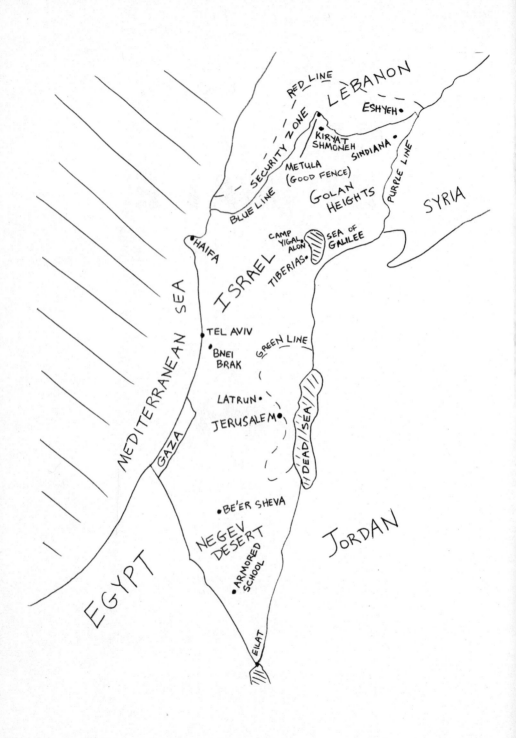

THE 188TH
CRYBABY
BRIGADE

A Skinny Jewish Kid
from Chicago
Fights Hezbollah

A MEMOIR

JOEL CHASNOFF

FREE PRESS

NEW YORK   LONDON   TORONTO   SYDNEY

FREE PRESS
A Division of Simon & Schuster, Inc.
1230 Avenue of the Americas
New York, NY 10020

First Free Press hardcover edition February 2010

FREE PRESS and colophon are trademarks of Simon & Schuster, Inc.

For information about special discounts for bulk purchases, please contact Simon & Schuster Special Sales at 1-866-506-1949 or business@simonandschuster.com.

The Simon & Schuster Speakers Bureau can bring authors to your live event. For more information or to book an event contact the Simon & Schuster Speakers Bureau at 1-866-248-3049 or visit our website at www.simonspeakers.com.

Designed by Mspace/Maura Fadden Rosenthal

Photos courtesy of iStockphoto.com

Certain names and identifying characteristics have been changed.

Manufactured in the United States of America

10   9   8   7   6   5   4   3   2   1

Library of Congress Cataloging-in-Publication Data
Chasnoff, Joel.
    The 188th Crybaby Brigade: a skinny Jewish kid from Chicago fights Hezbollah: a memoir / Joel Chasnoff.—1st Free Press hardcover ed.
        p.   cm.
    1. Chasnoff, Joel.   2. Israel. Tseva haganah le-Yisra'el—Biography.   3. Israel. Tseva haganah le-Yisra'el—Military life.   4. Soldiers—Israel—Biography.   5. Americans—Israel—Biography.   6. Arab-Israeli conflict—1993– —Personal narratives, Jewish.
7. Arab-Israeli conflict—1993– —Personal narratives, American.   8. Hezbollah (Lebanon).   9. Jewish youth—Illinois—Chicago—Biography.   I. Title.
U55.C475A3 2010
956.05'4—dc22
[B]   2009033835

ISBN 978-1-4165-4932-1
ISBN 978-1-4391-7180-6 (ebook)

This book is for S and N—
but only when you're old enough.

CONTENTS

INDUCTION

THE RUSSIAN

The Russian is poking my balls.

It's awkward.

I've been trapped in this dank examination room since nine o'clock. In five minutes it'll be nine-thirty, and I feel like a dope, what with my boxer shorts at my ankles and my dick in my hand so the Russian can get a good view.

"Hmm," he says.

It's Tuesday morning, the eighth of July, and I'm at the Israel Defense Forces Induction Center outside Tel Aviv. I arrived in Israel three weeks ago. Today is my first pre-army checkup.

The Russian says something in Hebrew, but I can't understand him through his thick Russian accent.

"Huh?" I say.

He switches to broken English. "You pee-nus . . . hurt you?"

"*Lo!*" I say in Hebrew, and shake my head. "*Penis tov!* My penis is fine."

The Russian scoots forward on his knees. He's about sixty years old and bald. Even though he's a doctor, he's dressed like a plumber—plaid short-sleeve shirt, dirty jeans. I imagine that back in Russia he was a brain surgeon. Now he checks gonads for the Israeli Army.

"Up," he says.

I lift my penis until it's flat against my stomach.

He squeezes my testicles gently as if trying to pick the perfect peach. His forehead is inches from my belly. I'm a hiccup away from a dishonorable discharge.

"Cough," he says.

"Huh-*hem.*"

He pulls his enormous Clark Kent eyeglasses off the crown of his head, presses them onto his nose, and jots a note on his clipboard, while I, in the meantime, try to think about anything in the world besides how much I hate holding myself while a nearsighted, balding Russian takes notes.

I try to name every team in the National League.

Cubs. Phillies. Mets.

My visit to the Induction Center began at eight this morning, when I showed up at the front gate without so much as an appointment. "I can't let you in without draft orders," said the soldier guarding the entrance. He was a chubby kid, with blond hair, sunglasses, and an Uzi. He stood in a white booth next to a chain-link fence. A hundred yards behind him were the three redbrick buildings that made up the Induction Center complex.

I explained in Hebrew that because I'd immigrated to Israel less than a month ago, I hadn't yet received my draft orders. "But here," I said, pulling out my brand-new national ID card. "I'm Israeli."

The soldier scrutinized my ID card. Then he looked at me, then back at the card, and then back to me. "Where're you from?" he asked suspiciously.

"The United States," I said.

"America," he purred. "Where?"

"Chicago."

"Chicago Bulls!" he cried. "Michael Jordan!"

"I've driven past his house," I said.

He handed me my ID. "Straight ahead. Inside the middle building."

The Russian grabs the edge of his desk and hoists himself to his feet. "Bend over," he orders. He must see the look of horror that flashes across my face, because he quickly adds, "You can put on your pants first."

Thank God.

I bend over and touch my toes. The Russian taps my spine. "Your back's crooked," he says.

"It is?" I shout through my legs, trying to sound surprised.

"You ever have back pain?" he asks.

The way I see it, I have two options. Option One: tell the truth, that is, confess to the Russian doctor that I was diagnosed with mild scoliosis when

I was nine and that, three months ago, during a pickup basketball game at the JCC, I collapsed to the gymnasium floor with back pain so severe it took the paramedics thirty minutes just to roll me onto the stretcher. I would then have no choice but to inform the Russian that my personal physician in the States, Dr. Zielinski, had advised me not to enlist in the Israeli Army—not that Zielinski had thought the IDF would take me. "I can't speak for Israel," he'd said, "but a back as messed up as yours would never be allowed in the Marine Corps."

The problem with Option One is that if the Russian finds out about my back, he will assign me to a noncombat desk job. But I don't want a desk job. I didn't immigrate to Israel to type memos or change tires. I'm here because since I was seventeen years old, I've dreamed of jumping out of planes, charging up mountains, and hiking the desert with a pack on my back as a combat soldier in the Israeli Army. For this reason, I choose Option Two:

Lie.

"My back's perfect," I say.

"Hmm," says the Russian.

He massages the glands in my neck. He studies the soles of my feet like they're a map of the sunken treasure. He sticks an icy stethoscope into my chest and orders me to breathe.

"Ah-*huh*."

"Sit."

I sit. He sits across from me at his desk. "Tell me about your family," the Russian says. "Any medical history I should know about?"

I shake my head.

"Your mother?"

My mother has multiple sclerosis, walks with a cane, and at times is confined to a wheelchair. "Nope."

"Father?"

My dad's back is worse than mine—so bad that he's had surgery on it twice. "Nothing comes to mind."

"Siblings?"

One of my younger brothers has Crohn's disease. The other had croup, two hernias, and an undescended testicle. "Not that I can think of."

The Russian scribbles on my chart. "You're going combat," he says.

I pump my fist and smile. My scoliosis has been overlooked! My feet are arched! My balls are worthy of a medal!

I skip to the door. "Chasnoff!" the Russian barks.

I freeze.

"Don't do anything stupid," he says.

Too late.

HERO OF THE JEWS

I'm the last guy you'd expect to join an army. For starters, I'm a Jew. And let's face it, we Jews aren't known for our military prowess. Jews make movies about war. In the case of Kissinger, we helped escalate a war. But when it comes to actually fighting wars, that's not our gig. We prefer to leave that to the Gentiles.

Then there's the issue of my body. I'm five foot eight and weigh 130 pounds soaking wet, which I rarely am since I don't know how to swim. Where manly men have chest hair, all I've got are ribs showing through in a way that makes it look like I just barely survived a famine. And as for that big, mean tattoo most U.S. Marines have on their biceps, I could never have that—not just because I'm afraid of needles, but also because it'd be impossible to draw on anything that small.

Psychologically, I'm no more of a warrior. In college, at the University of Pennsylvania, I was an actor in the Mask and Wig Club, an all-male comedy troupe in which we played the women's parts by dressing in drag. My svelte figure, high cheekbones, and willowy arms made me an ideal candidate to play any female lead. The comment I heard most often after shows, from old men and sorority sisters alike, was "Nice ass."

Not exactly military material.

Nor do I have the stomach of a soldier. I pass out when I see blood. If I see somebody throw up, I throw up. I'm something of a worrywart, a trait I inherited from my maternal grandmother, Gramma Ruth, who has spent her life warning me about everything from botulism and flammable pajamas to poisoned Girl Scout cookies and fitted bedsheets. (She'd read in *Reader's Digest* that a child could get strangled by the elastic in fitted bedsheets that hadn't been properly tucked under the mattress.)

But the main reason you'd never expect me to join an army is that I'm a peacenik. I hate guns. I've never been in a fistfight in my life. I grew up listening to Peter, Paul & Mary and Simon & Garfunkel, and I truly believe that, as John Lennon said, we should give peace a chance.

In other words, I don't hate Arabs.

So why would a peace-loving, left-leaning, lactose-intolerant Jew from the suburbs join the Israeli Army?

I grew up with a strong Jewish identity. Like most of my friends, my family was what's known as Conservative Jews, which basically meant that we picked and chose which rules to follow and made up others as we went along. Friday nights, we ate Sabbath dinner and refrained from watching television, unless there was a Cubs game on. We ate only kosher food at home, but on vacation we ate pretty much everything except pork. This made being Jewish easy and fun: we simply followed God's commandments until His laws became a pain in the ass.

From kindergarten through eighth grade, I attended a Jewish day school called Solomon Schechter, where I began learning Hebrew at age five. I was always at the top of my class in Hebrew and Torah studies, and not because I was smarter than my classmates, but because for as far back as I can remember, I genuinely loved being a Jew. At school, I volunteered to lead morning prayers as often as I could—so often that my teachers nicknamed me "Little Rabbi." At the grocery store, I scrutinized the labels on packages of food to make sure every ingredient was kosher. And I couldn't wait to have a bar mitzvah—not because I was excited for the party, but because it meant I could finally wear the tallis prayer shawl and leather tefillin in synagogue.

When I was six years old, my father's parents, Zayde Daniel and Bubbie Rose, gave me an illustrated children's Bible for Hanukkah. I loved my kiddie Bible. Every night, after my parents turned out the lights, I curled up under my blanket with a flashlight to read it. I loved the blood-curdling confrontations with evil Pharaoh, the breathtaking encounters with whales that swallowed men whole. When I read these stories, I imagined I was one of my Bible heroes, marching through the parted Red Sea and turning my staff into a serpent while Pharaoh gasped in fright. When I was eight, I dressed as Moses for Halloween. "T-t-t-trick or t-t-t-treat!" I stuttered, but my neighbors didn't get it. They didn't know Moses had a speech impediment.

What I loved most about my Bible was that these weren't just stories, these were *my* stories. Abraham, Isaac, and Jacob were my ancestors. All these wonderful tales were things that had happened to people in my family. And where did all the action take place? In a magical, far-off land called Israel. The thought that I might one day visit this wondrous land was, in my mind, like being told I might one day visit Oz.

Then, in second grade, a miracle happened:

Israel became real.

It was my second-grade Hebrew teacher, Ruti, who made Israel come alive.

Ruti was the first Israeli I'd ever met. She was tall with dark skin, honey-colored eyes, and black hair down to her waist, shiny like a horse's mane. Ruti was unlike any other teacher I'd ever had. During snack, she ate grapefruits with her bare hands. Unlike my other teachers, who dressed fancy in pantyhose and skirts, Ruti wore sweaters and blue jeans, like us. In spring, when she wore sandals, I could see the cracked, weathered soles of her brown feet—feet that looked as if they'd wandered forty years in the desert on the way to the Promised Land. As far as I was concerned, Ruti wasn't just Israeli, she was an Israelite, straight out of my illustrated Bible.

Ruti loved Israel, and her love was contagious. Her classroom was decorated with posters of Israel and Israelis: a cluster of Hasidic Jews dressed all in black at the Western Wall; a full moon rising over the Dead Sea; freckled, gap-toothed kibbutzniks in overalls and floppy hats, smiling in the sunshine. Fridays, just before we lit the Sabbath candles, Ruti called us up to her desk, one by one, to sound out Hebrew words in Israeli newspapers. It thrilled me to no end that there was a real, live country out there where the people spoke Hebrew and used money called shekels, just like in the Bible. That I, a Jewish kid in Chicago, could read their newspaper made it even sweeter. Sitting next to Ruti at her desk, her hand guiding mine over the Hebrew letters, I felt connected to this faraway land. I felt as if even though I'd never been to Israel, I had a place there.

Ten years later, I fell in love with Israelis.

I was seventeen years old and visiting Israel on a six-week teen tour. I'd been to Israel twice before, the first time with my father when I was nine, and again four years later with my parents and rabbi. But it was this third trip, as a teenager, that hooked me for life. Like most seventeen-year-olds, I was trying to figure out who I was and who my role models were going to be. Within days of arriving in Israel, I discovered my new heroes: Israelis.

They were the coolest, most exciting Jews I'd ever met. Back home, all the Jews I knew were doctors and lawyers, professors and accountants. But Israelis were different. They rode motorcycles. They smoked. The men were muscly hunks with tattoos and the women were gorgeous. It boggled my mind: here were these people with the same roots as us—yet they looked like supermodels, and we looked like Jews.

Most captivating of all were the Israeli soldiers. Here they were, just a year older than me, flying F-16s, carrying Uzis, and strutting around Jerusalem in olive-green uniforms and Ray-Bans. Compared to them, I felt like such a putz: they defended the homeland like Jewish Rambos while I walked around Israel in sunscreen and a fanny pack. All my life, I kept hearing about how Pharaoh had enslaved us, Hitler had killed us, and the Arabs wanted to wipe us off the map. In these Israeli soldiers, I saw a new narrative: Jews who kicked ass.

By the end of that enchanting summer, I'd decided two things. First, that it wasn't fair that we American Jews called Israel our homeland but left Israelis to defend it. Second, I made up my mind that I, too, would one day be a soldier standing at the side of the road, hitchhiking with an Uzi slung across my back. Instead of just praying for Israel, I would fight for it. I, too, would be the hero of the Jews.

But there's one more reason I joined the Israeli Army—and it's about a girl. Her name is Dorit. She's a Yemenite-Persian Israeli, with dark skin, curly black hair, and almond eyes—exactly the kind of Mediterranean princess I drooled over when I was seventeen. I met Dorit in January of my senior year of college. She was the Israel programs director at Brooklyn College Hillel, the organization for on-campus Jews; I'd been hired to perform stand-up comedy at the National Hillel Staff Conference in New York. During my show, I noticed her giggling in the back. Afterward, I found her at the pool table and delivered the single greatest pickup line in the history of man:

"Uhm."

At first, we spoke a couple times a week. Soon, it was every night at eleven on the dot, our conversations lasting into the early hours of the morning.

Dorit was unlike any Jewish girl I'd ever known. She was outspoken and fearless, a firecracker of a girl who'd backpacked across America on her own the summer she turned eighteen. After high school, she was a drill sergeant in the Israeli Army. When Saddam Hussein dropped thirty-nine Scud missiles on Israel, it was Dorit's neighborhood that was bombed—a traumatic experience, no doubt, but for a reason I can't quite explain, I found this incredibly attractive.

If Dorit and I end up staying together for the long haul, there's a good chance we'll live in Israel one day—and I told Dorit that I could never live in Israel without first serving in the Israeli Army. Every Israeli gets drafted when he or she turns eighteen. If I lived in Israel without serving, I'd feel like a freeloader and an alien.

I'd assumed Dorit would be thrilled that I wanted to join the Israeli Army—especially because part of the reason I'd be going was her. Instead she tried to talk me out of it. "The Israelis you'll meet in the army aren't the lovey-dovey Israelis they send to your Jewish summer camp," she warned. "Real Israelis are animals. They'll eat you alive."

MR. BAY CITY HIGH SCHOOL

When I told my father I wanted to join the Israeli Army, he slammed both hands on the table and yelled, *"What?!"*

It was April of my senior year of college, and we were sitting in an IHOP. Any time my dad wanted to discuss something important, he took me to breakfast at an IHOP. Past IHOP conversations included Where Your Mom and I Think You Should Go to College, and I Think Your Friend Neil Smokes Pot. Today, the final Sunday morning of spring break, we'd come to discuss Your Future.

For a few seconds, nobody spoke. From across the table, my father glared at me like I'd just announced that I was Republican. And Muslim. And gay. When he finally regained the power of speech, my father sputtered the only argument he could think of: "You realize if you move to Israel you'll have to pay double taxes the rest of your life."

"That's not true," I countered. "I went to the consulate—"

"Consulate?"

"The Israeli consulate in New York."

"You went to the *consulate*?"

"To look into it."

"How long have you been cooking this up?"

My dad and I have a complicated relationship. On the one hand, I worship him for his accomplishments. On the other hand, I resent these accomplishments because it's impossible that I could ever achieve as much.

A quick look at my father's intimidating curriculum vitae:

He was born in a Houston housing project and raised in a Podunk town called Bay City, Texas. By age twelve, he was an Eagle Scout; at fourteen, a lifeguard. He was valedictorian of his high school class and played Curly in *Oklahoma!* Senior year, he was voted Mr. Bay City High School. He then put himself through college and medical school and is currently one of the world's leading experts on babies born addicted to cocaine. In 1986, he was a guest on *Oprah*.

In high school, if I had trouble falling asleep, I'd tiptoe downstairs to my dad's office and read his yearbook. I'd stare at the photo of my father on the first page. With his buzz-cut hair and chiseled jaw, he looked like a prince. Then I'd read the caption—"Mr. Bay City High School, 1965"—and wonder what challenges I might overcome to achieve his level of greatness. I, too, wanted to be a self-made man. But how the hell was I supposed to pull myself up by my bootstraps when my ass was already strapped so firmly into the saddle?

"It's not definite," I hedged.

"What about acting, and comedy?" my father asked. It was an ironic thing for him to say. The last time we'd spoken about career plans, in December, I'd told my dad I wanted to be a comedian and actor, and he hadn't been thrilled. "How in God's name are you going to support yourself?" were his exact words. But compared to the Israeli Army, show business sounded as stable as med school.

"I'll pursue comedy when I come back," I said. "The comedy clubs will still be there in a year."

My dad took out a pen. On a napkin, he wrote the word MOMENTUM. "Right now, your career's headed in the right direction," he said. "You've got momentum."

He had a point. The previous fall, I'd begun touring college campuses with my stand-up comedy act. I'd just been cast as Dave the Wife Beater in an educational theater company that would perform in battered women's shelters across Pennsylvania. And I was about to begin my second season with the Philadelphia Phillies as an on-field and in-the-stands performer in their new improv troupe. Not exactly Broadway, but the ball was rolling.

"But you know what happens if you go to Israel?" my dad asked.

I shook my head. My father drew a big X through MOMENTUM.

"Got it?"

So I moved to New York. I rented a "furnished garden studio," as the *Village Voice* had called it, in a Brooklyn neighborhood of Hasidic Jews. The apartment was a dungeon. It came with a beat-up futon and a black-and-white

TV. The kitchen sink belched rusty water in spurts. There was one window, but it was plastered over with cement. And all for only four hundred dollars a month.

To make ends meet, I temped at a trade magazine called *Dressings and Sauces*. "We're the *New Yorker* of condiments," the publisher, Bruce, explained to me my first day on the job.

"Neat," I lied.

Nights, I pursued my plan to become an A-list comedy star. I figured this would take about a year. First, I'd do my act in the clubs. A couple of months later, around November, I'd land an agent. A few months after that, I'd book a spot on Letterman or Leno. Then in May, at the start of pilot season, a network scout would fly me to L.A., cast me in a sitcom, and I'd be set.

Four months after college graduation, I walked into New York's most prestigious comedy club, the renowned Comic Strip, and signed up for the next available audition spot—a Monday night nine months later, in early June. Seinfeld, Sandler, and Rock had all started out at the Comic Strip, and rumor had it that once a comedian passed the Strip, he could work any club in the city. I was sure I'd pass my audition because like most beginning comics, I was pretty certain I was God's gift to comedy. The way I saw it, the only difference between me and Jerry Seinfeld was not that his jokes were funnier, but that he had more of them: whereas Seinfeld could perform for an hour, I could do nine minutes.

You should've seen my audition. I killed. When the MC brought me off-stage, the crowd went wild, cheering and whistling as I left the showroom.

Around eleven, an emaciated man with a black mustache appeared next to the bar. It was Lucien Hold—the legendary booker of the Comic Strip.

Lucien motioned me into his office. The room was cramped, his desk littered with Chinese take-out containers. My heart pounding, I sat on a wooden stool next to the door.

"So, Joel," he said in a raspy voice. "You said onstage that you're from Chicago. Is that true?"

"Yes, sir," I said.

"In your opening bit, you talked about how people in Chicago are nicer than people in New York."

"That's right."

"Something about how, in Chicago, people will actually say 'Excuse me' when they run into you with their cars."

"Exactly," I said, beaming. I was proud that he'd remembered my joke.

Lucien shook his head. "Nothing original there. Everyone knows New Yorkers are tough. Then you did a bit about *Wheel of Fortune* in China. Not an ounce of truth in that joke. Soon as I heard it, I knew you were amateur."

"But people laughed," I said, my heart sinking.

Lucien pulled a folded-up piece of paper from his pocket. "This is my roster," he said. "I've got three hundred comics on here. Most are white guys with dark hair, like you. Now, if you were black, or a woman, or gay—are you gay?"

I shook my head. For the first time in my life, I was genuinely disappointed I wasn't gay.

"If you were gay, maybe I'd pass you. But if you're a white guy with dark hair, you need to show me something original. Talk about your family. Every comic who's made it big talks about his family."

"Seinfeld doesn't talk about his family!" I blurted out.

"But Jerry's so goddamn cute," Lucien replied.

I stood up and slumped to the door.

"One more thing," Lucien called. "Look at me."

I turned around.

"You've got really thick eyebrows," he said. "Much too thick for Hollywood."

Outside the Comic Strip, it was midnight and warm. Since I had nowhere to be, I walked in big circles through the Upper East Side, past delis and bakeries, through the park, and then south on Central Park West to Times Square.

When I was in high school, my dad and I visited New York every winter for an annual father-son getaway. With no wheelchair to push and no little brothers dawdling behind, we'd conquer the city on foot at superhuman speed. Then, after dinner and a Broadway show, we'd walk to Times Square and stare up at the lights.

Alone this time, I jostled my way past the peanut sellers and Black Hebrews shouting biblical quotes into megaphones, past throngs of tourists and policemen on horseback. At 1 A.M. Times Square was a jukebox. High above, Joe Camel lit up and disappeared.

I walked to the pay phone on Forty-fifth Street, picked up the receiver, and dialed.

"I didn't pass," I said.

"Oh," said my father. For a couple of moments, neither of us said a word. Then my dad said, "It's a tough business. Even the great ones take years."

I hung up the phone. Two weeks later, I was on a plane to Tel Aviv.

BASIC TRAINING

SUMMER

FIFTY-EIGHT SOLDIERS IN FORMATION,
ONE SOLDIER GUARDING THE BUNK,
AND CLEMENTE'S TAKING A SHIT

I am Israeli soldier number 5481287. I've been assigned to Platoon Two, Company B, Battalion 71 of the 188th Armored Brigade. I'm at the Armored School, in the south, halfway between Jordan and Egypt. It's the 30th of July, day one of basic training, and I'm in shock that I'm actually here, in uniform, on a military base, a soldier in a foreign country's army.

I'm dressed like a soldier but I look like a clown. My uniform's three sizes too big, and it's stiff, so it looks like I'm wearing a suit of green construction paper; I'd thought I would look sexy in uniform, but I don't. I've also got a new look—I'm buzz-cut and shaved—and a new name: instead of Joel, I am now my Hebrew name, Yoel, and my last name, according to my dog tags, is Shetznitz.

"You misspelled my name," I said to the guy at the dog tag machine.

"So don't die," he said, and shooed me out the door.

Yesterday morning, back at the Induction Center, I sat in a gated courtyard with hundreds of other new recruits, each with an entourage of family and friends who'd come to see him off. The atmosphere was like a tailgate party. Families picnicked and sang songs. At one table, friends took turns shaving their buddy's head. When, finally, a soldier's name was called over the loudspeaker, his friends marched him to the bus with claps, songs, kazoos, whistles, tambourines, and in one case, a trumpet. As they hugged goodbye, his parents—and sometimes even the new recruit—cried. Then the boy climbed onto a bus and rode off to become a man. It was a much more genuine coming-of-age ceremony than the typical American bar mitzvah.

Inside the Processing Center, teams of girl soldiers fingerprinted me,

X-rayed my teeth, and cut my hair. I was then handed a paper cup and in-structed to fill it. Behind the locked door of a bathroom stall, I unzipped my backpack and pulled out a Coke bottle one-third full with urine. The bottle was warm. I've got this strange condition called paruresis, a.k.a. "shy pee," in which I can't pee when I'm nervous. I knew the army would ask me to piss into a cup. So instead of taking my chances, I brought pee from home.

As I exited the bathroom stall, someone called, "Hey, bro." Ambling toward me was a short kid with buzz-cut blond hair, an eyebrow ring, and baggy jeans much too large for his tiny frame. His eyes were bloodshot. He looked like a tripped-out Friedrich von Trapp.

"Smoke grass?" he whispered.

It was like I was right back in Brooklyn. "No thanks," I said, and shook my head, but not too violently—I didn't want to spill my cupful of piss. I slithered out and started for the door, but the kid pressed his hand into my chest and pinned me to the wall.

"How about it, brother?" he begged. "Can I borrow some piss?"

It wasn't an issue of quantity—I had a Dixie cup nearly overflowing with healthy pee. A few drops of my piss could've meant one more Israeli soldier and a safer Jewish homeland. But if the girls in the urine lab found out, I'd have been kicked out of the Israeli Army before I was ever in. And what would I do when word of the scandal found its way back to Chicago?

You see, Rabbi, my son was all set to defend the Jewish state when he got caught sharing his pee with a reefer addict . . .

"Sorry," I said, and bolted past him, my piss sloshing beneath the rim of my cup.

Three hours later, I found myself staring up at a leathery-faced officer from the Manpower Division.

"Nu?" he barked. "Have you decided where you'd like to serve?"

"Paratroopers," I declared. I'd always dreamed of being a paratrooper, just like my idol, Yoni Netanyahu, the leader of the infamous Raid on En-tebbe in July 1976, where a crack squad of Israeli soldiers rescued hijacked airline passengers in Uganda. After Yoni died in the raid, his letters were collected into a book called *Self-Portrait of a Hero*. In high school, I read Yoni's book twice a year.

The officer opened a manila file folder and immediately snapped it shut. "Paratroopers is full. How about Tanks?"

I cleared my throat. Dorit had warned me that part of being an Israeli soldier was knowing how to stand up for myself. "With all due respect, sir," I said, "I came from America to be a paratrooper. I refuse to leave this office until you grant my request."

"You can go to Tanks, or you can go to jail," he said.

"How about Tanks?" I said.

Which is why I'm now standing in bedroom 3, bunk 6 at the Armored School. The room is small, the size of a dorm room. Five rickety bunk beds stand pushed against the freshly whitewashed walls in the shape of a U. Above the door there's an air-conditioning unit—one of the perks of the Armored Corps. ("Join Armored!" an Armored sergeant barked at the Induction Center. "You'll get air-conditioning in your room!") Scotch-taped to the doorway is a six-inch plastic mezuzah—the tiny case containing a piece of Torah parchment on the doorposts of Jewish homes and, apparently, army barracks. On the bed opposite the door, a kid named Ronen Peretz sits with his head in his hands. He has brown skin and thick eyeglasses. *"Lo ma'amin!"* he groans in Hebrew. "I can't believe it."

"What's with him?" says one of my new roommates, a skinny kid who stuffs a pillow into a pillowcase.

"He lost his kit bag," says a guy with glasses and a bumpy nose.

"I didn't lose it—someone stole it!" Ronen Peretz whimpers. "It had my cell phone, my keys. I knew I never should've joined Armored!"

"Poor Ronen Peretz," says the skinny guy. He unwraps a chocolate bar, shoves it front of my face. "Chocolate?"

I shake my head and walk outside into the courtyard and the ovenlike heat of the Negev Desert.

The Armored School is a four-square-kilometer island in an ocean of sand. The base is bordered on three sides by a chain-link fence topped with concertina wire; the fourth side, directly behind my bunk, is a firing range that opens onto miles of brown nothingness. On the far end of the base, near the front gate, are the dining hall, administrative offices, and an obstacle course consisting of red-and-white-striped climbing equipment that looks like giant candy canes. Behind those is a city of dormitories, classrooms, ammunition sheds, and a parking lot where thirty battle tanks sit in a line with their cannons pointing into the desert. A paved service road snakes through the various buildings. Olive-green jeeps zoom around the road at speeds well over ninety miles an hour. In the middle of the base is the town square—a concrete parade ground with an Israeli flag and a Coke machine. Every half hour, an air-conditioned bus screeches to a halt in the courtyard and spits a fresh batch of eighteen-year-old recruits into the steaming heat.

My platoon is one of three assigned to Company B of the 188th Armored Brigade, the brigade responsible for defending Israel's north, including the Golan Heights and the border with Syria. Three other Armored brigades protect the Galilee and Israel's center and south. All told, about one thousand eighteen-year-old Israeli boys will arrive at the Armored School today for two months of basic training, followed by two months of Tank School, three months of advanced warfare training, and a tour of duty in Gaza, the West Bank, or Lebanon.

From the looks of it, the Armored School has everything a soldier might need. There's a weight room, a canteen, a barbershop. There are even women—every now and then, a female soldier wanders into our bunk to check up on us and chat. The only thing missing are adults. I keep looking for some kind of authority figure, maybe a general with a chest full of ribbons, a clipboard in his hand, and a whistle around his neck—I imagine him looking like a camp director—someone who's unequivocally in charge of the commanders, who are all nineteen and twenty years of age. But there is no such authority figure to be seen. Even the officers, designated with a silver bar or two on their shoulders, are a mere twenty-one years old. What's clear is that I'm the oldest one here by a long shot—a proposition I find unnerving. In fact, although I've dreamed of serving in the Israeli Army since I was seventeen, I am, at the moment, shit scared.

A dark-skinned kid with black hair and long eyelashes shoves a piece of paper under my nose. *"Ata po?"* he says in Hebrew. "Is your name on this list?"

I take the paper. "What is this?"

"The Guard Duty List."

I check the page. "No."

"Then you're guarding," he says.

"Guarding what?"

"The bunk."

"How do I guard the bunk?" I've got no rifle, no bayonet. Just a pocket notebook and a pen.

"How should I know?" he says with a shrug. "Just walk back and forth through the courtyard. Make sure no one goes in our rooms except guys from our platoon."

"How do I know who's in our platoon?" I say.

He puts a hand on my shoulder. "Look. Some sergeant told me to post a guard in the bunk. So just guard. *Beseder?*"

Since I don't have a choice, I pace the open-air courtyard in the middle of the two-story concrete bunk and try my best to look important.

At one end of the courtyard is an orange pay phone; at the other, the showers and latrine. Our bedrooms line the courtyard, lengthwise, three per side. At this particular moment, the bunk is a circus. Eighteen-year-old Israeli boys chase each other in and out of doorways, whooping and hollering like freshmen on the first night of college. Rock music blares from a boom box. In the corner near the bathroom, twenty soldiers sit in a clump and swig Coke from one-liter bottles while one of them strums a guitar. Next to them, two guys kick a soccer ball back and forth as hard as possible, nailing the occasional passerby in the head. Everyone looks alike, as if we're genetic mutations of the same creature—a creature with closely cropped hair and Semitic features in a starchy green uniform two sizes too big.

As I watch my new platoon mates yelp and bounce off the walls like wild monkeys, I get the sick feeling that this is all a big mistake. I always thought it'd be so cool to be a gun-toting Israeli soldier. But now that I've done it, it's obvious I have no business being here. I look at their faces, which are so foreign, and I wonder if I will ever know them. I have this sinking feeling I will spend this year as the outsider of the platoon, alone, constantly reminding people of my name. It's like Dorit said: these Israeli kids will eat me alive. If I wanted to help Israel, I should've mailed a check to the Jewish Federation like everyone else.

As I wander back and forth, I notice two posters on the wall by the pay phone. The first poster says, in big Hebrew letters

KNOW YOUR ENEMY: HAMAS

Below the headline is a photo of masked Hamas gunmen, rifles raised high in the air. Some of the gunmen hold children dressed in black headbands with red tubes taped to their chests, like kiddie suicide bombers. Together, fathers and children burn an Israeli flag.

I've seen this kind of scary photo before—usually in ads for pro-Israel organizations that try to raise money by scaring the bejesus out of American Jews. In the past, I dismissed photos like this as propaganda. But today, I have a different thought:

Holy shit—these people want to kill me.

The second poster is titled

KNOW YOUR ENEMY: HEZBOLLAH

I lean in for a closer look. The poster is a crude, hand-drawn sketch of a Lebanese hillside. In the picture, three Hezbollah guerrillas set booby traps under a full moon. The guerrillas have dark skin and beards. They wear sneakers, white T-shirts, and jeans. One guerrilla stuffs dynamite into a fake rock. A few yards away, his buddy covers a land mine with a branch. The third guy holds a remote control device that, I suppose, will blow up the explosives in the rock.

I peer at the three guerrillas. In their sneakers and jeans, they look more like high school riffraff than enemies of the Jewish state. I try to imagine what it's like in that nightmare called Lebanon, where monsters in T-shirts and jeans set booby traps by the light of the moon. Suddenly, I'm overcome with a fresh wave of fear. It hits me that my stint in the Israeli Army isn't just some crazy adventure. It's real.

I'm jolted from my reverie by frantic shouts of *"Meesdar!"*

Meesdar means "Formation." It's a chain reaction: one soldier shouts *"Meesdar!"* and sprints to the courtyard, then the few who heard him all shout *"Meesdar!"* and sprint to the courtyard, and so on, until every soldier in the platoon is running hysterically, like a pack of headless chickens, frantically shouting *"Meesdar! Meesdar!"* in each other's faces, while they begin the impossible task of lining up in formation.

Lining up in formation should be simple. All we have to do is stand in three parallel rows:

PLATOON FORMATION—BIRD'S-EYE VIEW

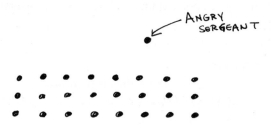

If the number of soldiers present is not divisible by three and there are, consequently, one or two leftovers, the extra soldier(s) stand(s) in the second to last column on the left:

PLATOON FORMATION WHERE THE NUMBER OF SOLDIERS PRESENT IS NOT DIVISIBLE BY 3—BIRD'S-EYE VIEW

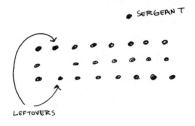

Easy, right?

Actually, it's impossible. Because in our haste to line up quickly, we behave like morons. Five soldiers cram into the same column instead of just moving over to a different column in the formation. Guys fight for the right to stand in one spot instead of another as if their very lives depend on where they stand. This cramming and pushing leads to name-calling and a barrage of insults concerning one another's mothers' vaginas, and all while three angry sergeants stand off to the side and shake their heads at our incompetence.

We, the soldiers of Platoon Two, Company B, Battalion 71 of the 188th Armored Brigade, will train together for the next seven months. These are the comrades with whom I'll learn to survive under the bleakest of conditions. It is for these brothers in arms that I may one day sacrifice my life. For the moment, however, we kick and whine like angry dogs.

"*Nu, zuz, ya hatichat hara!* Move over, you piece of shit!"

"Fuck you! I was standing here!"

"Your mother's cunt."

"*Your* mother's cunt!"

I remind myself they're only eighteen years old.

But still, wouldn't I have been able to stand in a column of three when I was eighteen? Or fourteen? Or ten?

"Enough!" shouts one of the sergeants.

We freeze.

"Guard!" he snaps his fingers and calls me over from where I'm standing watch by the pay phone.

I scurry over. The sergeant has a husky chest voice like a Harley rider. Physically, though, he looks like an infant. His pale blue eyes, soft features, and wisp of blond hair make him look like the Gerber baby.

"Listen to me, soldier. In exactly thirty seconds, this platoon will be standing in three perfect rows. Go."

I face my new platoon mates. The formation is a mosh pit. I run around back, grab two guys by the elbows, drag them to the front row. "Stand here," I say. Next, I push two guys, one skinny and the other chubby and wearing a yarmulke, into place behind the first two. "You stand here." I grab more guys by the elbow and line them up, one by one, into rows like a kid setting up dominoes. Finally, we stand in three perfectly parallel rows.

"What's your name?" barks the sergeant.

"Yoel," I say.

"Yoel what?"

"Chasnoff."

The sergeant shakes his head.

"Shetznitz?" I say.

"No. Yoel, Staff Sergeant. When you speak to me or your other commanders"—he points to the two sergeants standing behind him—"you address us as Staff Sergeant. Everyone hear that?"

"Yes, Staff Sergeant!" we shout.

"Yoel," he says, "how many soldiers here?"

I run to the far left side of the formation, count the soldiers, one-two-three-four—

"Yoel!" the sergeant screams.

I freeze.

"How many rows in this formation?"

"Three, Staff Sergeant."

"So if you were smart, you'd count the number of soldiers in the first row and then multiply by three. Right?"

"Yes, Staff Sergeant."

"So how many in the front row?"

I speed-walk past the formation and count.

"Eighteen, Staff Sergeant."

"And eighteen times three is . . ."

I open my mouth.

Air.

"Are you an idiot? Eighteen times three! Let's go!"

I was a math minor at Penn. In high school, I got a 5 on my BC Calculus AP test. And yet I cannot, for the life of me, figure out eighteen times three.

"Well?" the sergeant barks.

"Uhm . . . fifty-four?"

He scrunches his face into a scowl. "Really? That's it? Fifty-four?"

I stare at him bug-eyed. What the hell does he want from me?

"There are sixty soldiers in this platoon, Yoel."

I nod.

"So where the hell are they?" he roars.

I face the platoon. "We're missing six guys!" I shout.

My comrades mumble among themselves, discussing in earnest, and finally word reaches me that three soldiers are in the dining hall setting up for dinner, two soldiers are in the infirmary, and another soldier is off somewhere else.

I face the sergeant. "Three are in the dining hall," I say, "two are in the infirmary—"

"No, no, Yoel. From the beginning."

"Fifty-four soldiers here, Staff Sergeant. Three in the dining hall, two in—"

"Wait!" the sergeant barks. "Do not! Make me! Do the math! Tell me the exact total each step of the way."

I feel a bead of sweat trickle down my cheek. "Fifty-four soldiers in formation, Staff Sergeant. Three in the dining hall, that's fifty-seven."

"Excellent."

"Two in the infirmary, fifty-nine. And one . . . one . . ."

I face the platoon.

"Who's not here?" I whisper.

They mumble.

"Ronen Peretz!" shouts a voice in the back row. "Ronen Peretz is looking for his bag!"

The sergeant orders me to step forward. "Platoon Two, open your ears!" he barks. "At all times, each of you must know the exact whereabouts of every soldier in the platoon. In six months, you could be in Lebanon. God forbid you'd be in Lebanon and don't know exactly where each of your friends is."

A hush falls over the platoon as we process the word: *Lebanon.*

"For the next two months of basic training, Yoel is the platoon scribe. You know what that means, Yoel?"

Yes. Bad news.

"It means that you, Yoel, are responsible for keeping track of every soldier in this platoon. If I wake you up at three in the morning—and I will— you'll be able to tell me who's guarding, who's sick, and who's lying in bed awake because he's scared of the dark. Clear?"

"Yes, Staff Sergeant," I say.

"The rest of you: When you go somewhere, you tell Yoel first. If you go to the infirmary, tell Yoel. If you go to take a shit, tell Yoel you're going to take a shit, and the minute you're done wiping your ass you tell Yoel you're back. Understood?"

"Yes, Staff Sergeant!"

"Now everyone stand straight. Tuck in your shirts. You're about to meet your platoon commander. You will address him as Lieutenant. You will not, ever, speak to him unless he speaks to you first. Take one minute to prepare for the platoon commander." We dive into a frenzy of button checking, shirt tucking, and shoelace tying. I feel a hand inside my pants, on my ass— the kid in back of me tucking in my shirt from behind.

I decide to neither ask nor tell.

"Sir!" the sergeant shouts and salutes.

A tall, muscular, blond-haired officer struts into the courtyard. His uniform, crisp forest green, fits perfectly. His posture is perfect. His body is perfect. He is Charles Atlas. Only this Charles Atlas wears thin-framed eyeglasses, adding an aura of intelligence to that of his power. On his head he wears a knit white yarmulke.

This is fantastic news. If he's wearing a yarmulke, that means my officer is a religious Jew. If he's a religious Jew, that means he has Jewish values. This means he'll be nicer than the typical combat officer. If he believes in God, eats only kosher food, and keeps the Sabbath holy, how much of a jackass can he be?

"My name is Lieutenant Yaron," he says in a warm tone of voice. "I want to be the first to welcome you to the One Hundred Eighty-eighth Armored Brigade, the best brigade in the Israeli Army. Your tank, the Merkava Three Baz, is the best tank in the world. That means your brigade is the best brigade of any military on the planet. I expect every one of you to live up to the honor of serving in the One Hundred Eighty-eighth. Those of you who know how to give one hundred percent will succeed. Those who do not, I will rip your ass to pieces. Good luck."

We stand frozen while he exits the courtyard. So much for the yarmulke.

Once our officer is out of sight, our three squad commanders introduce themselves.

Sergeant Eli is tall and stocky with thick eyebrows that connect at the top of his nose. He looks like a pudgy Pete Sampras. Sergeant Hanoch is thin with blue eyes. From the way his mouth hangs open, he looks to be a bit of a dolt.

Sergeant Eran is the tough one. Despite his Gerber baby looks he's the one we instinctively fear most. "Tomorrow," he shouts, "we'll divide you into squads. Now, prepare to meet your platoon sergeant. He's in charge of discipline. If you work hard, you'll see little of your platoon sergeant. If you slack off, you'll curse the day you were born."

That's all it takes: the instant we hear the word *discipline*, we fly into another round of frantic shirt tucking, button checking, and hands inside the backs of each other's pants. "Platoon Two, Company B: prepare to greet your platoon sergeant!"

A short, crew-cut first sergeant darts into the courtyard.

"Good afternoon, Platoon Two!" he barks.

"Good afternoon, Staff Sergeant!" we reply.

We barely get the last words out of our mouths when the pint-size platoon sergeant jabbers in. "Platoon Two, listen up and listen good because I'm going to say this one time and one time only: I am First Sergeant Guy Ben-Gur, and I am not your squad commander, so you will not call me 'Staff Sergeant.' I am your platoon sergeant, which means you will call me 'Platoon Sergeant' or 'Sergeant' but never, ever 'Staff Sergeant.' Clear?"

"Yes, Platoon Sergeant!" we shout.

"Good," he barks. He is a short, wound up mini tornado who spins, points, whispers, and screams during a single sentence. His eyes dart left, up, down, right as he keeps his eyes on every single one of us and no one in particular. "In the Israel Defense Forces there are rules, and as your platoon sergeant it is my job to make sure you A) know them and B) follow them. One: when you are told to be somewhere at a certain time, you will be there on time. Two: when you see the platoon commander or any other officer, you will stop what you're doing and salute. Understood?"

A hand shoots up in the back row. "What happens if I see the platoon commander when I'm eating?"

"Offer him a bite and ask if he'd like some hummus to go with it," the platoon sergeant snaps, cracking us up. "Don't waste my time with stupid questions. Clear?"

"Yes, Staff Sergeant!" we shout in unison.

The platoon sergeant nearly has a heart attack. "I am not a staff sergeant, I am your platoon sergeant!" he roars. "Is that understood?"

"Yes, Platoon Sergeant!"

"Good! Tomorrow, each of you will receive a Glilon assault rifle and five clips of thirty-five bullets each. Your rifle goes with you everywhere. You will sleep with it, eat with it, shit, shave, and shower with it. If I see anyone without his rifle, you will lose your next Sabbath leave. Dog tags: you must wear one dog tag around your neck and one in each boot. Is anyone either missing a dog tag or have a dog tag whose name or personal number is incorrect?" I and a few others raise our hands. "Fine. Who's the platoon scribe?"

"I am, Platoon Sergeant."

"Your name?"

"Yoel, Platoon Sergeant."

"Yoel—make a list of soldiers who need tags. Give me the list after dinner. Clear?"

I nod.

"It is now"—he checks his watch—"six twenty-six. At six-thirty, you're lined up outside the dining hall with a full count. Dismissed."

We sprint off to dinner, driven not by hunger, but by fear of our cold-blooded platoon sergeant.

"Yoel!" someone shouts.

I turn. The platoon sergeant beckons me over with an index finger. "I hear an accent, Yoel," he barks. "Where you from?"

"Chicago, Platoon Sergeant."

He smiles, wide and friendly. "My dad's from Queens," he says in perfect English.

"I lived in Brooklyn," I say.

"You know Forest Hills?"

"Of course. Right by Queens College. Your dad still there?"

"No. L.A." He puts a hand on my shoulder. "So tell me—how old are you, Yoel?"

"Twenty-four."

He whistles. "What, you thought it'd be cool to be an Israeli soldier?"

"Something like that."

"Good for you," he says and pounds me on the back. "I admire that. Now be at the dining hall in thirty seconds or else I'll open your asshole so wide you can shove a tank in it."

After dinner, we change into sport clothes and gather on the basketball court for a fitness test.

My Israeli comrades show up in white undershirts, cheap soccer shorts, and off-brand sneakers. One kid named Eldad doesn't even wear sneakers—he says he can't afford them—and does the two-kilometer run in combat boots.

Then there's me, in my knee-length U-Penn lacrosse shorts ($39.99 at the university bookstore), my Champion smart-wick breathable running jersey ($26, Sportmart), and brand-new Nike Air Pegasus cross-trainers ($74.95 at the Nike Store, Michigan Avenue, Chicago).

I feel like such a goddamn stereotype.

• • •

That night, ten minutes after lights out, someone knocks on the door of bedroom 3. "Yoel?" he whispers.

I scurry out of bed and hop down. Standing in the courtyard is a short kid in tight red underwear and chunky glasses.

"I'm Clemente," he says with a Russian accent. "I'm going to take a shit."

"Thanks for telling me," I say, "but I think the sergeant was joking about that. You don't really have to tell me every time you shit."

Clemente's face turns as red as his shorts. "Sergeant Eran said he might wake you up. I didn't want you to get in trouble."

"Well, then you did the right thing, Clemente. If he wakes me up, I'll remember: fifty-eight soldiers in formation. One soldier guarding the bunk, that's fifty-nine. And Clemente's taking a shit."

AVIVA

You'd think it'd be difficult for a foreigner to join the Israeli Army. In fact, it was as easy as signing up for a library card. The only hard part about it was convincing the immigration officer at the Israeli consulate in New York that I wasn't out of my mind.

"Are you out of your goddamn mind?" she screamed at me in Israeli-accented English. Her name was Aviva. She had short blond hair and eyeglasses that she wore on a cord around her neck. Since her job was to help American Jews move to Israel, I was surprised when she spent the entire meeting trying to convince me not to move to Israel.

"You don't want to go to Israel," she said. "There's terrorism. The economy's a mess. The people are rude. What business does a nice American boy like you have in Israel?"

"Actually," I said, squirming in my seat, "I was thinking about joining the army."

"The *army*?" she cried. She rolled her eyes, clutched her head, then shook her hands at the ceiling. "What, you think you're Rambo or something? The Israeli Army doesn't need you."

She stood up and walked me to the door. "You think about what I said. If you're still interested in two weeks, call. But I think it's a big mistake."

I thought it over. I wasn't a hundred percent sure. But I figured I could always start the process and then back out later.

I called Aviva to make a second appointment.

"Mazel tov!" she yelped.

"You're not mad?" I asked.

"I'm thrilled!" she said.

"Then why'd you give me such a hard time?"

"Listen," Aviva said. "A lot of American Jews think Israel's paradise. They visit on some synagogue trip, fall in love with the country, and decide to move there. Then reality sets in. The last thing Israel needs is a bunch of whiny Americans who don't know what they're getting into."

With Aviva on my side, the rest was easy. All I had to do was fill out a form, submit two passport photos, and prove I was Jewish.

"And how exactly do I prove I'm Jewish?" I asked.

"Is at least one of your parents Jewish?" she said.

"Both," I said.

"One's enough. Just fax over your bar mitzvah certificate. If you don't have that, have your rabbi write a letter on synagogue stationery. Or you could always just send over a copy of your bris certificate."

"You mean birth certificate," I corrected her.

She shook her head. "Bris certificate. From your bris, when you were circumcised. You're circumcised?"

I nodded. And blushed.

"You have the certificate?"

"I didn't realize there was such a thing," I said.

"If there was no certificate, how would you prove it?"

"Well—I could always just—"

"No." She interrupted me. "We need to know it was done by a mohel, at a ceremony. Not in the hospital."

"I'll see if I can dig it up," I said.

Aviva nodded. "You never know when you'll need a bris certificate."

Once I'd finalized the paperwork with Aviva, I spent two weeks packing and saying good-bye to family and friends. My Jewish friends understood why I wanted to serve in the Israeli Army, even if they thought I was off my rocker. My one close non-Jewish friend, a devout Protestant named John, was even more enthusiastic. "May the Lord bless you in your defense of Zion," he said.

"Thanks," I replied.

When I told my father that my decision was final, he didn't offer his blessing. Instead, he switched tactics. First, he tried to convince me to work on a kibbutz. Then, once my dad accepted that I really would be joining the army, he tried to steer me into a support job, something like a military spokesman or a job in the Education Corps, helping soldiers from broken homes to finish high school. What my dad didn't understand was that, important as those jobs were, they were all what Israelis called *jobnik* roles—support tasks, devoid of glory, just a tad more honorable than being a cook. Finally, my father told me the story of his fraternity brother, Denny MacLean. "I sat next to Denny at college graduation," my dad said, his voice cracking. "Six months later, he was dead in Vietnam."

It was the closest my dad ever came to saying, "I'm scared."

When I told my mother I'd be joining the army, she patted my hand and said, "Be safe." I wasn't surprised she reacted so casually. I knew she'd support me if for no other reason than to contradict my father. Family tradition dictates that when my dad expresses an opinion, my mother must stake out a position in the opposite camp. Over the years, I've watched my mother disparage trade unions, defend pro-life demonstrators, and badmouth *Schindler's List,* all because my dad had first professed the opposite. My brothers and I joke that the day can't be far off when our father will rant angrily against Adolf Hitler, at which point Mom will pipe up, "Now, Ira—Nazis are people, too."

On June 19, I flew to Israel on a one-way ticket paid for by the Israeli government. I flew alone; once Dorit finished her job at Brooklyn College in early August, she'd move back to Israel to live with her parents.

The immigration literature promised that upon my arrival in Israel, I'd be met by an entourage of government officials who'd escort me to the New Immigrant Lounge inside Ben Gurion Airport, where I'd be showered with a welcome kit and refreshments. But when I landed, there was nobody to greet me. Instead, I wandered the bowels of the airport until I stumbled upon the Immigration Office. After I filled out the requisite forms, I asked the clerk if she had any refreshments.

She cocked her head at the water fountain.

Welcome to Israel.

The Israeli Army defines a Lone Soldier as any soldier whose parents live outside Israel or a soldier who's estranged from his family and has no parents to rely on for support. I spent my first week in the country running from one government office to the next, filing the paperwork I needed to prove I qualified for Lone Soldier rights, including the $200-per-month apartment rental subsidy so I'd have somewhere to stay when I went home on leave.

My original plan was to pocket the subsidy and instead just shack up with Dorit and her family in Bnei Brak whenever I came home on leave. I'd met Dorit's parents a month earlier, when they visited New York, and we got along great. Dorit's father, Menashe, is a short, sixty-year-old Yemenite with bushy white hair—he looks like a combination of Joe Pesci and Albert Einstein—and an endless supply of stories about everything from his days as a professional soccer player to the four wars he fought as an Israeli infantryman. Dorit's mother, Tzionah, wears long dresses and a headscarf and has a heart of gold. It was a no-brainer: if I lived with Dorit's family when I came home on leave, I'd have no utilities to pay, no groceries to buy, and, best of all, access to Menashe's car—since Dorit's parents are religious Jews who don't drive on the Sabbath, I figured Menashe's '88 Subaru would be mine on any Sabbath I was home.

Then Menashe told me about the *Shomer Shabbos* car insurance.

"Excuse me?" I said.

"*Shomer Shabbos* car insurance," he said. He explained that because he didn't drive on the Sabbath, he qualified for a discounted *Shomer Shabbos* (Sabbath observer's) insurance policy. And since most traffic accidents in Israel happen on the Sabbath—the day Menashe never drives—"I save more than twenty percent!" he cried.

Bummer.

Worse, though, was Tzionah's nonstop pressure to marry Dorit. Tzionah is dying to see her children married. Literally. Once a week, she has chest pains related to the heart attack she's afraid she'll have if her children stay single. To twist my arm, Tzionah used every tactic from guilt—

"Please don't let me die without grandchildren!"

—to bribery—

"If you marry Dorit now, the army will double your salary!"

—to subliminal messages, such as the night her neighbor dropped by and Tzionah introduced me using a Hebrew word I didn't understand, at which point the neighbor hugged me and yelped, "Mazel tov!"

So after two weeks with Dorit's parents, I opened the Yellow Pages and connected with a real estate agent named Mickey. Mickey drove me around Tel Aviv on his motorcycle, dodging buses and nearly running over numerous children, until, finally, I found a furnished one-bedroom at 60 Ben

Yehudah Street in Tel Aviv, two blocks from the beach, for only $300 a month. Which means that between my monthly $80 military salary and my Lone Soldier rental subsidy, I'm losing only twenty bucks a month by defending the Jewish state.

Once I received my draft date, July 30, I began to train. I ran twenty minutes every morning, and then another forty at night. I ran not because I wanted to be the most fit soldier in the platoon, but because I was certain I'd be the runt. I envisioned my future comrades as a platoon of Israeli tigers, each with rippling abs, forearms like bricks, and bushels of chest hair, like Ari Ben Canaan in the movie *Exodus*. I feared I'd fall behind on hikes, and then the animal Israelis that Dorit had warned me about would punish me with code reds, pummeling me with fists and bars of soap rolled up in their socks. In eighth grade, I was the only kid cut from the Solomon Schechter basketball team—a humiliating experience made all the more shameful by the fact that I'd been cut not just from a sports team, but from a Jewish sports team. In the weeks leading up to the army, I ran so that I would not be humiliated in the platoon of Israeli he-men I was about to join.

OUR FATHERS

Tomer's father drives a taxi. Next Sunday, on Parents' Day, Tomer's father will drive his taxi down from Haifa, more than two hundred miles away. If Dorit needs a ride, Tomer's father will pick her up at her parents' house in Bnei Brak and drive her to the Armored School, free of charge.

Elran's father sells ladies' shoes. Elran says that if Dorit ever wants a deal on shoes, I should send her to his father's store on Akiba Street.

Dror's father has a Ph.D. in physics and lectures on string theory at the Technion. Twice a year, Dror's father flies to Toronto, first class, and consults a team of engineers building a semiconductor.

Our fathers are locksmiths and lawyers. Our fathers patch tires, program computers, and teach English literature at Hebrew U. They are bank tellers, factory foremen, pharmacists, and high school principals. Our fathers deliver babies, and they deliver the mail.

A typical day of basic training goes something like this:

At 4 A.M., whoever's guarding the bunk sticks his head into our bedrooms, flicks on the lights, and shouts, "*Boker tov*, Platoon Two. Everyone up!" We respond by telling said guard to go fuck himself.

At 4:29, one of us notices it's 4:29 and shouts, "*Yallah!* Four twenty-nine! Formation!" We sprint to the courtyard, line up in three rows, and argue over our first dilemma of the day:

Sleeves up or sleeves down.

The rule is, we can wear our sleeves either rolled up, above the elbow, or down, buttoned at the wrists, as long as we all wear our sleeves the same way.

"Everyone! Quick! Sleeves down!" I shout. As platoon scribe, my job is to decide how we wear our sleeves.

"*Koos emok!* It's gonna be hot! Sleeves up!" someone shouts. As eighteen-year-old Israelis, their job is to challenge anyone who tells them what to do.

The sleeves argument lasts anywhere from two to four minutes. Then, it takes another minute for those with the wrong kinds of sleeves to fix them.

A little after 4:30, Sergeant Eran moseys into the courtyard and shouts, "*Nu?*"

"Staff Sergeant, can I please have an extension?" I say. As platoon scribe, it is my job to ask for extensions when we are not ready on time.

"You kidding me?" Sergeant Eran shouts in my face. "It's four-thirty and you're still buttoning your sleeves?" As commander, it is Sergeant Eran's job to make me feel like a schmuck. "*Yallah*, Yoel. Give me the count."

As platoon scribe, I am responsible for presenting an accurate count at every formation. The problem is, I can never figure out the count because I can't keep track of the guys. The reason I can't keep track of the guys is that they wander off without telling me where they're going or when they'll be back. Therefore, every formation is a crisis. Uzi wanders off to the infirmary. Tanenbaum's in his bedroom, on hands and knees, looking for his boot. Doni's asleep on the toilet, pants at his ankles. And I get blamed.

Our fathers are rabbis and plumbers, policemen and architects, deputy mayors and chemical engineers. Most of our fathers are living, Hayim's father is dying, and Etai's father died when Etai was three.

From 4:35 until 5:30, we mop the floor, scrub the sinks, flush the toilets, collect the trash, beat our mattresses with broomsticks, and fold our blankets into eighths. We shave. Then we sit in the courtyard, Indian style, and polish our boots.

"Shoe polish!" someone shouts.

Someone tosses him a tin of shoe polish.

"Hey, that's my shoe polish!" shouts whoever's shoe polish just got tossed.

Each of us has his own tin of shoe polish, but on any given morning, only five of us bring shoe polish to the courtyard. The rest of us assume someone else will bring shoe polish and leave our shoe polish in our kit bags.

After we polish our boots, we clean our rifles with screwdrivers, old toothbrushes, and WD-40 that we borrow from the same five guys who brought shoe polish.

In Platoon Two, Company B, we have four Drors, three Liors, two Omers, and a Tomer. We have a Nir, a D'vir, and a Ya'ir. We have a Liran, an Elran, two Erans, and a Ron. We have a Gidi, a Gadi, a Gil, and a Gal. We have a Chen Tal. We have a Tal Chen. We have an Oren Idan or an Idan Oren—I'm not sure which one's his first name and which is his last.

We have a Pasha, a Nikolayev, a Vladimir, an Ofir, and a Clemente. They are the Russians.

We have two Moshes. Both Moshes are Yeshiva Boys and wear yarmulkes and have beards. Yaki, Yitzi, Hudi, Yudi, Gershon, Shimon, Shlomi, Shmuel, Uziel, and Issaschar also wear yarmulkes and have beards. I'm the only soldier with a biblical name who does not have a yarmulke and beard.

At 5:29, someone shouts, "*Koos-emok!* It's five-twenty-nine! Formation!" We throw together our guns—tubes into slots, pins into holes, spring into the buttstock, *click-clack.* In our bedrooms, we stuff underwear, socks, candy bar wrappers, and yarmulkes into kit bags and then scramble into formation while I try to figure out the count, which is altogether different from last hour's count because more soldiers have wandered off to God Knows Where without telling me.

"Staff Sergeant, can I please have an extension?"

"You kidding me?"

"We're missing one!" I shout to the platoon.

"Uri's in the kitchen!" someone shouts.

"No, Uri's in the infirmary!" shouts someone else.

"I'm right here!" shouts Uri from over by the pay phone, guarding.

Then we eat.

We are two-thirds Ashkenazi white guys with Eastern European roots. The rest of us are dark-skinned Sephardic guys with roots in Turkey, Yemen, Iran, Iraq, and Morocco.

Ashkenazi white guys live in North Tel Aviv, Haifa, and kibbutz settlements in the North. Dark-skinned Sephardic guys live in South Tel Aviv, Jerusalem, and Lod, near the airport. The Russians live in the south, in crumbling development towns on the outskirts of Be'er Sheva. A few of the Yeshiva Boys live on settlements in the West Bank, deep in the Occupied Territories.

Lieutenant Yaron, Platoon Sergeant Guy, and Sergeants Eran, Eli, and Hanoch are all Ashkenazi white guys. Every officer I've seen so far at the Armored School is an Ashkenazi white guy. The highest-ranking dark-skinned guy I've seen at the Armored School is the barber.

When I asked Dror, an Ashkenazi kid and the smartest soldier in the platoon, why it is that I don't see any brown-skinned officers, he explained that it was a result of complex sociological phenomena, including immigration patterns, weak school systems in traditionally Sephardic working-class neighborhoods, and a value system in certain dark-skinned communities that emphasizes religion over more contemporary fields of study, all of which lead to a self-perpetuating cycle of poverty and disproportionately, but undeniably, lower levels of achievement in dark-skinned Sephardic communities writ large.

When I asked my buddy Ido, who is Yemenite, dark, and a pretty sharp guy himself, the same question, he said, "Because this army is goddamn racist."

Breakfast is cottage cheese, hard-boiled eggs, and tea. We eat breakfast on blue dairy-meal plates. While the rest of us eat, the Yeshiva Boys pray. I find this strange: I'd expected that in the Jewish army, observant Jews would be given time to pray. But that's not how it works; if they want to pray, they have to skip a meal. It's like they're being penalized for being pious.

Since the Yeshiva Boys don't get to eat breakfast, the rest of us are supposed to make them sandwiches. Usually, we forget. When this happens, the Yeshiva Boys go hungry until lunch and Staff Sergeant Eran calls us self-centered pigs. This, in turn, makes us angry with the Yeshiva Boys.

Who knew it would be so tough to be a Jew in the Jewish army?

On the third morning of basic training, we hike into the desert for a tank show. To pump us up and get us excited for our service in the Armored

Corps, Colonel Avi, the commanding officer of 188th Armored Brigade, puts on a demonstration of our tank, the Merkava 3 Baz.

We march into the desert with Platoons One and Three until we reach metal bleachers set up on a cliff. Below us, in the valley, a Merkava battle tank sits with its engine idling.

Colonel Avi, a stocky officer with clipped gray hair, peps us.

"Tank soldiers! Welcome to the Armored Corps of the Israel Defense Forces. By show of hands, how many of you requested to serve in Armored?"

Only six of us raise our hands.

Problem One: nobody wants Tanks. Unlike paratroopers and navy SEALS, who compete for coveted spots in their elite units, we tank soldiers don't request Armored so much as end up here. We go to Armored because we have flat feet, heart murmurs, and asthma, or because the more popular units are full. In fact, the only guys in my platoon who asked for Armored are the ones whose fathers or brothers were tank soldiers before them.

"Hands down," Colonel Avi orders. "Whether you know it or not, tanks are the backbone of this army. Engineers build the bridge. Air force patrols the sky. But until there's a tank on that hilltop, we don't own the land.

"Now some people think tanks aren't sexy."

Problem Two: tanks aren't sexy. In the month and a half since I arrived in Israel, I've learned that each unit has its own distinct reputation: Paratroopers are heroes because they jump out of planes. Golani infantrymen are the shoot-first, ask-questions-later badasses for whom no mountain is too high to conquer. Navy SEALS are he-men. At the top of the food chain are the fighter pilots. They live in luxury dorms on air force bases that have swimming pools. And as for us Armored guys—we're a bunch of wholesome, intelligent, nose-to-the-grindstone soldiers who don't ask for attention and don't get it. Or, as my buddy Shai puts it, "Infantry guys are the ones your daughter wants to date, but tank guys are the ones you want your daughter to marry."

Colonel Avi points his finger in the air and continues. "Walk into any hotel gift shop in this country, and you'll see postcards of paratroopers praying at the Western Wall. You know why paratroopers pray at the Western Wall? Because they have to. In the Armored Corps, we don't pray—we win wars. Understood, tank soldiers?"

"Yes, Colonel!" we shout from our seats.

Then, it's showtime. For the next half hour, Sergeants Eran, Eli, and Hanoch crisscross the desert in our Merkava 3 Baz battle tank. The tank zig-zags up and over sand dunes at forty miles an hour, ejects a smoke screen, zooms forward, and fires a missile at a metal bull's-eye a kilometer away while my comrades and I ooh and ahh, whistle and cheer, like kids watching Shamu do tricks at Sea World.

"So who wants to be a paratrooper now?" barks Colonel Avi.

There are platoons within the platoon.

The Yeshiva boys pray three times a day. At night, after they pray the evening service, they join us in bedroom 2 and play guitar.

I am one of two Lone Soldiers in the platoon. The other is a kid named Eldad. Eldad's mother and father live in South Tel Aviv, but Eldad ran away from home when he was fifteen and hasn't seen his parents since. Next Friday, when we're furloughed home for our first Sabbath leave, Eldad will sleep in a shelter for troubled boys.

The Russians are an island within the platoon. At meals, they sit alone. At night, when we play guitar in bedroom 2, the Russians play checkers. We make fun of the Russians constantly. Or, rather, Ben Gerber makes fun of the Russians constantly and we laugh. The main way Gerber makes fun of the Russians is by imitating their accents and mimicking the way they sprinkle Hebrew military words into otherwise Russian sentences:

"*Vladimir! Nidnya blodnik vil nalfnik* grenade launcher?"

Poor Russians. For as far back as I can remember, they've suffered. It reminds me of third grade. That fall, we wrote letters to President Reagan demanding freedom for the refuseniks—the imprisoned Russian Jews.

Our letters worked. The next spring, Mrs. Gould announced that a former refusenik was joining our class. "This is Svetlana," Mrs. Gould said, holding the new girl's hand. Svetlana wore pink moon boots even though it wasn't snowing. She was ugly.

"Please make her feel welcome," said Mrs. Gould.

We welcomed her with a game called "Svetlana Disease."

Here's how it worked:

If Svetlana touched you, you got infected with Svetlana Disease. To get rid of Svetlana Disease, you had to touch someone else and say, "Svetlana Disease." The antidote to Svetlana Disease was crossed fingers: if you touched someone and said, "Svetlana Disease," and the other person held up crossed fingers and said, "Crossies," then you were stuck with Svetlana Disease.

Most days, Svetlana threw up during lunch.

We live ten to a room, where we sleep on rusty bunk beds that creak when we breathe. The inhabitants of my bedroom, clockwise, bottom bunk to top:

DONI: A six-foot-four lumberjack with red hair and meaty hands that look like they should be drenched in motor oil. Loves Israel, hates Judaism—which is why he never had a bar mitzvah. Talks openly about his sexual conquests to the gleeful astonishment of the Yeshiva Boys, most of whom won't touch a girl until they're married.

TOMER: A scrawny, blue-eyed Tom Sawyer type with rimless glasses and a warm smile. Madly in love with his girlfriend back home, Tali, whom he talks about constantly.

GANZ: A stocky, blond smart aleck who's always ticked off about something. Classic middle child: older brother flies F-16s in the air force, younger brother's a soccer star. Plays saxophone. Hopes to one day start a rock band.

DROR BOY GENIUS: A clean-cut Ashkenazi kid with dark hair and the lean, angular face of an Austrian skier. One of three in Platoon Two to score above the 99th percentile on his high school A-levels. He's that rare breed of genius who's both wicked smart and socially affable, equally adept at discussing quantum physics and *Animal House*. Prone to uttering annoying phrases such as "When I become an officer . . ." and "If I go to Harvard . . ."

NITZAN: A dark-skinned geek with a screechy voice, thick eyeglasses, and asthma. Sings constantly. In the shower, he harmonizes with Ganz on an Israeli pop song called "Boray'ach"—"Running"—by the rock group Shikler's List. Thanks to Nitzan and Ganz, the song is slowly becoming the unofficial anthem of the platoon.

GERBER: A hyperactive motormouth with a shaved head and the face of a pit bull. Like a boxer, he's constantly darting, jabbing—except instead of throwing punches, he pummels away with one-liners and insults that sock you in the gut. Hilarious, but like sugar, too much Gerber makes you sick.

SHIMON: A muscular Yeshiva Boy with a yarmulke and wire-rimmed glasses. Born in L.A., he immigrated with his parents and four older sisters at age three. Speaks perfect English. I turn to him for translations. Like Dror Boy Genius, he scored above 99 on his A-levels.

RONEN PERETZ: A chunky Sephardic kid from Tel Aviv. Still looking for his kit bag.

TANENBAUM: A smiley Persian with light brown skin, fashionable glasses, and an easy laugh. One of those guys who's impossible to dislike. A tad scatterbrained. Has a tendency to misplace his boots.

YOEL: A twenty-four-year-old Chicago native in a jungle of Israeli teens. Conceived: Florence, Italy, March 1973, after his parents spent the day at a winery. Joined the Israeli Army against the wishes of his father, though he harbors the secret hope that doing so will make his father proud. Keeps a journal—every night, after lights out, he sits on his top bunk with a flashlight and scribbles in spiral notebooks while his roommates wonder why in God's name he doesn't go to sleep. Despite his initial fears of being an outsider, he actually fits in quite well, to the point where you might even say he's made friends. Smitten by his Israeli girlfriend, a Yemenite-Persian beauty who at once reinforces and challenges everything he's ever thought about Israelis. Enjoys the camaraderie of training, but deathly afraid of combat. Torn by dueling impulses, on the one hand, to be a badass Israeli warrior and, on the other, his hope that he will never have to pull the trigger.

Lunch is meat: baked chicken, couscous and meatballs, chopped hot dogs in beans, on orange plates. Because the Israeli Army is kosher, and since one of the main rules of keeping kosher is that you don't mix milk with meat, our dining hall has two separate kitchens, each with its own color dishware. Once in a while, a blue dairy-meal plate ends up in the meat kitchen, and an orange in the dairy. Depending on whether or not there happens to be a Yeshiva Boy nearby, we either place the contaminated plate in a special box or sneak it back into the appropriate kitchen.

After lunch, we get an hour of free time. During this hour, we lie on our beds and eat snacks. If we have the energy, we crack jokes and make fun of the Russians. Most days, it's too hot to do anything but lie on our backs, comatose, and talk about the heat.

The conversation usually goes something like this:

TOMER: Uch. It's so hot.

GANZ: I can't believe it's this hot.

DONI: Fuck! So hot!

DROR BOY GENIUS: Uch.

TOMER: *Koos-emok!*

GERBER: How is it so damn hot?

A few minutes into this conversation, someone remembers that we have an air conditioner. We then fight over who should get up to turn it on.

Afternoons, we run the ropes course in full gear: rifle, flak jacket, combat vest, two canteens, five magazines, helmet on head. We climb ladders, skip through tires, tiptoe along a balance beam, and conquer other obstacles I doubt we'll ever see in combat. We run the obstacle course in pairs, and we cheer each other on—even the Russians.

"*Yallah*, Moshe! *Yallah!*"

"Come on, Clemente—up! Up!"

When Yitzi, Yaki, and a couple of other chubby Yeshiva Boys get stuck on the concrete wall, Lieutenant Yaron cups his hands under their butt cheeks and pushes them over. The rest of us applaud.

In Platoon Two, we speak a language all our own. This language is a combination of Arabic proverbs, modern Hebrew slang, military acronyms, English imports, and invented words. It's nothing like the Hebrew I learned in Jewish day school, yet I picked up this new language within days because the words so perfectly describe the life of a soldier.

First, there are the words we use to describe one another. A *Rosh Gadol*— "Big Head"—is a soldier who goes above and beyond the call of duty. Ask him to scrub the toilets, he'll scrub the toilets and then mop the bathroom floor while he's at it. The nemesis of the *Rosh Gadol* is the *Rosh Katan*— "Small Head." A *Rosh Katan* does the absolute minimum. Ask him to clean the toilets, and he'll flush each toilet once then lock himself in a stall so you can't assign him any more chores until morning inspection's over.

A *Laf-laf* is a nerd. A *Chik-mook* is a hapless slob—shirt untucked, bootlaces untied, drool dribbling off his chin. A *Dibeelee* is an imbecile, not to be confused with a *Shocko'ist*, who is a soldier who tends to say and do stupid things, but only under pressure.

An example: Moti Sasson sleeps in his clothes, boots included, so he can sleep later in the morning. Moti once went four straight nights without showering (to get more sleep at night) until, finally, Sergeant Eran threatened to take away his Sabbath leave if he didn't bathe. The kid's a *Dibeelee*.

My buddy Tomer, on the other hand, is a sharp guy who, once in a while, does stupid things that leave the rest of us shaking our heads. Like the other night, during our weekly platoon meeting, Lieutenant Yaron asked if anyone had any complaints, and Tomer stood up and said there were too many flies at the Armored School. Not untrue. But a totally idiotic thing to say. The only way to explain it is that Tomer was in shock. He's a *Shocko'ist*.

The easiest way to label a soldier is to just add -*nik* to his most prominent characteristic. A guy who's from a kibbutz is a *kibbutznik*. A guy like me, from outside Israel—*hutz la'aretz*—is a *hutznik*. A soldier who works a noncombat desk job is a *jobnik*. If he's got a medical excuse—a *p'tor*—he's a *p'tornik*.

Since army life is often frustrating, miserable, and downright disappointing, we've got plenty of expressions and words of disdain. Most of these are sexual in nature. The most popular is *koos-emok!*—Arabic for "your mother's cunt." In close second is *zayin sheli!*—Hebrew slang for "my dick." There's *rabak!* I have no idea what this means, but it sounds Arabic and we say it when we're angry. And then there's the English word *fuck,* which in army Hebrew means "mistake" or "fuck-up." Every night, before bed, we line up for our nightly *Meesdar Fuckim*—our "Fuck-up Formation"— where Sergeant Eran reads his *Reshimat Fuckim*—his "Fuck-ups List"— which contains all the times we messed up during the day, for which we're then duly punished.

Many of our words aren't words at all, but just sounds, hand motions, and facial tics that everyone understands. These looks and sounds express not just the meaning, but also the speaker's opinion of the other person. Usually, this opinion is that the other person is a moron.

A simple tongue click means "No—and how stupid are you for asking that?"

Pshhhh! means, "Wow—aren't you some kind of big shot!"

Yo! means "Incredible!"

Uf! means "Damn! I don't feel like it!"

Wallah! means, "You don't say!"

Nu! means pretty much everything—including, "So?" "Well?" "Now what?" "And then what?" "Come on already!" "You with me?" and "What the hell is the matter with you?"

An upturned hand with the fingers and thumb bunched together means "Hang on, you impatient son of a bitch!"

A finger wag, such as the one a parent might use to scold a child who snuck a cookie, means "You are *so* wrong!"

In fact, it's possible to have an entire conversation where nobody speaks a single word.

But probably our favorite word of all is the term *achi*—"my brother." Most of the time, we call each other *achi* and don't even bother with given names.

Dinner is breakfast: cottage cheese and eggs on blue plates. Then, our food still digesting, we change into sneakers and shorts for our date with Revital.

Revital is our fitness instructor. She has long legs that don't have hair. To us, this is incredible—we've already forgotten what legs without hair look like. She also has amazing breasts, an amazing butt, and a face we barely look at because we're too busy staring at her legs and breasts and butt.

"We'll start with the lower back," says the stretch leader. Then all of us bend over and stare at Revital's butt.

"Next—triceps." We put one hand behind our heads, push down on our elbows, and stare at Revital's breasts.

"Now right foot over left, bend slowly and stretch the calves."

This is our favorite time of the day.

After we stretch, we play an Israeli game called thirty-on-thirty basketball. It's just like regular basketball, except there are thirty guys on each team instead of five, and there are no fouls. Kicking, biting, pinching, eye gouging, and elbows to the groin are allowed and in fact encouraged. We play until eight-thirty or someone gets a bloody nose. Then Revital leads us in a postgame stretch where we stare at her legs, breasts, and butt.

We stare at Revital not because we want sex, but because we remember we're supposed to want sex. The truth is, after a week of army life, we're too tired for sex. If Revital invited me to her room, I'd ask her to tuck me into bed and sing a lullaby.

The Yeshiva Boys are virgins. Probably. Some of the other guys are also virgins, but most aren't. As far as we know, we are all straight, except for Gil Weitzman, whom we think is gay. We think Gil Weitzman is gay because:

A) He has a high voice.
B) He walks like he's fragile.
C) He's vegetarian.

and, most suspiciously,

D) He describes himself with the feminine form of adjectives and his actions with the feminine form of verbs.

Of course, it's entirely possible that Gil Weitzman is not gay but simply:

    E) Talks funny.
    F) Walks funny.
    G) Loves animals.

and

    H) Has poor grammar.

Before bed, our commanders punish us for our mistakes, called *fuckim*. Common *fuckim* include untucked shirts, untied boots, wearing sleeves up when the rest of the platoon has sleeves down and vice versa, falling asleep during a gun lesson, and forgetting to make sandwiches for the Yeshiva Boys.

Our commanders punish us with push-ups, wind sprints, and a grueling concoction called Position 2, which is a push-up without the down part: instead, you balance on straight arms, torso parallel to the ground, until your shoulders tremble, your neck burns, and you fantasize about shooting yourself in the face.

This is Sergeant Eran's favorite time of the day.

Our fathers speak Hebrew, German, Polish, Russian, Romanian, Arabic, English, French, and Farsi. Despite the many languages our fathers speak and the countries from which our fathers hail, the soldiers of Platoon Two, Company B are united by the one trait we all have in common:

We are Jews.

Except for the Russians. There's a rumor that next week, when the Russians go to Be'er Sheva to visit "the dentist," they're actually going to a surgeon to get circumcised. It's just a rumor, but Gerber swears it's true. To prove it, he says he'll look at their penises in the shower and check to see if they have foreskins.

Most nights, before lights out, I call Dorit on the orange pay phone.

"Sweetheart!" she says. "How are you?"

"Alive," I say.

She tells me about her job at the Vita Soup factory. Dorit landed in Israel two days after I started basic training, and already she's the product manager for an entire line of powdered soups. She gets a cell phone and maybe even a company car. I ask her if she'll have the car in time for Parents' Day. She says she's not sure, but that Tomer's father has already called and offered to drive her down in his taxi.

Then Dorit asks, "What'd you do today?"

"Well . . ." I say.

But I can never remember. Each day lasts a year and flies by in an instant. Every morning I wake up and wonder how I'll make it through another day. Every night I lie in bed and marvel at how I got from morning to here. It is like this every day—each day endless, the minutes fleeting, and the days topple one into the next like dominoes.

More and more, I feel like a soldier. My biceps are solid. For the first time in my life, my pectoral muscles have broken the plane of my breastbone. During our nightly two-kilometer runs, my pecs jiggle up and down and I feel a tremendous thrill.

I am wedded to my assault rifle. My gun is an appendage, as much a part of my body as my leg. In those rare moments when my rifle is not physically on me, I feel naked, and I panic—the way I might feel if I'd been stripped of my underwear in front of a crowd.

I have also begun to think like a soldier, often in ways I'm not proud of. I joined the army thinking I'd be the model cadet who always volunteered. But I quickly learned that a big part of being an Israeli soldier is not being what Israelis call a *friar*—a sucker, or dupe, who gets taken advantage of—and that it's every soldier's responsibility to look out for his own ass. So when, on the first Friday night of basic training, just minutes before the Sabbath, my platoon mate, Ro'ee Shemesh, announced that he needed three volunteers for a twenty-four-hour stint of base guard duty, I ran to the latrine and locked myself in a stall. As I sat there cowering on the toilet, I thought about how Yoni Netanyahu would never have acted so selfishly. Obviously, I wasn't Yoni Netanyahu. But I also wasn't about to be a *friar*.

Army life is maddening in ways I didn't anticipate. We are always in a rush, always sprinting from one location to the next so as to not be late. And yet we waste hours and hours of time, waiting for equipment to arrive, for our commanders to show, for orders to be cleared before we can march out to the field.

The biggest time killer of all is guard duty. I can't count the number of hours I've wasted guarding items I never dreamed could be guarded. Since basic training began, I've guarded pup tents, toilet paper, crates of bullets, sleeping bags, gasoline, a soldier with a fever, old berets, an empty jerry can, tent stakes, a pile of tires, and tomato sauce. As far as I can tell, the rule is this: if it's important, we wear it, and if we can't wear it, we guard it.

The question I've never been able to answer is, Just whom are we guarding against?

I cannot say. Not because it's a secret. I mean, I literally cannot say because I don't know. We are guarding against Arabs, I suppose. But down here in the Armored School, a hundred kilometers from Eilat and half an hour from the nearest gas station, there's little chance even the most resourceful Arab would find the place.

So one night, I asked. We were lined up in formation, just as we do every night, and had just reviewed the Nine Rules of Guard Duty (No sitting, No sleeping, No writing, No reading, No smoking, No leaning, No music, No eating, No drinking except water from your own canteen) and discussed the Procedure for How to Handle an Intruder (Shout "Stop!" Shout "Stop!" again, Point your rifle, Cock your rifle, Fire at 60 degrees, Point your rifle, Cock your rifle, Shoot to kill) when I called out, "Sergeant Eran—just who are we guarding against, anyway?"

"Enemies," said Sergeant Eran.

"But how do I know he's an enemy?" I asked. "What if it's a soldier from another company, or an Arab dressed up like an Israeli soldier so I think he's one of us?"

For five very long seconds, Sergeant Eran glared at me. Then he ordered me to drop and give him twenty push-ups for talking without raising my hand.

After hours of thought—all of it during guard duty—I've decided that the reason we guard is because the alternative, not guarding, makes even less sense. The Israeli Army is full of these insanities, ridiculous tasks we do because not doing them would be even more ridiculous. To wit: every Sunday night, we take a true-false Rifle Safety Test. The questions are asinine—"During guard duty, you should keep your rifle pointed at your head." Absurd. But the alternative—never taking a true-false Rifle Safety

Test—would be even more absurd in the unlikely but potentially terrible event that some *Dibeelee* assumed he was supposed to point his rifle at his own head as he guarded the bunk.

What I'm beginning to wonder is how far up the chain of command this kind of logic goes. The army sends soldiers to Gaza to protect a couple of hundred Israeli settlers who live among a million-plus Arabs. Ludicrous.

Not protecting the Israeli settlers: even more ludicrous.

What's obvious is that there are cracks in the army system. Nobody has the answers, but nobody want to admit to that. So in the army, the buck stops nowhere, and shirking responsibility becomes not just a sometime activity, but a pastime, for basic trainee and commander alike. More often than not, it comes down to laziness. But it leads to dangerous situations—such as the day I throw my first grenade.

The morning we learned to throw grenades, I missed the entire lesson because Ro'ee Shemesh forced me to guard the bunk instead. I wasn't worried—I was certain I'd get a private lesson later on, because there was no way an army would allow a soldier to throw a grenade without first teaching him how.

Problem is, I forgot which army I was dealing with.

After the class, we marched to the firing range to throw our grenades. As we walked, I scurried up to Sergeant Eran and explained that I'd missed the lesson because I was guarding.

"Ask Sergeant Eli," he said.

I ran down the line until I found Sergeant Eli. "Don't worry about it," he said. "It's easy."

"Could you show me?" I asked.

Sergeant Eli huffed. "Stick your finger in the ring, twist, pull, throw."

"Okay," I said. "But could you show me on an actual grenade?"

"I don't have an actual grenade!" he roared. He bent over and picked up a rock. "See this? Pretend it's a grenade. Now go ask one of your friends to explain it."

I asked my buddy Shimon because he's extremely smart and speaks English.

"It's easy," Shimon said. "Put your finger in the ring." He demonstrated on an invisible ring on our rock that was a grenade.

"Okay."

"Twist your hand toward you, like you're checking your watch."

"Okay."

"Pull out the ring . . ."

"All right."

"And then throw."

I nodded.

Ten minutes later, Shimon tapped me on the shoulder. "One more thing," he said. "Be sure to keep your thumb on the safety button so the grenade doesn't blow up in your face."

CUB SCOUTS

Tomer can't believe I'm twenty-four.

We're in the dining hall, in the kitchen, singing Beatles songs. My roommates and I have been here since 4:15 this morning. I'm at the sink with Tomer. We are scrubbing frying pans with steel wool and pink soap. Behind us, Doni and Ronen Peretz mop; Ganz and Dror Boy Genius transfer plates onto a conveyor belt; Shimon, Nitzan, and Tanenbaum scoop guck out of the floor drain; and Gerber sits on an upturned trash can and bangs a twenty-liter soup pot with a spoon. We are doing this because at 3:45 this morning, our platoon mate Ro'ee Shemesh, who's in charge of the kitchen work schedule, stuck his head into our room and assigned us a daylong stint in the dining hall. Twenty hours later, we are out of our minds. So we've been trying our best to entertain each other—Gerber with his imitations of the Russians, Ganz with his spot-on impression of Sergeant Eran, and me with a very neat trick in which, when nobody's looking, I thread a rubber hose up my pants and out my fly and then turn on the sink full blast so it looks like I'm urinating with the force of a water cannon.

When, finally, the laughing dies down and the kitchen falls silent, Tomer says, "So, Yoel—how old are you, anyway?"

"Guess," I say.

"Nineteen?"

I wipe my hands on my pants—my hands are filthy, caked with cottage cheese, cucumbers, egg yolk—reach into my pocket, and pull out my national ID card.

Tomer checks it out. "What?!" he shrieks.

"Yep," I say.

"Ronen!" Tomer shouts.

Ronen looks up from his mop.

"Guess how old Chasnoff is?"

Ronen shrugs.

"Twenty-four!"

"What?!"

Tomer waves my ID card like it's a winning lottery ticket. Ronen struts over to the sink, snatches away my ID. "Gerber! Chasnoff's twenty-four!" Ronen shouts.

Gerber ambles over, and then Ganz and Dror Boy Genius, seeing that this is now an official meeting, abandon their plates and join us at the sink.

Gerber peers at my ID card. "Nice hair," he says.

"Let me see," says Ganz.

"What's up?" says Dror Boy Genius.

"Chasnoff's twenty-four," says Ronen.

"Really?" says Dror. "He looks sixteen."

"You want to see hair?" says Ganz. "Check this out." He pulls out his own ID.

"You look like Jim Morrison," I say.

"Let's go, everyone—ID check," says Gerber.

We pass around our national ID cards.

"Oh my God!" we say to each other.

"Your hair!"

"Your beard!"

"Holy shit, that's you?"

In his photo, Tomer has a ponytail. Gerber—lamb chops and a goatee. The only one who's the same is Dror Boy Genius, who looks exactly like the clean cut, goody-two-shoes teenager he is now.

"Are you in college?" Ronen asks.

"I graduated," I say.

"Were you in a fraternity?"

"What's a fraternity?" says Gerber.

"It's when a bunch of guys live together and throw parties, and have sex with lots of girls," says Ronen.

"*Sababa,*" says Gerber. Cool.

"Were you?" says Ronen.

One of the nice things about being a complete stranger here is that I can edit my biography at will. For example, instead of telling my roommates that I rushed AEPi—the "Jewish Fraternity"—but wasn't offered a bid, I can just say, "I don't believe in fraternities."

"If you're not in a fraternity, can you still have lots of sex?" says Gerber.

"Absolutely!" I say.

"Did you?" says Ronen.

Their horny teenage eyes sear into me like lasers. "Of course!" I edit again.

"Stud!" shouts Ronen, and slaps me on the back.

"Where'd you go to college?" says Dror Boy Genius.

"University of Pennsylvania."

"Good school," says Dror.

"Never heard of it," says Ronen.

"It's in Philadelphia," I say.

Ronen shrugs.

"*Nu!*" says Dror Boy Genius. "You know the movie *Philadelphia*?"

Ronen shakes his head.

"It's where Tom Hanks is a homo," says Gerber.

"Gay," I correct him.

They all glare at me.

"What's the difference?" says Gerber.

"Well, it's not about the difference, it's just a nicer way to say it," I explain.

"Does he suck dick?" says Ronen.

"I mean, maybe." I hem and haw. "I don't know, probably—"

"Then he's a homo!" says Ronen.

I'd love to be the guy who enlightens them on political correctness. But since it's nearly midnight, and there's no such thing as PC in Israel to begin with, I'm thinking this might not be the best time to start.

"So you're from Philadelphia?" says Dror.

"Chicago," I say.

"Chicago Bulls!" Gerber yelps. "Michael Jordan!"

"Michael Jordan," I say and nod. "You know, I never once saw him play."

Gerber's face crumples. "Why not?" he asks.

"Well, I mean, I saw him play on television all the time." I flail at an explanation. "But I never made it to an actual *game* game."

"But—you're from Chicago," Gerber says.

"True," I say. "But it's actually quite hard to get tickets. You see, they have this thing called season tickets, so the same people go to every game . . ." My voice trails off. Gerber stares at me with his mouth open. Suddenly, I feel like a fool. All those years, I had the greatest athlete in the world playing in my own backyard, and I never saw him play. I'm like the guy who orbits the spaceship around the moon while the other astronauts climb out and bounce around on the surface.

"I've driven past Michael Jordan's house." I try to salvage any last scrape of honor.

Gerber shakes his head. "I'd give anything to see him play."

We stand for a couple of seconds in uncomfortable silence. Then Ronen says, "Are your parents Israeli?"

"Nope," I say, happy for the change in subject.

"So why didn't you just join the American Army?"

Again, this mind-boggling question. At least once a day, one of my Israeli platoon mates asks me why, if I'm from the United States, I didn't just join the American Army. I'm astounded that they have to ask. My whole life, Israelis have been practically begging me to move to Israel. My Hebrew teachers at Solomon Schechter, the Israeli Scouts who sang at my summer camp, and the Israeli counselors on my teen tour all pounded me with the same message: "Jews belong in Israel! The Jewish state needs you! Come home!"

And now these Israeli kids want to know why I didn't just join the American Army.

"Because I'm a Jew," I say.

"But you live in America," he says.

"But my history's *here*," I say. "America's where I live. But Israel's who I am."

From the look on his face, you'd think I'd just told Ronen Peretz that my grandfather was Moses.

Why don't these Israeli kids get it?

So I tell them the Cub Scout story. It's a silly story, and a bit painful, but it's the best way I know to explain why I sometimes feel like a stranger in America—and what's so special to me about Israel.

When I was nine, I joined the Cub Scouts. It was a mutual decision: my parents wanted me to meet public school kids in the neighborhood, and I liked the uniform.

It was a disaster from the start. From the moment I joined, I felt intimidated. The public school boys were huge. They had names I'd never heard of, like Torby, Dylan, and Darnell. They picked on me mercilessly. During the Scout oath, they'd kick me in the back of my calf so I'd topple over. On the playground, during outside time, they hung me from the jungle gym by my underwear. "Man, you *sorry!*" screamed a kid named Todd as I bicycle-kicked my legs though the air, my Underoos somewhere between my ass and my neck.

"Sorry for what?" I whimpered.

Todd found my response hilarious. "Sorry for what!" he cackled. "Man, you really *are* sorry!"

I told my mother I wanted to quit the Scouts. But Mom had a better idea:

Synagogue.

In December, when we reached the religion chapter of our Scout manual, my mom called the Scoutmaster, Mr. Bevan, and asked if the Scouts might like to visit our synagogue for a Sabbath morning junior congregation service.

At first, I liked the idea. Finally, my fellow Scouts would see who I really was. Because if there was one spot on earth where I was completely in my essence, it was Sabbath morning junior congregation. To put it bluntly, I was a junior congregation superstar. Since I went to day school and knew all the prayers, I stood up front with Rabbi Mike and led the service. Some Saturdays, I delivered a sermon on the Torah portion. After the service, I stood next to the dessert table and flirted with Becky Engelbaum. Becky was gorgeous. She had frizzy red hair, a bumpy nose, and a terrific smile that I was sure would be even prettier once she got her braces off. "Good Shabbos, Becky," I'd say.

"Good Shabbos," she'd say, and blush. "You're a really great Torah reader."

"Oh, that?" I'd say, my voice full of swagger. "That was nothin'." Then I'd hand Becky a cup of grape juice. With everybody watching, I'd recite the kiddush blessing over the wine.

"Hungry?" I'd say.

"Sure," Becky giggled.

Then I'd bless the brownies.

At 10 A.M. sharp, the Scouts arrived on a yellow school bus. They wore their navy blue uniforms and red kerchiefs. I greeted them at the door and handed each Scout a yarmulke. Once they were seated in the first two rows, Mr. Bevan asked me to explain the headwear.

"It's called a yarmulke," I said.

"Yarmul*what*?" shrieked a kid named Damon. The other Scouts snickered. I blushed.

"And why do Jews wear yammahkees?" asked Mr. Bevan.

"To remember that God's above us," I said, immediately realizing how stupid I must sound.

I fumbled with my prayer book and dropped it. Without thinking, I picked it up and kissed the cover.

"He kissin' the book?" cried Damon.

I froze, as if I'd just been caught doing something private.

"Why did you kiss the book, Joel?" asked Mr. Bevan.

My lips quivered. I knew what I was about to say would sound ridiculous. "Because it has God's name in it and we want to show God respect."

The Scouts howled in laughter as I lowered my head in shame. I'd thought I'd be proud to have the Scouts see me in my element. Instead, I felt like my special world had been invaded.

The service was a catastrophe. The Scouts turned their yarmulkes into sailor hats and surgical masks. Anytime a Scout dropped his prayer book, he kissed it with a loud, wet smooch.

I wanted the Scouts to leave. I hated them, but even more, I hated us. I'd always loved being Jewish, but with the Scouts in the room, I suddenly saw what we Jews looked like to the outside world: ridiculous. I mean, just look at us! Swaying back and forth like idiots, whining prayers in this ugly language while we wore magic beanies on our heads. I looked around the room at my Jewish friends, and suddenly they all looked like such Yids. Rabbi Mike, with his beard and clunky glasses, looked like one of those weakling Jews in Holocaust movies. Becky Engelbaum's nose looked enormous, like a beak. And me, in my gray yarmulke and tallis prayer shawl—I felt like such a moron in my Jew costume. Now I knew why Jews lived alone in shtetls all those years. Who wanted to look that foolish in public?

"But in Israel," I explain to my kitchen work buddies, "I don't have to feel like a stranger in my own country. I can wear a yarmulke and not have to explain what it is. Nobody's gonna laugh if I kiss my prayer book. I can be me. I can be Jewish without feeling like such a . . ."

"Such a what?" says Ronen.

"Without feeling like such a goddamn Yid," I say in English.

Ronen shakes his head. "That's great you love Israel, but I don't get why anyone would do the army if he doesn't have to. I think you're nuts."

"Well what about you?" I turn the tables. "Why are you in the army?"

He shrugs. "It's what we do after high school."

"What about, defending the Jewish homeland?"

Ronen looks at me like I'm out of my mind. "All I know is, the day I get out of this army, I'm on the first plane to New York."

BUTTONS AND SNAPS

The problem with serving in an army run by twenty-year-olds is that I sometimes feel like I'm serving in an army run by twenty-year-olds. My commanders and even Lieutenant Yaron are just a couple of years out of high school. So despite the stripes on my sergeants' arms and the bars on my officer's shoulders, they're still just kids. For example, if I were in charge of this platoon, I would have demonstrated how to build a tent, when there was plenty of light, instead of assuming my soldiers would figure it out on their own in the dark. I would have warned them ahead of time that some tents had buttons and others had snaps.

But I'm not in charge of this platoon.

It's week three of basic, and we're in the desert for five days of survival training. The sun's long gone, the sky a giant purple bruise. Far ahead, the moon, swollen and silver, hovers above the dark silhouette of a mountain range. Every few minutes, a vicious desert wind blows a swirl of sand into our mouths and eyes.

We stand quietly in formation while Platoon Sergeant Guy paces before us. He is furious. Our pup tents were supposed to be up an hour ago, but instead we're standing in formation with our tents in our hands. The reason: each pup tent comes in two halves, and no matter how hard we try, we just can't seem to fit the two halves together.

It's an issue of buttons and snaps.

"Platoon Two, I'm going to say this one time and one time only so open your ears and listen like your life depends on it!" the platoon sergeant barks. "Now I'd assumed since you all graduated high school and one of you even finished college that you'd figure it out by yourselves. But since you did not, I will explain this once. In this platoon there are two types of tents—Israeli tents and American tents. Israeli tents have buttons. American tents have snaps. With me so far?"

"Yes, Platoon Sergeant!" we shout.

"Each half of each American tent has male snaps along one edge and female snaps on the other. This means that any two halves of any two American tents will snap together as long as you line up male snaps with female
snaps. However—if you're building an Israeli tent, one half needs to have
buttons and the other must have holes. So—if you and your partner both
have American tents, stay partners. If one of you has an American tent and
the other has an Israeli tent, or if both of you have Israeli tents with buttons
or holes, you must either trade partners or trade tents with someone who has
the type of tent you need and needs the type of tent you have. It is now six-
fifteen. At six-thirty, I want a campsite with tents in a perfect U, doors open
to the middle. Let's move!"

Immediately, the desert turns into the floor of the New York Stock Exchange.

"Buttons! Who's got buttons?"

"Holes! Holes!"

"I need snaps!"

"I've got snaps. What do you got?"

"Israeli tent."

"Buttons or holes?"

"Holes."

"Fuck."

"What do you have?"

"Buttons."

"So you need holes!"

"I need buttons!"

"You said you had buttons!"

"I mean I need buttons! I have holes!"

"Moshe had buttons!"

"Rosenbaum or Schwartz?"

"Schwartz!"

"Schwartz had buttons?"

"Schwartz had snaps."

"You said he had buttons!"

"No I mean he needs buttons."

"Fuck!"

Lucky for me, I'm sharing a tent with Dror Boy Genius. Dror's smart:
instead of sending me to search for buttons while he searches for snaps, he

just takes both our tent halves and trades for the first match he can find. Within a minute, he swaps my Israeli tent with holes for an American tent with snaps.

"So what now?" I shout.

"I'll put the tent together. You pound stakes!"

I open the kit bag and dig out our six orange stakes. I try pushing the first one in the ground, but it won't go in. The ground's too rocky.

I sit on my ass, take off my boot, and use my boot like it's a mallet. "Mother! Fucking! Stake!" I hammer out the syllables. The stake topples over. It's no use—it's like trying to push a golf tee into cement.

"Get a rock!" Dror Boy Genius shouts over the cacophony of our screaming platoon mates. I run off to a sand dune and return with a rock the size of a baby's head.

I pound, but again the stake topples over. I'm not surprised. I'm horrible at camping. At summer camp, when we'd go on our overnight, I never put up the tent, never built the fire. I applied bug spray and told jokes during dinner.

Dror grabs the rock from my hand. "You retarded?" he shouts. "Pound at an angle!" He steadies the stake at a 60-degree angle and pounds. The stake slides in like a toothpick into butter.

The campsite is absolute mayhem. My platoon mates, many of them still searching for corresponding tent halves, shriek and curse into the howling desert wind. Gerber and Uri's tent blows away completely, hurls through the desert like tumbleweed while they chase after it shouting, "Get back here!" In all this pandemonium, the word I hear most is *mefager*—"retard." Usually, it's in the form of a question: "*Nu, ata mefager?* You a retard?" Often, it's a declarative statement: "*Mefager!* You retard!" And sometimes, it's just a curse, directed at no one, or maybe God: "*Mefager!* Retard!"

Just when I think it can't get any crazier, a tall kid named Shai hands me a piece of string.

"What's this?" I say.

"String," he says.

"What's it for?"

He shrugs. "Sergeant Eran told me to pass it out." He walks on to the next tent.

I stare at the string. "What the hell am I supposed to do with this?" I say to Dror.

"You retarded?" he shouts. "It's to tie the tent to the stakes." He yanks the string out of my hands, pulls it taut in front of his teeth, and cuts the string into six smaller pieces. A couple of feet away, Kobi, at the tent next door, shouts, "What the hell am I supposed to do with this string?"

"You retarded?" I shout. "It's to tie the tent to the stakes!"

Then, when nobody's watching, the sky turns black.

Say what you want about the boys of Platoon Two, Company B. Say that we're foolish, and incompetent—a collection of half-wits and merry prank-sters who couldn't build a pup tent, much less a campsite, to save our lives. Say that we're reckless and irresponsible. Because we are. We lose bullets like they're paper clips, we fall asleep during gun lessons, and we never, ever remember to make sandwiches for the Yeshiva Boys.

And while you're at it, go ahead and say that we're selfish. Because we're that, too. When Ro'ee Shemesh assigns us kitchen work, we claim to have diarrhea. When he posts the nightly guard duty list, we remind him that Pasha the Russian hasn't guarded in, oh, maybe three nights now, and wouldn't it make sense for Pasha to guard that dreaded 3 A.M. shift instead of me?

Say what you want about the boys of Platoon Two, Company B of the 188th Armored Brigade. But the fact of the matter is, we have fun.

For example—watch us eat.

It's noon on our first full day of desert survival training. The sun is blaz-ing, the sky sapphire blue. We sit Indian style in a clump, everyone mixed in with everyone else—Russians with Yeshiva Boys, dark-skinned Sephardic guys with Ashkenazi kibbutz kids, and me with my usual gang of Tomer, Doni, Gerber, Dror Boy Genius, and Ganz.

Lunch is combat rations: tuna, corn, kosher Spam-like canned meat called Luf, suck-candies, and chocolate spread in tin cans stamped KOSHER FOR PASSOVER—1985. We also get a loaf of bread.

We have utensils—each soldier has two sets, in fact: one for dairy meals and one for meat meals. But we do not use utensils because, frankly, eating with utensils is not fun.

Instead, we eat like Vikings. We scoop tuna with our bare hands, drop it into our mouths like it's peanuts. When we do this, tuna juice dribbles down our chins, onto our shirts. We drink corn straight from the can, and when somebody shouts "Corn!" we pass the can to whoever asked for it. We hold the Luf, which is ground beef crossbred with Jell-O, like an apple. We chomp off one bite each and then pass it on to the next guy. We make sandwiches in ridiculous combinations—corn with Luf, chocolate spread with tuna, or, my personal favorite, chocolate-spread-tuna-corn-Luf—all of which are surprisingly tasty and, more importantly, allow us to consume every last morsel as efficiently as possible. We trade handfuls of tuna for chunks of Luf, a swig of corn for a lick of chocolate spread. We perform these transactions with our hands. And if, by accident, we drop a handful of tuna in the sand, we open a canteen and rinse off the grit. Nothing is wasted.

Today, the laughs begin the same way they always do. First, Gerber makes fun of the Russians. When that gets old, Doni imitates Sergeant Eran, and then I perform my impersonation of Ziv, the redheaded kid with a learning disability who was kicked out of the platoon last week after he tripped and cut his forehead on his rifle. One of us, I think it's Shai, mentions that since basic training started, there's something different about his snot. "Yes!" we all shout in agreement. It is universally agreed upon that our snot is perfectly dry, so that long chunks of crystalized snot slip out of our nostrils with just a gentle tug. Dror Boy Genius says, "It's meteorological." He explains, while we listen, rapt, that the Negev Desert is one of the driest spots on earth—so dry that a person can dehydrate without sweating.

"Awesome!" we say.

Through all of this, we laugh. When we laugh, bits of corn, tuna, and Luf shoot out of our mouths and onto one another's cheeks and shirts. We then flick these bits of foodstuff into the sand. We laugh because in Platoon Two, Company B, we are never not laughing, not mimicking one another, not entertaining many at the expense of one, usually a Russian, though in truth, we're all fair game.

After every can of tuna has been licked clean and every last morsel of Luf plucked off our shirts and either eaten or flicked into the sand, we go back to our pup tents, open our kit bags, and dig up our *chooparim*—Israeli slang for "treats."

We return with armloads of *chooparim*—chocolate wafers, pound cakes, jelly beans, sunflower seeds, candy bars—without taking into account that this is only day two of our week in the field, so maybe it'd be a good idea to ration our sweets.

We tear into our treats with our fingers. Since the chocolate bars are melted, we smear the chocolate directly onto our teeth and tongues, straight off the wrapper. Any chocolate that ends up on our shirts we lick off directly. We do this by pinching the shirt between two fingers and biting our shirts.

We eat like monkeys.

After dessert, we sing the "188th Armored Brigade Song." Gershon, one of the Yeshiva Boys, wrote the lyrics to the tune of the famous Jewish folk song "Hava Nagilla":

THE 188TH ARMORED BRIGADE SONG

One hun-
dred eighty eight the
Brigade that Syria
Fears most in times of war.

In Leb-
anon we'll crush Hez-
bollah and show them
The meaning of terr-or.

The only problem with Gershon's fight song is that it takes less than thirty seconds to sing, and we're getting a bit sick of repeating ourselves.

After ten or so rounds of the 188th song, we switch to "Breakfast at Tiffany's," by Deep Blue Something. My platoon mates love this song—it's in the top five in terms of play time on the Platoon Two, Company B tape deck—and a few of them, Uzi Zamoosh in particular, want desperately to learn the words. I've taken it upon myself to walk them through the lyrics.

Picture it: sixty green dots in the desert, sitting in a clump, singing "Breakfast at Tiffany's" while I wave my hand through the air like a maestro:

ME

You say that we've got nothing in common

THEM

You zay zet vee've got nussing in cowmon

We sing the chorus together, the chorus being, on the one hand, the strongest part—it's the part of the song they know best—but also the weakest, because they mangle the otherwise catchy, feel-good ballad with their horrendous accents:

THEM

And I sed vut about
Br'chekfist et Teefoony
She say I sink I
Ch'remember'ch ze film end
Ez I ch'ricol I sink
We boze kindeh likes it end
I say vell zets
One sing we got.

Then Uzi Zamoosh says, "Yoel—what does it mean?"

"Well," I say. "It's about a guy and a girl. The girl breaks up with the guy because she thinks they don't have anything in common. But the guy says, what about the movie *Breakfast at Tiffany's*?"

"It's a movie?"

"Yes, Uzi! Audrey Hepburn! You didn't get that?"

Uzi shakes his head.

"So the guy says, well what about *Breakfast at Tiffany's*? We both like that movie—so that's something we have in common."

"Because he doesn't want the girl to break up with him."

"Exactly. But what the song's really about is how sometimes people might love each other but just don't belong together because they're too different."

Uzi nods. "That's sad."

Then, quite suddenly, it's too hot to move. The sun is directly overhead, and we're baking. So Tomer, who's sitting in front of me, lies back and rests his head on my thigh. I lie back with my head on Gerber's stomach. Gerber lays his head on Doni's chest, and so on, until we're reclining back on each other, cuddled up on one another the way everyone does at summer camp, like a giant game of Ha.

We lie, perfectly quiet, in the heat.

"We're such homos," says Gerber.

"You're a homo," says Nir.

"Your mother," says Gerber.

Then we doze off in the sun.

After lunch, Sergeant Eran teaches us the Hitchhike Shot. We sit on a sand dune while he explains.

The point of the Hitchhike Shot is to kill a terrorist in the blink of an eye—before he has a chance to attack. It's called the Hitchhike Shot because in the past couple of years, Hamas and Islamic Jihad have tried countless times to kidnap hitchhiking Israeli soldiers. When the terrorists succeeded, it was because the Israeli soldiers didn't react fast enough.

In the Hitchhike Shot, a soldier has three seconds to snap in a magazine, switch to semi, cock a bullet, set the buttstock on his shoulder, and pop three shots into the terrorist's face. It's a serious exercise with serious consequences.

Except, of course, for the boys of Platoon Two, Company B, for whom everything must be fun.

After Sergeant Eran demonstrates, we stand in a big circle, facing out, and practice the moves. When we think we've got it down, Sergeant Eran sets up the drama.

"So it's Friday afternoon," he shouts. "You're hitchhiking home for a Sabbath leave. A car pulls up. The driver rolls down his window, and . . . he whips out a gun!"

"Nooooo!" we shout in mock panic. Then we shove in our magazines, flip to semi, cock the bullets, and shout, *"Esh! Esh!"*—Hebrew for "Fire!"

"Too slow!" says Sergeant Eran. "You're all dead. Let's try again."

We take out our magazines, swivel our rifles across our backs. "You're next to the highway," says Sergeant Eran. "You're hitchhiking home for the Sabbath when—"

"Staff Sergeant!" Nir cuts him off. Nir's a kibbutz kid from up the Galilee, and he's an absolute riot. He's an Israeli Buster Keaton who's constantly entertaining us with fake falls, sound effects, and goofy faces. "If it's okay with you, can I make up the situation?"

"Make it good," says Sergeant Eran.

"So it's Friday night." Nir shouts loud enough so we all can hear. "You're home on leave. You're horny. So you go to Alozorov Street and find a Romanian whore. You take her back to your place. She unzips your fly and starts sucking you off. Then, just when you're about to finish—she pulls out a gun!"

"No!" we simultaneously shriek and crack up. Because we're laughing, it takes a long time to shoot the imaginary terrorist whore.

"You're all dead," says Sergeant Eran. "But at least you're happy. Who's next?"

"I am!" shouts Gerber. "So you're home from the army. It's Saturday morning, and you're exhausted. You were up all night screwing Uri's sister."

"You son of a bitch," shouts Uri, who supposedly is Gerber's best friend.

Gerber continues. "You walk to the bank, to get money so you can pay her," says Gerber.

"Son of a bitch!" shouts Uri.

"You ask the teller for fifty shekels. That's how much it costs to screw Uri's sister five times."

"I'm gonna kill you, Gerber!"

"The teller reaches into his desk. He pulls out his hand. But instead of money—he's got a gun!"

"No! *Esh! Esh! Esh!*"

What disturbs me about our endless fun isn't just that it's so often misogynistic, racist, and, in the case of Ziv the redhead, outright insensitive, but how easily I go along with it.

On the one hand, I know this isn't the real me. The real me is the resident advisor at Penn who organized workshops on domestic violence. The real me is the actor who toured women's shelters in an educational play.

And yet, that can't be the whole story. Because here I am, standing in the desert with no women around—and I'm laughing at this stuff.

This army is changing me. But am I becoming less like me, or more?

That night, curled up in my pup tent, I sleep deeper than I've slept in years. The earth's wild energy creeps into my body, and I have fantastical dreams, full of silvers and maroons. And then I'm on a beach, with people from high school. We're laughing, chasing each other on the shore. I'm rolling in the sand, tumbling, and there's a woman—I can't see her face, but she's laughing, and then she's on top of me. I hug her tight, squeeze, and then water, warm, gushing—

I wake up with a start.

At first, I don't know where I am. Then I remember. The pup tent. With Dror. There he is, right next to me. Purring like an infant.

I sit up and peek outside. Still dark. But that smell? What is that? Like freshly cut grass. And why is my leg all wet? Did I just—?

I reach down, pat my shorts. Oh, God. I did.

I check my watch: 3:30. That leaves half an hour to air out the evidence.

I unlatch the tent, crawl outside into the cool desert breeze.

I pull my sleeping bag through the door, and as I do I remember the first time this happened, when I was fifteen, at Camp Ramah, in the top bunk. While my bunkmates snored, I stuffed my Muppet bedsheets into my laundry bag, startled but also relieved that, finally, I'd joined the club.

I unzip my sleeping bag and shake it. I notice Assaf, one of the Yeshiva Boys, standing guard over the camp about a hundred feet away.

I wave hello. *Hello, Assaf! This is normal! It's three-thirty in the morning and I'm standing in the desert in my boxer shorts, shaking a sleeping bag and it's normal!*

Assaf waves back. Then he shouts, in a loud whisper, *"Nu?"*

"Jookim!" I shout the first Hebrew word I can think of. Cockroaches.

CARDBOARD ARABS

The first time I almost die it's a Tuesday.

It's our third day out in the field. I'm in the firing range with nine other guys. We're on our bellies, shooting cardboard Arabs. *Pop! Pop!* Suddenly, the kid next to me, a Russian named Ofir, screams, "Owww!" Then he jumps up, points his loaded rifle at my face, hops back and forth like a schoolgirl skipping Double Dutch, and yelps, "Ow! Ow! Ow! Ow!" in Russian.

As he jumps and screams, Ofir points his rifle straight at my face, then chest, then balls, then knees, then balls, and then back at my face.

"Fuck," I say. "Oh fuck Ofir fuck Ofir what the fuck stop Ofir what the fuck!"—which, given the circumstances, i.e., a Russian teenage psychopath skipping like a monkey while he points a loaded rifle at my face, is a logical thing to say.

"Stop fire!" shouts Lieutenant Yaron.

"Stop fire!" we shout—except Ofir, who continues to shout "Ow! Ow!" in Russian, and me, because for the life of me I cannot stop saying "Fuck Ofir fuck stop Ofir fuck!"

What happens next happens fast.

Lieutenant Yaron charges full-speed down the firing platform and bear-hugs Ofir from behind. Then he pushes Ofir's rifle up and away from my face just as—

"Pow!"

—Ofir's finger accidentally grazes the trigger and a bullet zings past my ear.

Lieutenant Yaron wrestles the rifle out of Ofir's hands and switches it to safe position while at the same time Ofir rips off his shirt, Superman style, and cries, "Owwwwww!"

A second later, a hot shell casing tumbles out of Ofir's shirt and clinks to the cement.

Ofir collapses on the firing platform, and we crowd around and gasp at the sight of the huge red welt on Ofir's stomach.

"Everyone back!" shouts Lieutenant Yaron.

We don't move.

Lieutenant Yaron pours cold water on the welt, causing Ofir to shout "Ow!" one last time before passing out.

After Ofir comes to, Lieutenant Yaron calls an emergency platoon meeting and explains what happened.

On the Israeli-made Glilon assault rifle, hot shell casings discharge on the right. When a soldier pulls the trigger, the bullet shoots out the barrel, toward the target, and the shell casing—the metal cylinder that holds the bullet—exits through a tiny trapdoor on the right side of the rifle and flies away from the shooter.

Unless, Lieutenant Yaron explains, the shooter is left-handed—in which case the hot shell casings discharge toward the shooter, not away from him. On occasion, these hot shell casings discharge directly into the shooter himself. In Ofir's case, the scorching metal shell discharged out the trapdoor and flew between two buttons on his shirt, searing his skin with the heat of a branding iron.

But the soldier most in danger of being killed wasn't Ofir. It was the soldier lying next to him while Ofir jumped up and down like a maniac with a loaded rifle in his hands.

In other words—me.

Later that afternoon, I almost die again. Only this time, it's not an accident.

I'm in the supply tent. I'm seated Indian style, reading *Sports Illustrated*. Next to me is a wooden crate filled with one thousand bullets. The crate's open. Every twenty minutes, another ten soldiers return from the firing range and refill their magazines with bullets from the crate.

Sitting on the other side of the crate is a chubby kid named Chen Tal. Chen is short and plump with dark skin and a trim black beard. He looks like a Mexican Santa Claus. He is what Israelis call an *arse*—a greasy-haired, gold-chain-wearing, cigarette-smoking hoodlum from South Tel Aviv. As Chen tells it, most kids in his neighborhood don't even get drafted—the army figures such hooligans are a waste of time. Practically all Chen talks about is how next Friday, when we're home for our first Sabbath leave, his father's going to parade him around town in his army uniform so all the neighbors will know that Chen Tal made it big.

I'm engrossed in my *Sports Illustrated*, miles away from the army, when all of a sudden Chen lights a match. He holds the lit match over the open crate of bullets.

"Chen—what the hell are you doing?" I say.

"Scared?" he says. He blows out the match.

"That's not funny," I say. "You'll kill everyone in here."

Chen chuckles.

If I were smart, or less lazy, I'd get up and walk away from this rascal. But I'm tired, and I'm comfortable. And anyway, he'd have to be a complete imbecile to pull that kind of stunt a second time.

What I forgot is that Chen Tal is a complete imbecile.

He lights another match.

"Chen—"

"Move and I drop it."

I watch the flame flicker down the match. At the last possible second, Chen leans forward and blows.

Poof!

Smoke swirls up from the blackened match.

"You're sick," I say.

Chen cackles. Then he drops the match in the crate.

I gasp. Freeze. Wait—for the explosion that doesn't come. Then I lean forward and, my fingers like tweezers, pull out the match where it sits between two bullets—the most ludicrous game of pick-up sticks I've ever played.

Before dinner, I pull Lieutenant Yaron aside and tell him about Chen Tal and the match. Fifteen minutes later, a jeep speeds up to our campsite. Chen Tal climbs inside, the jeep drives away, and we never see the bastard again.

That night, I lie awake in my pup tent and think about my two close calls. The more I think about it, the more I think it's a miracle that hundreds of Israeli soldiers aren't accidentally killing one another every day. I think about the situation in Platoon Two, Company B. With Chen Tal gone, we're now fifty-eight soldiers in the platoon. Each of us has one rifle and five magazines that hold thirty-five bullets each.

I open my notebook and sketch it out:

58 scatterbrained teenagers x 1 assault rifle x 5 magazines x 35 bullets = approx. 10,000 scatterbrained bullets

teenager   assault rifle   magazine

With ten thousand bullets in our platoon, the likelihood that one of those bullets will end up inside one of us isn't just plausible—it's statistically probable. There are simply too many teenagers walking around with too many guns and too many bullets for one of those bullets not to end up inside someone else.

I think about all our mistakes, or *fuckim*—stuff like untucked shirts, unlaced boots, and showing up late for formation. I'd assumed that the longer we were in the army, the less *fuckim* we'd make, because we'd know the rules. That graph might look like this:

PLATOON TWO, COMPANY B *FUCKIM*: HYPOTHESIZED

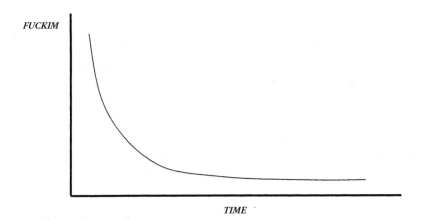

But in fact, it's the opposite. Between the stress, the fatigue, and our commanders' never-ending demands, we're actually making more *fuckim* now than we were the first few days of basic training. So the graph actually looks like this:

PLATOON TWO, COMPANY B *FUCKIM*: ACTUAL

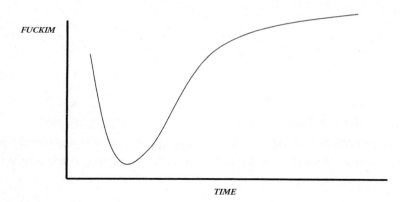

—where, after an initial dip in *fuckim*, our mistakes increase in any given amount of time at the rate

$$\Delta\, fuckim$$

and the sum of expected fuck-ups in any given period of time is

$$\int (t\text{-}b)^2 + k \cdot d\,fuckim$$

where

b = the number of soldiers present at any point in time, t,

and

$$k = (\sqrt[4]{b\text{-}t})^{-1}$$

which comes to an awful lot of potentially lethal *fuckim*.

While I'm journaling in the pup tent, Dror Boy Genius, who had guard duty, opens the flap and scoots in. "Why you still awake?" he asks.

"Someone's gonna die," I say. I show Dror my equations and explain my graphs. I tell him about our increasing rate of *fuckim* and how, eventually, one of those fuck-ups will involve an accidental bullet in one of us.

Dror Boy Genius chuckles. "That's why they draft us when we're eighteen," he says as he slides into his sleeping bag. "We're too stupid to know the difference."

My buddy Tomer is bummed.

It's Thursday morning—our last day in the field. For the past three hours, we've been practicing War 101—the most rudimentary, bare-bones technique for fighting a gun battle. In War 101, a team of three soldiers advances across a battlefield by alternately sprinting, diving, rolling, and shielding one another with cover fire. The entire time, we communicate by shouting a series of predetermined commands. It sounds complicated, but it's actually simple. All you have to do is listen to your instinct and then do the opposite. Because if there's one thing I'm learning about war, it's that the rules that help you stay alive in the real world are the ones that will kill you in battle.

For example, your instinct probably tells you that to survive a firefight, you should tiptoe across the battlefield as quietly as you can, hide behind bushes and rocks as often as possible, and move in a direction away from your enemy.

But in War 101, you do the opposite: charge straight at your enemy, as fast as you can, while firing your weapon and shouting "Ahhhh!" The idea, I suppose, is that if your enemy sees you running straight at him, firing your weapon, and shouting "Ahhhh!" he'll be so freaked out that he'll be less likely to stand up and fire back.

At least, that's what I tell myself.

During a quick water break, Tomer and I look for a quiet spot to sit and practice the oral battle commands. Our third team member, Hayim, won't be joining us—he's been recruited to help Platoon Sergeant Guy break down the camp.

"How about the mountain?" says Tomer.

Adjacent to our campsite is an enormous red mountain. It looks like the quietest place around.

We climb fifty feet up, at which point Tomer plops down on the rocks. I sit next to him, panting. The heat is devastating.

"Water?" Tomer says. He hands me his canteen.

I gulp. The water's hot. It's like I'm drinking from a Jacuzzi.

From where we sit, the view is spectacular. Far ahead, a kilometer in the distance, our platoon mates take turns running through the mock battle-field. Below us, at the foot of the mountain, Platoon Sergeant Guy barks or-ders at soldiers who help him break down the camp. While he curses them and calls them little girls, they scurry about the desert like mice through a maze as they count kit bags, fetch jerry cans, and stack cardboard Arabs into an idling supply truck.

I lie back on the rust-colored rocks. The mountain is covered with mil-lions of them. "Look at all these rocks!" I exclaim.

"Um-hm," says Tomer.

"I mean—there must be *billions* of rocks on this mountain!"

"Yep."

"And you know what's wild? There are more people in the world than there are rocks on this mountain. Isn't that wild, Tomer?"

"Wild," he says. He's not into the rocks.

"What's with you?" I ask.

Tomer picks up a rock. "I'm just thinking about the rock I want to be with."

I sit up. "What does that mean?"

"Tali," he says.

"Your girlfriend?"

"Ex."

"Oh. Sorry," I say.

I'd met Tali last Sunday on Parents' Day. She was a perky teenager, bubbly and smiling, with pink nail polish and pigtails. I thought she was Tomer's little sister until they French-kissed.

Tomer shakes his head. "She called the other night. She said it's too hard with me in the army. She said she wants to enjoy high school." He tosses the rock he'd been fiddling with. We watch it tumble down the mountain. "Goddamn army," he says. Then he looks at me. "What do you think that means, Yoel? 'Enjoy high school'?"

I've been a soldier for three weeks, but I've been a big brother for twenty years. "Tomer," I say, "let me tell you something about women." This is a strange thing for me to say since I know close to nothing about women. But Tomer doesn't know that. "When I was in college, I had a girlfriend named Annie. We dated pretty much my entire first year. I thought we'd be to-gether forever. Then, in April, Annie dumped me. She said she wanted to enjoy college. I'm telling you, Tomer, I was crushed. I couldn't eat. I cried. Honestly, I wanted to kill myself." I catch a glimpse of Tomer's assault rifle. "Not that I would. Anyway. The next couple weeks were the worst weeks of my life. I couldn't study. At night, I'd go for long walks through the most dangerous parts of Philadelphia. I was heartbroken. So over the summer, I came up with a plan for how to win her back. The day school started, I showed up at Annie's door and knocked. She answered the door in her bathrobe. I told her we had to talk. She said she was going to a party and asked if we could talk later. But I begged her, so she said I could sit on her couch and wait and she'd talk to me after her shower. And you know what I did when she was in the shower?"

Tomer shakes his head.

"I read her diary. It was sitting right there on the coffee table. It was page after page about how excited she was to finally date other people. She had a list of guys she wanted to go out with, including one of my roommates. Just horrible. When I finished reading, I just stood up, walked out the door, sat outside under a tree, and cried."

For a couple of seconds, Tomer and I sit quietly in the sun. Then he says, "Is there a point?"

"Yes," I say. "The point, Tomer, is that if she doesn't want you, then you don't want her." I squeeze his shoulder and pull him close. "Look at all these rocks, Tomer," I say. "Half of these rocks are women—and one of them is the rock for you. There's too many rocks on this mountain to be crying over just one."

We stare at the desert. "She was my first," says Tomer.

"Girlfriend?"

"Sex," he says.

I drink some water. "How old were you?"

"Fifteen," he says.

"Wow."

"I know. I was late."

"Right."

"How about Annie? Was she your first?"

"Annie? Oh, no. She was my—"

I drink more water. Lots.

"Honestly, Tomer, it's been so long I don't even remember."

"How old were you the first time?"

"The first time?"

I finish off the canteen.

"I don't know. Probably about the age you were. Give or take—"

Five years.

When we get back to camp, Platoon Sergeant Guy is ripping my friend Hayim a new one. "Hayim Goldstein! You piece of shit!"

I've never seen the platoon sergeant this angry. "Oh my God!" Tomer says in horror.

We watch the scene unfold. Hayim, who'd been sitting on a nearby sand dune, sprints over to Platoon Sergeant Guy.

"Where in God's name were you?" he explodes in Hayim's face.

"I was—"

"Shut your mouth, you lying shit! I told you to load the supply truck, and where do you go? Off to make a cup of Nescafé?"

"I thought I was supposed to—"

"Shut! Your! Mouth!" the platoon sergeant roars.

I cringe. It'd pain me to watch the platoon sergeant rip into anyone like this. But especially Hayim. He's such a quiet soul—one of those kids who just doesn't belong in the army. He's a funny-looking boy with a face full of mismatched features. He has dark skin and freckles. He has blue eyes and black hair. His most noticeable trait is the pink splotches on his face and arms—patches of raw, unpigmented skin. I can only imagine how much teasing Hayim Goldstein took as a child in a classroom of malicious Israelis. Worst of all, though, is that Hayim's father has cancer and is dying.

"I'm so furious I don't even know what to do with you!" the platoon sergeant shouts.

Hayim bows his head.

"Look at me when I'm speaking to you, do you understand me? What's so interesting on the ground, anyway—ants fucking?"

"Poor Hayim," Tomer chuckles.

"Sit down until I think of what to do with you—and don't move!" the platoon sergeant screams.

I watch Hayim sit at the foot of the mountain with his head in his hands. From the way his body shakes, I can tell he's crying.

I used to think it was great that every Israeli served in the army. I liked the idea of national service and common sacrifice. But now I'm starting to think it's not so great. If you take every eighteen-year-old in your country, scream at him, punish him, and tell him he's a worthless piece of shit for three years, that can't be good for the psychology of the nation. I worry about all my platoon mates, but especially the soft ones, like Hayim. He's a gentle, quiet guy in a country where it's virtually impossible to be gentle and quiet. Before the army, kids like Hayim are like sweet fruit. Then the army comes along and mashes them into a pulp.

As I watch Hayim bawl, I suddenly feel much older than my comrades. They annoy me when they bitch over whose turn it is to guard, and they frighten me when they nearly shoot me in the face. But when I see them mourning their girlfriends and sobbing into their sleeves, I have the urge to comfort them. Sometimes it becomes so clear they're all just boys.

TIM BAILEY

Halfway through basic training, I'm in the shower, soaping up and singing the 188th Armored Brigade Song with my buddies, when Uzi Zamoosh, the stuttering Yeshiva Boy, gallops into the bathroom and shouts, "Y-y-y-oel! Y-y-y-ou here?"

I peek my head around the stall. Uzi breaks into a wide smile. "C-c-c-c-come! Q-q-q-q-quick!"

The thing about Uzi's stutter is, it's conditional. Usually, he talks fine. But when Uzi's excited, angry, or speaking to one of our sergeants, he can't get out a word.

Since he's smiling, I assume it's good news.

I towel off while Uzi jumps up and down like the proverbial kid on Christmas. He follows me to my room and watches me dress. No sooner do I pull on my boxer shorts than he yanks me out the door and pulls me through the courtyard to bedroom 6.

The bedroom is packed with soldiers. An overflow crowd spills into the courtyard. "Yoel's here!" someone shouts.

The crowd parts. Uzi points. In the middle of the floor, a soldier sits on his knees and rummages through a kit bag.

I have never seen this soldier before. He has dark hair, a black beard, and thick glasses. He's dressed like a hardened vet in a Vietnam movie—naked from the waist up, and below, combat boots and pants. His pecs are enormous. Thick blue veins ripple through his biceps like rivers.

Uzi Zamoosh smiles. *"A-m-m-m-m-m-erica'ee!"* he explodes.

American.

The soldier stands up and looks me square in the eye. "You the American?" he barks in English.

I nod. He breaks into a grin the size of Texas. "Well I'll be!" he shouts. He sticks out his hand. "Tim Bailey. Syracuse, New York."

I stare at his hand. I haven't shaken hands in a month. I greet my platoon mates with hugs and arms around their shoulders. Shaking hands is so formal, so—

American.

I shake his hand. "Yoel. Chicago. I mean, Tel Aviv."

He pumps my hand up and down so hard my shoulder hurts. "They told me about you!" he barks. "Thought they were crazy. I mean, another American? Here? What are the odds?"

I'm speechless. I can't believe this cowboy.

"How's your Hebrew?" he yaps.

"Good," I say.

"Perfect! You'll translate. I don't speak a word. I mean, I know the basics—hello, good-bye, mother, father, flak jacket—I took a Hebrew class up north, I was actually drafted a month ago, into infantry, but turns out my eyesight's so bad I don't even qualify, here, check it out"—he hands me his glasses—"I'm actually legally blind without these, go ahead, put 'em on . . ."

I try on his glasses. I feel like I'm looking through a kaleidoscope. "How do you see with these?" I say.

"How?" he cackles. "Shit! I can't see without 'em!" Then he slaps me on the back so hard I stumble forward. "So I could've worked a desk job in the Paratroopers, but I wanted a gun—right? I mean, how'm I gonna pick up chicks if I don't carry a gun?" He drops to his knees, goes back to digging through his kit bag. "So they offered me Artillery or Tanks, and I figure, Artillery, you're behind the lines, but Tanks, you're smack in the middle of the action, right? So I said Tanks, and I asked for the Merkava, because, you know, the Merkava's pretty much a carbon copy of the American M-1 Abrams, except with isolated treads instead of modular and the hundred-twenty-millimeter cannon. So I ended up here, which is pretty sweet, right? We'll see action, kick ass in Lebanon . . ."

He rambles on for ten minutes, hops from one topic to the next like he's on a verbal pogo stick. My platoon mates, meanwhile, stare at us with big, goofy smiles, thrilled to witness the interaction of two real, live Americans right here in their bunk.

I can read their minds: *So this is what it's like in America!*

They probably think I'm ecstatic to have another American around. But I'm not.

My plan since basic training began has been to fit in seamlessly. I don't want to be the American who gets along with Israelis; I want to be the Israeli who the Israelis didn't even realize was American. If I start hanging out with an American, speaking English, that'll stunt my Israeli growth.

Besides, I know what Israelis think of Americans. For as much as Israelis love American culture and can't wait to live in America, they think Americans are spoiled, pampered, and materialistic. In fact, in Israel, *American* isn't just an adjective to describe nationality, it's an adjective to describe behavior. When a soldier hordes food or doesn't immediately share the contents of a care package from home, my comrades shout, "Don't be such a goddamn American!"

The first time an Israeli called me American, I was thirteen years old, visiting Israel with my parents. I was in a gift shop on Ben Yehudah Street, in Jerusalem. I was checking out a baseball-themed menorah when one of the candlesticks snapped off in my hand. Panicking, I did what any morally competent teenager would do.

I ran.

"Hey, you!" the owner shouted. He chased me out the door and followed me halfway down the block. Then he stopped, raised the broken menorah over his head, and shouted, "Fucking American!"

I turn my back and walk to the doorway of bedroom 6. "Good luck," I call over my shoulder.

Fuck Tim Bailey. The American's on his own.

GLORY

I'm God. No—I'm bigger than God. And badder. I'm Clint Eastwood. I'm Jesus Christ, Captain America, and the Beatles.

I mean, look at me. Do you see me? Do you see me in my olive-green uniform, beret, and shiny black boots? Do you see the assault rifle slung across my chest?

That's me! Finally! I am the badass Israeli soldier at the side of the road, in sunglasses, beret, forearms like bricks. And honestly—have you ever seen anything quite like me?

It's Friday, 2 P.M., and I'm in Tel Aviv on my first Sabbath leave. I'm on the number 4 bus to Ben Yehudah Street. There's an open seat, but I stand.

I must be seen.

A couple of feet away, two college-aged American girls chat in English. They're Yeshiva girls, decked out in ankle-length denim skirts and long sleeves. They giggle. Whisper. Then one of them—I think—yes!—checks me out. I turn my head and catch her staring at my uniform and gun. She's smitten. She is thinking thoughts that would get her kicked out of Yeshiva. I flash a smile. She blushes, looks away. I am the Israeli soldier who makes American girls swoon. I am fireworks. A one-man ticker-tape parade.

I am glory.

At my apartment, I drop my bag, lock the door, and head right back outside. Sure, I could have changed out of my uniform and locked up my gun. But then nobody would know I'm a hero. And what fun is it to be a hero if nobody sees?

I check my watch: 3:00. Dorit's on an all-day Vita Soup field trip to a food plant in Tiberias. At six, I'll take a cab to her parents' place, and then we'll walk to her aunt's for dinner. Until then, I have one goal:

Be seen.

Since I have nowhere to go, I walk. I walk into a grocery store and buy an ice cream bar. In the checkout line, a filthy Canadian couple stares at my rifle. He has dreadlocks, she has legs hairier than mine. Both have maple leaves sewn prominently on their knapsacks. "Brian!" the woman shrieks. "Do these soldiers *really* have to bring their rifles into grocery stores?"

Silly Canuck. You're so naïve. Don't you know it's because of guys like me that you can sleep at night?

I head west, to the beach, then turn south and walk along the waterfront promenade.

Understand, I am *not* a gun guy. I hate guns. I never played with toy guns. As a kid, I wasn't allowed to see movies with guns. I can't tell you how many classic American films I've missed because I was forbidden to see movies with guns, but here are a few: *Scarface, Chinatown, Tron,* the *Godfather* movies, the *Star Trek* movies, every *James Bond* movie, all three *Star Wars* movies, all three *Indiana Jones* movies, and *Witness.* I've missed out on Harrison Ford's entire career.

But this is different. What I love about my rifle isn't the violence or my capacity to kill. It's the feeling of power. Manliness. Walking around Tel Aviv with my rifle, it's like walking naked with a twelve-inch penis.

Last night, at the Armored School, the mood was positively giddy. Lieutenant Yaron announced we'd depart for Tel Aviv at six the next morning—but only if the bunk was spotless. So we scoured the bunk in thirty minutes in a display of platoon teamwork the likes of which I'd never seen.

The only one who wasn't overjoyed was my roommate, Nitzan. While we mopped and sang the 188th Armored Brigade Song, Nitzan lay on his bed and sobbed. Unlike the rest of us, Nitzan would be staying back at the Armored School to guard the bunk—his punishment for showing up at the firing range without his rifle, which he'd forgotten in his pup tent. Last night, our bedroom was like a shiva call. We sat on Nitzan's bed, patted his back, and promised to bring him treats. Outside, we spoke in hushed tones.

"How is he?"

"Terrible."

"Poor guy. But still—"

"I know."

"I mean, who shows up at the rifle range without his rifle?"

• • •

The Tel Aviv Promenade runs north-south along the coast of the Mediterranean Sea. On the Promenade, couples hold hands while they munch ice
cream cones, push strollers, and yap into cell phones. Young Thai nurses
push old men in wheelchairs. Twenty feet away, on the beach, two bare-
chested Israeli guys in cutoff shorts play bongos and smoke. I walk past the
usual peddlers: the old violinist, case open at his feet; the Russian caricature
artist who stands proudly next to an exaggerated drawing of Tom Cruise;
the Black Hebrew fortune teller who sits on a stool with her tarot cards.

When the Promenade ends, the road slopes up into the ancient city of
Yafo. With its narrow, brick streets and stone houses, Yafo feels authenti-
cally biblical. I walk past Abu Lafia, the twenty-four-hour pita bakery, and
Zacharia's Restaurant, where an old Yemenite man with no teeth serves cow
testicle soup in chipped white bowls. On the waterfront, Arab and Israeli
fishermen cast their lines into the Mediterranean, which, at four in the afternoon, shimmers like orange stained glass. And then I turn west, toward
the Carmel Market in the heart of Old Tel Aviv.

There are so many reasons to hate this country. The bureaucracy is crippling. Government offices operate when they want, for as long (or short) as
they want, usually something like 8 A.M. until noon Mondays, Wednes-
days, and alternate Thursdays. Each week, another group goes on strike—
schoolteachers, garbage men, postal workers, phone operators, cable guys,
bus drivers, doctors, nurses, paramedics, airport baggage guys, and the old
men in blue jumpsuits who walk the streets of Tel Aviv stabbing pieces of
trash with meter-long spears have all struck in the past year—so the country never runs at full power. In big cities, there's dog shit on the sidewalks.
The Knesset, Israel's fifteen-party parliament, is trapped in a state of perpet-
ual gridlock. And as for the economy, it's defective, backward, and in even
worse condition than the shit-covered sidewalks—a predicament I'm forced
to deal with on the first of every month when it's time to pay rent. Like all
Israelis, I pay rent in dollars but get paid in shekels. So when the shekel falls
against the dollar—as it does pretty much daily—my rent goes up even as
my pay holds steady.

This country!

And yet, when I step into the Carmel Market and hear the shopkeepers
hawking their wares, smell the mixture of frying lamb, goat cheese, and human sweat, and watch the people lined up to buy flowers for the Sabbath, I
remember why I love Israel so much. And now that I'm a soldier, I can enjoy

it without feeling guilty that I'm taking without giving back. When I was seventeen and visiting Israel with my American friends, I felt like a fraud calling Israel my homeland when it was the Israelis, and not me, who defended it. I remember how, junior year of high school, I watched Saddam Hussein's missiles fall on Israel during the Gulf War, and it felt so wrong that we American Jews did nothing but pray and mail checks while the Israelis holed up in shelters with gas masks on. Walking through this market in uniform, I feel vindicated. After twenty-four years, I've earned the right to call Israel mine.

"Hey, soldier!" a shopkeeper beckons me over. "Where you serve?"

"Armored," I say.

"Kol ha kavod!" He commends me. "Here—free falafel, just for you."

Because it's Friday, the market is packed. I inch along, crushed in the throng of human mass. At pushcarts and stalls, middle-aged men with gold chains and raspy smokers' voices sell mangos, lemons, whole and quarter chickens, cow lungs, cow tongues, cow testicles, sheep brains, fifty-plus varieties of fish, calculators, knockoff Nikes, carnations, sponges, girdles, bras, batteries, and men's and ladies' underwear. With only a couple of hours until sundown, the peddlers shout their last minute, pre-Sabbath bargains:

"Tangerines, one shekel, one shekel!"

"Pita, hummus, chickpeas—*yallah*! Shabbat, Shabbat!"

I love the excitement of this market, but also the Middle Easternness of it—the barking, the bargaining, the haggling that's at once friendly and brutal. When I walk here, I think about all those American diplomats who call Israel the America of the Middle East. If those diplomats really want to understand Israel, they should leave their fancy Jerusalem hotels and take a stroll through the Carmel Market.

Here and there, a shopkeeper shouts, *"Hayal!"*—Soldier!—and offers me a doughnut, a cookie, a wedge of baklava on the house. At the flower stand, I pick up roses for Dorit's aunt, who's hosting us for dinner. "How much for twelve?" I ask.

"Ninety shekel."

"Pshhhh," I say.

"How much you want?"

"Fifty."

"Serious? Eighty, best price."

"Sixty."

"You want me to be poor?"

"Sixty-five."

"*Yallah*, sixty-five. Here. Go. Good Sabbath, soldier."

That's the other thing I love about Israel—for all their shouting and arguing, Israelis are as warm and generous a people as any on earth. There's this incredible bond between Israelis, and they take care of one another. Maybe it's a remnant of shtetl life in Europe, or perhaps it has something to do with living so close to your enemy. Whatever the reason, Israelis act as if everyone is everyone else's next-door neighbor.

The first time I experienced this unique bond was the week I arrived. I was driving to Tel Aviv—Dorit's father, Menashe, had lent me his car—when a guy pulled up next to me at a stoplight and beeped his horn. "Hey, brother!" he called. "My girlfriend's thirsty. You got water?"

Beside me, on the passenger seat, was a bottle of water. But it was half empty.

I held up the bottle. "It's already open," I said.

"No problem," he said. He stuck out his hand.

A week later, I was at Dorit's family's apartment with her parents. It was dinnertime and we had ordered pizza. Finally, after two hours, the pizza guy showed up on his motor scooter. He was disheveled and sopped with sweat. "I got lost," he whimpered.

"So come inside! Sit!" said Dorit's mother, Tzionah. "Coffee or tea?"

"Coffee. Milk and two sugars," he said.

While Tzionah made the coffee, Menashe opened the pizza box. "Please take." He offered a slice.

The pizza guy waved him off.

"*Nu!* You're offending me!" said Menashe. "What's your name?"

"Oren," said the delivery guy.

"Oren. I insist. Eat."

And I'll be damned if Oren the pizza guy didn't sit down at the kitchen table and eat the pizza he'd just delivered. As we ate, I thought about all those porno movies where the lonely housewife invites the pizza boy inside and screws him on the kitchen table. In the Israeli version of the story, the pizza boy doesn't make love to the housewife. Instead, he sits down with the family and eats pizza.

The longer I'm in the army—and it's been three weeks now—the more I think mandatory army service is the reason why Israelis are the way they are: aggressive, hotheaded, and stubborn on the one hand, and, on the other, unbelievably generous and community minded. It's because these are army values. And since just about every Israeli comes of age in the army, these values become national values. Sometimes it feels like Israel is just one big army base, what with everyone shouting at each other, barking commands, refusing ever to back down—and passing around their water bottles when their buddy (or his girlfriend) needs a drink.

Just after sunset, I meet Dorit and her parents at their apartment in Bnei Brak. I haven't seen Dorit in a month, and I'm thrilled to finally hold her in my arms. My new haircut aside, I can tell she's pretty happy to see me, too. Together, we walk to her aunt Nachama's apartment in nearby Pardes Katz.

Like most Israeli neighborhoods named after rabbis, Pardes Katz is a slum. Dorit says it's just a coincidence, but I've got my own theory: the poor cling to religion because they don't have access to that other god— money.

The residents of Pardes Katz are almost all working-class, dark-skinned Sephardic Jews. They live in crumbling gray cinder-block apartments with their laundry hung out to dry below their windows. On street corners, green Dumpsters overflow with trash. Stray cats dart in and out of garbage cans while kids kick a soccer ball in the street. As we walk through Pardes Katz, I think about Ruti's classroom back in second grade, and how neighborhoods like this never showed up in her posters. Those posters all showed the same thing: smiling children on Masada, smiling soldiers at the Western Wall, smiling kibbutzniks picking oranges in the sunshine. You'd never guess there were Israelis who weren't happy, or rich, or white.

When we reach Nachama's building, Dorit and I are greeted with much excitement. Here in Pardes Katz, Dorit and I are all the rage—not only because we're a dashingly handsome young couple, but because there's an element of jungle fever about us: it's not common for a Yemenite-Persian girl like Dorit to date a white guy, and an American no less. It's strange: back in America, all my parents and my friends' parents cared about was that our girlfriends and boyfriends were Jewish. It didn't matter if they were light-skinned or dark, religious, secular, convicted felons, or addicted to crack. As long as she or he was a member of the tribe, it was cool. But here, where practically everyone's Jewish, Israelis have the luxury of judging their kids' relationships based on other criteria. So by American Jewish standards, Dorit and I are an exemplary couple, while in Israel we are an anomaly.

Nachama's apartment door is wide open. The moment Dorit and I step inside, Nachama shrieks, "Aiihhh!" This is Nachama's way of saying hello. She's dressed as she's always dressed—long pink gown, sandals, and a white headscarf. She shuffles over from the stove, clutches my shoulders, and plants a violent kiss on each cheek.

"*Hultan shi'dobray, Jigar?*" she screams in Persian.

"I'm fine," I say.

"*Yofi!*" she cries. "How's Clinton?"

Nachama thinks that my father, who is tall and white, looks exactly like Bill Clinton.

"Clinton's good," I say.

"Mommy? Brothers?"

"Everyone's good."

"*Yofi*, sweetheart!" she says. Then she slaps my cheek so hard it hurts. "Sit! Eat!"

Like Dorit's mother, Nachama is a fantastic cook. Maybe it's because all she ever does is cook—whenever I drop by, I find Nachama at the stove, brewing up a pot of Yemenite soup, baking pita, or marinating six dozen chicken wings for the kids and neighbors.

Tonight, we eat a traditional Sephardic Sabbath meal: chicken legs simmered in paprika sauce, Persian rice, fried potatoes sprinkled with rosemary, a breaded meatball slathered in chickpea-and-beet sauce called *ghondi,* and for dessert, baklava and tea. I'd always assumed that Jewish food was, by definition, bland and tasteless. When I was a kid, my mother and her friends cooked Sabbath dinners consisting of chicken, rice, and potatoes, just like Nachama. The difference, I now realize, is that we Ashkenazi white folks do nothing exciting to our food. Nachama and Tzionah, meanwhile, utilize a combination of spices I until recently had never even heard of—cumin, turmeric, *hawayij, za'atar*—to create Jewish food that I actually enjoy eating.

Joining us for dinner are Nachama's five children, three of whom live with Nachama in her two-bedroom apartment. The meal is loud and raucous. Nobody speaks. Instead, we shout, even when we're talking to the person right next to us. The minute we sit down, Nachama turns to me and shrieks, "*Nu?*"

"*Nu* what?" I shout back, even though I know perfectly well what she's talking about.

Nachama grabs my arm. "Marriage! Babies! You and Dorit are meant to be—so what are you waiting for?"

"Leave him alone, Nachama," says Dorit.

"What, it's not a fair question? You're together two years, so what's keeping you?"

"I'm in the army, Nachama," I say. "Too complicated."

Tzionah clicks her tongue. "Listen, Yoel—my friend's son got married as a soldier, and the army gave him free bedsheets."

"I already have bedsheets."

"But what's the point of bedsheets if you haven't got a wife to share them?" Nachama cries.

I find this an ironic comment from a divorced mother of five.

I don't know the details of Nachama's divorce. I do know that her ex-husband is a man named Boaz who, supposedly, wore a glass eye and couldn't keep the other from looking at other women.

After I deflect their marriage pestering, Nachama brings up their next favorite topic—the Arabs.

"The Arabs are donkeys!" Menashe shouts.

"The Arabs are dogs!" Nachama agrees.

"Get serious!" shouts Dorit. "They can't all be donkeys and dogs."

Tzionah shakes her head. "Never trust an Arab," she says, clicking her tongue.

"Come on, Dad," says Dorit, "I bet there are some good ones who just want the same thing as you."

"No chance," says Menashe.

"Really?" I say. "You're telling me there's not a single Arab out there who wants peace?"

"Peace?" cries Menashe, nearly flying out of his seat. "*Peace?* They say they want peace, but you know what they want?"

"Tell me."

"Tel Aviv! Fifty years they've been trying to drive us into the sea, and now they want peace? Don't be a fool."

"But not all Arabs," says Dorit. "If you look hard enough—"

"Nonsense!" Menashe shouts, and slams his fist on the table. "Do you know what the Arabs did to me when I was a boy?"

"Yes," I say. It's one of Menashe's favorite stories—which is why he tells it anyway.

"They threw rocks at me on my way to school! Rocks, at a seven-year-old boy! What kind of animal throws rocks at a boy on his way to school?"

American diplomats don't get it. They think the Palestinian-Israeli conflict is about land for peace and pre-1967 borders. But it's not. It's about what the Arabs did to Menashe when he was seven. And somewhere in Ramallah, there's a sixty-year-old Arab slamming his fist on his own table, calling the Israelis donkeys and dogs, furious because of what an Israeli bulldozer did to his father's olive tree in 1948. In the Middle East, politics is personal. So if there's ever going to be peace, it's going to have to be personal, too.

After dinner, I sit on the front steps and chew sunflower seeds with Nachama's middle child, Nadav.

Nadav is a fourteen-year-old straight-A student who likes to program computers. Of all Nachama's children, he's my favorite. I've made it my mission to make sure he turns out all right, and maybe even be like the father he doesn't have. I ask Nadav about school. He tells me about his computer class and a girl he likes and he thinks likes him. "And how about the army?" I ask.

Nadav shrugs. "I haven't thought about it much. Maybe I'll be a cook."

"A cook?" I cry. "No, Nadav. You will not be a cook. You'll go combat, and you'll be an officer."

Nadav laughs. "You crazy? My mom doesn't even want me to go in. She says she's going to burn my draft orders."

I believe him. If Nadav does serve in the army, he'd be the first of Nachama's children to go. The others never made it to the Induction Center—Nachama torched their draft orders on the family grill and slammed the door when the draft officer came calling in person, and the army finally gave up.

I grab a handful of seeds and chew. I think about Chen Tal, the kid who nearly killed me when he lit a match over the crate of bullets. The army was Chen Tal's chance to move out of the slum, but he blew it. I don't want Nadav to make the same mistake.

"Nadav—promise me when you get your draft orders, you'll talk to me first, before you talk to your mom. Otherwise . . ."

"Otherwise what?" he asks.

• • •

After dinner, Dorit and I walk to Jabotinsky Street to find a taxi. I'm over-flowing with joy. It's a beautiful night. Dorit's at my side. I have thirty-six hours of free time ahead of me.

And then Dorit has to ruin it.

"So what do you think about what Aunt Nachama said?"

"About Arabs?" I say.

"No." She squeezes my hand. "About us."

The way I see it, there are two types of married couples: the 50 percent that get divorced, and the 50 percent that would get divorced if only they had the balls.

I put my arm around Dorit. "Honestly, babe—I kinda like things the way they are."

She slithers out of my grip. "Wait a second. You know I'm not twenty-four, Joel. Nachama's right—we've been together two years—"

"A year and nine months."

"Who cares? It's long enough to know if I'm the one."

"And you know I'm the one?"

"Yes."

"Impossible!" I can't believe any woman would think I was the one.

"I don't get it," she says. "Do you really think we'll be unhappy?"

"Think? No. I don't think we'll be unhappy. I *know* we'll be unhappy. Because that's what marriage is—two people totally miserable because they're stuck with one another until they die."

"There are plenty of happily married people."

"Name one couple."

She mulls it over. "Your grandparents."

"You serious? Bubbie and Zayde?"

"They've been married fifty years, and they're happy."

"She's got Alzheimer's and he's deaf. Of course they're happy."

It's my own damn fault I'm in this conundrum in the first place. When I met Dorit and she told me she was twenty-eight, I knew she'd never give me a chance if she knew I was twenty-two. So I told her I was twenty-four. She never would've found out, either, except that a month later she came to my family's house for Passover. My mother insisted on dragging out my bar

mitzvah album. Before Dorit saw a single picture, she noticed the date em-
blazoned on the front in gold foil:

The Bar Mitzvah of Joel Aaron Chasnoff

January 24, 1987

"Were you fifteen at your bar mitzvah?" she asked.

I'm against marrying young on principle: I simply think it's a bad idea
for a guy to get married before he's had a chance to figure out who he is. But
there's another reason, too. When I was ten, my mother was diagnosed with
multiple sclerosis. It's excruciating to watch my mother suffer. I'm afraid of
having a sick wife.

At Jabotinsky Street, I take Dorit's hands in mine.

"I just need time," I say.

"How long?"

"Enough to think it over."

Dorit sighs. "Rosh Hashanah?"

"Rosh Hashanah? That's in a month!"

"Yom Kippur?"

"Too soon. I'm thinking—"

"Sukkot?"

"Passover."

"Passover? No. I'm not waiting six months for you to decide what you
should already know." She storms off down the sidewalk.

"Purim?" I shout after her.

She keeps walking.

"Tu Bishv'at?"

Silence.

"New Year's?"

She stops.

"I mean, the Gregorian one."

She turns around. "Hanukkah. Final offer."

• • •

Saturday flies by way too fast. I wake up and check the clock—6:30—and tell myself I'll sleep another hour. The next time I open my eyes, it's noon, and I panic as I realize my vacation's half over. I spend the rest of the day immersed in quiet activities I hope will keep the sun from setting. I read. I sit on the beach and stare at the waves. Despite my efforts, the sun, with its typical chutzpah, sets. As I watch it sink into the Mediterranean, I get a sick feeling in my stomach—the same sick feeling I'd get in elementary school, on Sunday nights, when the Bears game finished and the sky turned dark and I realized with dread that tomorrow I'd be back in school, my freedom gone.

After sundown, Dorit goes to Bnei Brak to pick up her dad's car. In my apartment, I call my parents in Evanston.

I want my mother to answer the phone. That way, I'll get to speak to each parent separately. If my dad answers, though, then my mom will insist on listening in on the extension, and this will lead to bickering and an awkward conversation where I play referee.

Seven thousand miles away, a phone rings.

"Hello?"

Damn.

"Dad?"

"Joel! Where are you, is everything all right?"

"I'm fine. I'm in Tel Aviv, on leave."

"Who is it?" my mother shouts in the background.

"Joel," says my father. "He's on leave."

"Wait for me!" my mother cries.

"Are you safe? Are you going to Lebanon?" my father says.

"I'm still in basic training, Dad. We don't—"

"Hello!" my mom cuts in. "I'm here! What'd I miss?"

"Nothing, Mom. I was just telling Dad I'm on leave."

"I asked about Lebanon," says my dad.

"I'm sure you'll be safe," says my mom.

"So what are you doing with your free time?" asks my dad.

"Dorit and I might see a movie tonight. *Ice Storm*."

"Kevin Kline's great in that," says my dad.

"I didn't know you saw *Ice Storm*, Ira."

"I didn't, Carol."

"Then how do you know Kevin Kline's good?"

"I read a review."

"So now you believe everything you read?"

"Anyway!" I say.

My youngest brother, Gabe, fills me in on the Cubs and life at his new high school. Then my middle brother, Ari, tells me everything else.

Ari's my opposite in pretty much every way. Whereas Gabe and I look like Chasnoffs—that is, Semites—Ari, with his curly blond hair and light eyes, looks like my mom's father, Grandpa Jim. Psychologically, Ari and I are nothing alike. If life is a train, then I'm the engineer, up front in the locomotive, frantically pushing buttons, pulling levers, keeping it on course. Ari, meanwhile, is camped in a boxcar, feet dangling out the side, curls blowing in the breeze, munching a sandwich. Because Ari's so calm, he's an amazing observer—which is why, whenever I call home, he's my mole.

"So what's the story?" I say.

"Where shall we start?" says Ari.

"Mom and Dad. What's the scoop?"

"Dad's fine."

"And Mom?"

Long pause. "She didn't tell you?"

My stomach goes sick. "No."

"She relapsed."

Shit.

In the thirteen years since my mother was diagnosed with multiple sclerosis, she's been alternately paralyzed, blind, tingly all over, completely numb, too weak to stand, too dizzy to sit, walked with the aid of canes, and confined to a wheelchair. Then, at other times, she's been so functional you'd never guess she was ill. Every time she relapses, I worry it's forever. And each time her symptoms vanish, I hope that this time it's for good. But it never is.

I slump down to the floor, sit with my back to the wall. "What happened?" I groan.

"The heat," Ari says. "It was in the nineties last week. Totally fried her."

"What's she like?"

"Tired. Dizzy."

"Walking?"

"Barely. She's using the canes."

"And Dad?"

"He's going nuts."

"Christ." I lie back, stare at the ceiling. "You know, I don't understand why she doesn't just get a scooter."

"Because the minute she's in a scooter, it's over!" Ari snaps. "It's not about what's easiest for you!"

That's the other way Ari and I are different. He's so goddamn selfless. Drives me nuts. I guess that's why our conversations always leave me hot with shame.

After I hang up the phone, I do something very unsoldierly.

I weep.

I weep for my poor mother. I also weep for myself. I suddenly feel overcome by terror. I'm scared of death. Stray bullets. Hezbollah. Most of all, I'm scared I'll end up in a wheelchair like her.

WALKING MIRACLES

Sunday morning, the platoon meets at Tel Aviv Central Station for the bus ride back to the Armored School. We're glum. Having tasted freedom, we're loath to return to 4 A.M. wake-ups, grouchy commanders, and running back and forth between poles.

But just as we're settling into our seats, Lieutenant Yaron picks up the microphone and greets us with the two most beautiful words a soldier could hear:

Holocaust Museum.

"Yes!" we erupt into a spontaneous cheer. This is awesome news. Three hours at the Yad Vashem Holocaust History Museum in Jerusalem means three less hours of push-ups, wind sprints, and Platoon Sergeant Guy busting our balls. And as if that weren't enough cause for celebration, my buddy Issaschar, who lives in Jerusalem and knows Yad Vashem like the back of his hand, informs us that next to the Walk of the Martyrs there's a coffee shop that sells ice cream.

Yippee!

The ride to Jerusalem is boisterous. We sing, pass around snacks. In the museum parking lot, we meet our tour guide, a cute, redheaded female soldier named Sigal. She explains that she'll lead us on a one-hour tour, after which we'll have an hour to explore the museum on our own and contemplate our feelings about the death of the six million martyrs.

In other words, ice cream.

We line up and follow Sigal onto the museum grounds. The campus is packed with soldiers. Almost all are basic trainees, like us, who've been brought by their officers to Yad Vashem after their first Sabbath leave. The atmosphere reminds me of Spring Fling at Penn. Soldiers stand in clusters, kick a hacky-sack, smoke. On the grass, two navy guys play-wrestle while their buddies egg them on. A paratrooper and his girlfriend, also a soldier, make out with long, slow kisses outside the Hall of Camps.

Inside the museum, it's the usual Platoon Two, Company B shenanigans. While Sigal describes Hitler's rise to power, Gerber pinches Uri in the ass. *"Koos-emok!"* Uri whispers, then he stuns Gerber with a quick knee to the nuts that sends him stumbling into a display case of Zyklon B.

"Bitch!" whispers Gerber.

"Your mother," Uri whispers back.

Doni and Tanenbaum step between them, try to break it up, but only get sucked into the melee. Then Ganz jumps in, then Nir, and suddenly six, seven of them are attacking one another with headlocks and noogies, Three Stooges-style, next to a wall-size photo of Jewish corpses.

My first thought is to scold my platoon mates. *Show some respect!* I want to shout. *For the sake of the six million dead!*

But as I watch my comrades roughhouse, I suddenly have another thought:

This is awesome.

I grew up with so much Holocaust. It started in second grade, when Abby Cohen's grandmother, who survived Auschwitz, visited our class. She told us that her parents were cooked in an oven. Then she rolled up her sleeve and we took turns rubbing her concentration camp tattoo.

A year later, in third grade, Mrs. Gould showed us a slide show of black-and-white photos of naked Jews with their hands in the air. In fourth grade, we watched a film where dead Jews are bulldozed into a pit. It was all very important. And yet—I feel guilty saying this—I got sick of it. Sick of the victimhood, the message that we Jews are cowering weaklings who got gassed, shot, beaten, and burned by pretty much anyone who wanted to.

When I was seventeen, I visited Yad Vashem with my Israel teen tour. My friends and I walked through the museum in silence. We shook our heads. We sobbed. We mumbled the usual phrases.

"How could it happen?"

"Where was the world?"

"Never again!" we promised. Then we boarded our air-conditioned bus and rode back to the hotel.

Three years later, I co-led a six-week Jewish teen tour to Poland and Israel. We visited five concentration camps in seven days. We stood inside gas
chambers, saw the crematoria, the train tracks, the piles of ash. At Birkenau,
we walked the infamous train tracks. My fifteen-year-old campers were a
mess. I was a mess. Some of us cried, and some of us were too stunned to cry.
We sang songs. We scribbled in our journals trying to make sense of it all.
We shook our heads and said, "Never again." It was a passive response, but
we had no other answer.

Then, after a week of this horror, we flew from Warsaw to Israel. We
landed in Tel Aviv at 3 A.M., boarded a bus to Jerusalem, and watched the
sun rise over the Old City from Mount Scopus. With Jerusalem glowing
gold before us, we recited the morning prayers. As we finished our service,
an Israeli Army transport truck pulled into the parking lot beside us. A
team of soldiers jumped out, clipped magazines into their M-16s, and set
off on a foot patrol. And I bawled. All of us did. The minute we saw those
soldiers, each and every one of us broke down into tears. After a week of gas
chambers and ash, these Jewish soldiers were a glorious sight. They repre-
sented redemption and hope. They meant that we Jews had more than our
terrible history; we had a future full of promise. The soldiers were a walking miracle: sixty years after our people were shoved into ovens, we had an
army of our own.

Today, I am one of those walking miracles. Standing here in Yad Vashem
in my olive-green uniform, with my Glilon assault rifle across my back, I
feel absolved of the Holocaust guilt I've been carrying since grade school.
Finally, I don't just have to whisper, "Never again"—I *am* Never Again!
Tomer, Doni, Tanenbaum, Dror Boy Genius, and I and the rest of Platoon
Two, Company B are the walking embodiment of Never Again. Unlike the
Jews in Auschwitz, we can fight. And unlike them, we will not starve. We
have ice cream.

As I watch my platoon mates wrestle, it occurs to me that I am witness-
ing a pivotal moment in Jewish history: not sixty years since Hitler tried
to annihilate us, there are now Jews for whom the concept of victimhood
is so foreign that they can give one another wedgies in a Holocaust museum.

So when Gerber licks his finger and sticks it in Uri's ear, I don't pull them apart and shout, "Stop—for the sake of the martyrs!" Instead, I grab Gerber by his collar, throw my arm around his neck, pinch his nipple, whisper, "Titty twister!"—and then shove him into a picture of the burning Reichstag.

Genocide has never been such fun.

DANIEL AND BERNARD

I'm the third Chasnoff in as many generations to serve in an army.

My dad's father, my Zayde Daniel, was an aircraft gunner in World War II. A month after he married my Bubbie Rose, he shipped off for a thirty-month tour in Okinawa.

A year later, Zayde Daniel's sixteen-year-old nephew, Bernard, lied about his age and enlisted in the 101st Airborne. He was shot down over Austria and held in a German POW camp. For two years, Bernard's Nazi captors starved and beat him. The head Nazi guard took particular delight in torturing Bernard when he found out Bernard was a Jew.

When finally the POW camp was liberated, Bernard raced through the camp in search of the Nazi guard who'd tortured him for being Jewish. Bernard found the guard outside an empty barracks, his arms and legs tied, as he and his fellow SS soldiers awaited interrogation by the Americans. Bernard pulled the guard out of line, marched him to the industrial-sized delousing machine, tossed him inside, hit the "On" switch, and steamed his Nazi captor to death.

After the war, Bernard married my Bubbie Rose's sister, Sylvia. This made Bernard, who was already my dad's cousin, my dad's uncle. And if you work it all out—and I have—it means that I am my own third cousin twice removed.

CAPTAIN BAD NEWS

Probably the nicest guy in Platoon Two, Company B is a dark-skinned kid named Ro'ee Shemesh. Unlike most guys in the platoon, who shout incessantly, curse nonstop, and often behave like animals, Ro'ee is soft-spoken and calm—a peaceful soul. When he talks, I have to lean in close just to hear him. Ro'ee is so nice that he actually *looks* nice—he has smooth, coffee-colored skin, big brown eyes, and long eyelashes that give his face a look of puppy dog sadness. He is, without a doubt, one of the kindest, gentlest, sweetest human beings I have ever met. And we hate him.

Not some of us. Not most of us. All of us. We hate Ro'ee Shemesh. And here's why:

On the first night of basic training, Sergeant Eran asked for a volunteer. Right away, Ro'ee shot his hand into the air. *Now that's a team player!* I thought to myself.

"What's your name?" barked Sergeant Eran.

"Ro'ee Shemesh, Staff Sergeant."

"Mazel tov," said Sergeant Eran. "Tonight, you're in charge of guard duty." He then ordered Ro'ee to compile a guard duty list covering the next twenty-four hours, the idea being that at all times there'd be a guard posted inside the courtyard of the bunk.

You can guess what happened next. Ro'ee did such a stellar job that the next night, Sergeant Eran made him do it again. By night three, the job was permanent—Ro'ee was officially crowned the Platoon Two, Company B Guard Duty Guy. Two days later, when it came time to send a team to the kitchen for a day of kitchen work, Sergeant Eran put Ro'ee in charge of that, too. Every night, poor Ro'ee suffers a routine that goes like this:

9:00 P.M.   Ro'ee Shemesh posts the guard duty list next to the orange pay phone.

9:00:20   We crowd around the guard duty list and check our slots.

9:00:27   Guys who got stuck with bad nighttime slots stomp their feet and curse Ro'ee's mother.

9:00:35   Guys who scored good nighttime slots or, better, didn't get assigned at all tell the guys who got bad slots to shut their mouths and leave Ro'ee alone because he's just doing his job.

9:00:45   Guys who got bad slots curse the mothers of the guys who got good slots or no slots.

9:00:52   Ro'ee Shemesh trudges off to his bedroom without a friend in the world.

Five weeks into basic training, we're sitting in a clump out in the field, waiting our turn at the rifle range, when Ganz asks me, *"Adayin omed lecha?"*

I don't understand the Hebrew.

"You know," says Ganz. He grabs his crotch and then lifts his hand, slowly, as if it's a rising balloon. *"Omed lecha."*

"Erection," says Shimon.

"You mean," I say, "do I still get—"

"Hard. Boners."

"Omed lecha," says Ganz.

It's a damn good question. One phenomenon of army life is the complete absence of erections. No morning wood. No spontaneous afternoon hardons. My debacle in the pup tent aside, I am all flaccid, all the time. And I'm not the only one.

"My dick's AWOL," says Gerber, and we chuckle. "Haven't seen him hard in three weeks."

"Ashkara," says Ganz. "Tell me about it. I wake up and he's lying there, snoring and curled up like a kitten just like he was when I went to sleep."

"How about guard duty?" says Tanenbaum.

The conversation creaks to a halt. Gerber glares at Tanenbaum. "Are you asking me if guard duty makes me hard?" Gerber says.

"No, no," says Tanenbaum, and clicks his tongue. "I'm asking you if you ever . . ." He makes a fist, slides it back and forth.

"You serious?" says Tomer. "During guard duty?"

"You're sick," says Ronen.

"Not in the bunk, you schmuck. During base guard duty. You know—six hours. In the ammunition bunker. Alone . . ."

Three days later, I'm assigned a stint of base guard duty. It's hell. For six hours straight, I do nothing but walk in circles around the perimeter of the Armored School. Then, after each lap, I exit the base, cross the road, and head down the canyon into the ammunition bunker to check the locks on the missile shed. These stints of base guard duty are boring, tedious, and devoid of stimulation.

Until now.

Usually, during these long stretches of guard duty, I entertain myself with mental games. I try to remember every U.S. capital and think up as many cereals as I can name.

But today, for the first time since basic training began, I think about sex. Which, in my case, means thinking not about all the great sex I've ever had, but about all the great sex I haven't.

For as far back as I can remember, I've been uneasy about sex. Part of it was my Jewish day school upbringing, where we learned that sex was a holy act involving husband, wife, and God, and was not to be engaged in outside the confines of marriage. What made it worse was that I was educated about sex by my father. I don't mean that my dad sat me down in the living room and explained the birds and the bees. I mean that my dad was the sex education teacher at my school, and that he taught sex ed to me and my classmates—for four years. Since my Jewish day school didn't have the money to hire a real sex education teacher, my dad, a pediatrician and member of the PTA, offered to teach sex ed for free. My principal, Mrs. Eckstein, loved the idea, and they came up with a plan: once a month, my father would come in on a Tuesday—his day off—and teach the sixth, seventh, and eighth graders for one hour each. I was in second grade when this started, and at that age, I had no idea what was going on. All I knew was that once a month, my dad came to school to talk to the older kids about doctor stuff that I didn't understand.

Now you'd think that when I reached sixth grade, the school would have found someone new to teach the course. Just a year earlier, my friend Stu

Blumberg had switched math classes so he wouldn't have his mom for pre-algebra. So it was logical that the school would find a new health teacher so Joel Chasnoff wouldn't have his dad for sex ed. Otherwise, the poor kid could be messed up for life.

But no.

At first, I liked that my dad taught sex ed. I felt like a celebrity. Everybody knew that was *my dad* at the head of the class. The pretty girls, who normally didn't pay attention to me, suddenly looked at me and whispered. When my dad made a joke, everyone laughed and then looked at me, like I'd said something funny. My dad and I were like a team. And there was nothing embarrassing about what he was saying. That first year, my dad talked about zygotes, recessive traits, and genetic mutations. It was biology, not sex.

Then, in seventh grade, it got awkward.

We filed into the science room for our first class. My dad stood up front, next to the blackboard. He wore a cardigan and khaki pants.

I winked at my dad.

He winked back. Then my father said, "Fuck!"

We gasped.

"Fuck," my dad said again. "Fuck. Fuck. Fuck. There. I said it. Now who else knows a word for sex?"

My classmates and I sat in horrified silence. I slithered down in my seat.

"Come on," said my dad. "You won't get in trouble. Who can tell me a word for sex?"

My friend Seth raised his hand. *"Screw?"* he said sheepishly.

"Excellent," said my father. "No need to raise your hand. Just shout it out. What else?"

"Bang," someone said.

"Very good. Who's next?"

"Nail," someone called.

"Good."

"Pork."

"Nice one.

"Lay."

"Bone."

"Shtup."

"Yiddish—fantastic!" said my dad. "More?"

"Pop the cherry," my friend Jeremy shouted.

"But only when you're married!" my dad said.

The most embarrassing class was the Q&A. To preserve anonymity, we wrote our questions on index cards. One by one, my dad read our questions aloud.

"Is sperm kosher?"

"Does penis size matter?"

"Does the Torah say you can't masturbate?"

This last one made us giggle especially loud. "Quiet down," my father hushed us. "I've got news for you. Are you ready?"

We got quiet.

"Everybody masturbates!" my dad shrieked with glee. My classmates erupted into explosive laughter. Then they turned to look at me.

Now, as I walk in big circles around the Armored School, I think back on all the fun I could've had if only I hadn't been such a good boy. Oh, what I wouldn't give for a sexual time machine, so I could go back and be fifteen again, except with the confidence of a guy who's twenty-four!

But since I can't go back in time, I do the next best thing:

I imagine it.

I picture the caressing. The undressing. Squeezing. Stroking. Quiet moaning, rubbing, nibbling, my heart pounding, and suddenly my mind is a rapid-fire collage of lips and legs and fingers and necks and hands and lace and smooth-shaven thighs and when I can no longer take it I jump into the ditch by the barbed-wire fence and jam my hand beneath my belt and pump until ten knee-buckling seconds later my heart slows and I return to the path along the fence and wonder, paranoid, if there are cameras set up in the ammunition bunker that may have witnessed my foray into the ditch.

HARD-CORE JEWS

Tim Bailey the American and I are on a bus. We're heading north to Tel Aviv for our last Sabbath leave of basic training. I chose a window seat, because I'd planned to sleep the whole ride. But then Tim plopped down next to me, started talking, and doesn't stop. He tells me everything, from his only-child boyhood in Syracuse, to the Boy Scouts ("Hell yeah, I made Eagle Scout!"), the heavy metal band he played in during high school, and his first serious girlfriend, a former Miss Teen Vermont. During college, Tim visited Israel and got hooked on the Israeli Army. "This was, like, two years after my mom told me I was Jewish and I was probably looking for a hero, and the minute I saw the soldiers I just knew I had to be one of them."

Tim divulges his life story in one long, unpunctuated sentence. Getting Tim Bailey to talk is like trying to convince the ocean to make waves.

On his sixteenth birthday, Tim found out he was a Jew. "My mom was a born-again Christian and my dad was a preacher, evangelical, and I was raised hard-core Christian, church camp, Communion, the whole deal, but when I was twelve my parents got divorced and four years later my mom sat me down and told me the truth, that she was born a Jew and had been Jewish when I was born, and since Jewish law says that if the mother's a Jew then the child's a Jew, that meant I was a Jew."

"You must have been shocked," I say.

"It was like finding out I was adopted," says Tim.

After Tim finishes his epic monologue, he turns to me and says, "How about you?"

I give him the short version: born in Chicago, married parents, two brothers, Jewish day school, kosher home, Jewish summer camps, five Israel trips by the time I'd finished college.

"Hard-core Jew," he says.

I shrug.

For a few minutes, I watch the desert, flat and brown, roll past the window. Then Tim asks me the strangest question I've ever been asked in my life:

"So both your parents were born Jewish?"

I could understand why a person would want to know if both my parents were Jewish. But *born* Jewish? Only a confused young man undergoing a major crisis of identity could think to ask such a bizarre question. And only an equally confused young man grappling with his own identity crisis would be so ashamed to answer.

I stare out the window. Who is this Tim Bailey guy that I've known all of one hour and already he's hit on my biggest secret? And who does he think he is that I'd tell him the truth when some of my closest friends in the world still don't know?

But for some reason—and maybe it's because I've only known him an hour and there's no history between us—I decide to come clean.

"My dad was born Jewish," I say. "But my mother converted."

"Oh," says Tim.

"She was twenty. It was before she met my dad."

"Okay."

"Her conversion was Orthodox."

Tim nods.

"Nobody knows," I say.

"Who would I tell?" says Tim.

It's true—who would Tim Bailey tell? But I can't risk it. I've spent my whole life burying this secret because I'm afraid of what people will assume: that my mother converted to satisfy the in-laws, that it was a shotgun conversion done to appease my father, the result of arm twisting and relentless pressure to raise the kids in a single-religion home, and that, consequently, my mother is a Jew on paper but not the real thing.

She was an only child, raised Protestant in Berwyn, Illinois, a blue-collar neighborhood west of Chicago. Her mother, my Gramma Ruth, is the daughter of Scotch-Irish immigrants and the niece of the Honorable William Dever, twenty-third mayor of Chicago, who notoriously drove Al Capone out of town. My mom's father, Jim, was a machinist who enjoyed bowling, cigarettes, and Stroh's Lite. When my mom was sixteen, her parents split. In college, my mother discovered Judaism and initiated a conversion. After three years of rigorous study, she dunked in the Jewish ritual bath known as a mikveh and received a new Hebrew name, *Leah bat Avra-ham Avinu*—Leah, Daughter of Abraham our Forefather.

I've always felt queasy about my mother's Hebrew name. The second part, "Daughter of Abraham our Forefather," is a dead giveaway that she's a convert. So in synagogue, when I stand for the Prayer for the Sick and recite my mother's name aloud, I say "Leah, Daughter of Ruth" instead. Who cares if the Ruth in question comes from Ireland, County Donegal?

My mother's conversion was Orthodox. Did I mention that, that it was Orthodox? I make such a point of it because I can't allow my identity to be disputed. I want Tim to know that my mother's conversion was the most stringent kind, that every *i* had been dotted, every *t* crossed. I want him to know that my mother is an absolutely legitimate Jew and that I, by extension, am equally legitimate.

I know my mom's conversion was Orthodox because I checked. Freshman year of college, when I told my then-girlfriend, Annie, that my mother had converted, Annie asked if the conversion was Orthodox. "Of course," I said, though in truth I had no clue. It hadn't occurred to me there might be different categories. I assumed a conversion was a conversion and that was that.

On my next visit home, I told my mother I wanted to see her conversion certificate. "My conversion was Orthodox," my mother said.

I told her I wanted to be sure.

She led me to a black file cabinet in the basement. In the top drawer, under a sheaf of old insurance bills, was an envelope labeled "CONV."

I pulled out the yellowing certificate. At the bottom were two signatures—my mother's and the rabbi's—and a fading blue stamp that read "Union of Orthodox Rabbis, San Antonio, Texas."

"Happy?" my mother said, her eyes welling with tears.

The other reason I don't tell people my mother converted is that I forget. Seriously—the same way a transgender person feels like a woman trapped in a man's body, I think of my mother as a Jew trapped in the body of a Gentile. My mom is the most religious Jew in our family, often to the chagrin of my father. It is she, not my dad, who forbids television on Friday nights and insists that on Sabbaths and holidays, we recite the twenty-minute Grace After Meals. My mother observes the kashrut dietary laws more rigorously than the rest of us—she waits four hours between eating meat and milk; my brothers and I wait three hours, my dad thirty to forty-five minutes. And it was Mom who decided that if I was going to attend public high school, I had to agree to take Confirmation courses at the synagogue, even if it meant missing a play rehearsal during Tech Week. After a lifetime of my mother's blessings, Yiddish expressions, and Jewish guilt, it is literally incomprehensible to me that she's ever been anything but a full-fledged Jew.

The only time I ever got a glimpse of my mother's old self was on Sundays.

Sundays, we lived like Gentiles. While my Jewish friends ate lox and bagels with their grandparents at the Jewish Home for the Aged, my family ate brunch with Gramma Ruth and her husband, Stan, at the most Gentile restaurant on the planet, a steakhouse called The Flame. Everything about The Flame freaked me out: the lobster tank by the front door, the elderly man in the tuxedo playing piano, the noxious smell of sizzling bacon. Then we'd visit Grandpa Jim in La Grange, where he lived in a trailer park off Interstate 55, and watch the Bears or Cubs while Grandpa Jim drank Stroh's from the can.

What amazes me is not just my mother's absolute commitment to Judaism, but the way my grandparents completely supported her choice. Grandpa Jim just wanted his only daughter to be happy. And after twenty-five years of Sabbath dinners and Hanukkah songs, Gramma Ruth is an honorary Jew. On Thanksgiving, she cooks kosher turkey. At the Passover table, she reads aloud about how we Jews are God's chosen people and doesn't even seem to take offense. Gramma Ruth's open-mindedness is all the more remarkable because, when it comes to ethnicity, she's a tad old-fashioned. I wouldn't go so far as to call Gramma Ruth racist, because she doesn't judge people by race. It's more like she categorizes everybody and uses the familiar slurs: Polish are Polacks, Italians are Wops, African-Americans are Colored. And Jews? I don't know what she used to call them, but now she calls them "grandkids."

"So we're both here for the same reason," says Tim.

"And what's that?" I say.

"To erase the doubts."

I laugh. "Doubts? No. I know who I am, Tim. I don't have any doubts."

But this is a lie. The truth is, I sometimes wonder how a convert—or the son of a convert, like me—can possibly be a Jew. So much about being Jewish is our history. We are defined by the three-thousand-year story of our people—the exodus from Egypt, the building and destruction of two temples, the horrors of the Holocaust, and the birth of the state of Israel. Our history makes us Jews who we are. Can a person dunk himself in water and just like that claim three thousand years of history as his own?

When I experience doubt, I remind myself that half my family was present for the story—even if it's not the half that Jewish law counts. And I remind myself that King David himself was the grandson of a convert. His grandmother, also named Ruth, converted as an adult. Since Jews call the Messiah *Moshiach Ben-David*—Messiah, Son of David—that means I'm in pretty good company. If conversion's good enough for the Messiah, Son of David, shouldn't it be good enough for me?

THE 188TH CRYBABY BRIGADE

Every night, before lights out, we line up in formation in the courtyard.

Except tonight. Tonight, six weeks into basic, Lieutenant Yaron orders evening roll call outside the infirmary.

"Anybody like to guess why we're standing outside the infirmary?" says Lieutenant Yaron.

We all know why. But no one wants to say.

"We're standing here because, as of tonight, there are twenty-three soldiers from this platoon inside the infirmary, including"—he pulls a folded paper from his breast pocket—"five soldiers with bad backs, three with fevers, six sprained ankles, two headaches, four stomachaches, two twisted knees, and one soldier who's too dizzy to stand." He crumples the list and stuffs it in his pocket. "In addition to those twenty-three, we have a number of soldiers right here, in this formation, who have medical excuses exempting them from physical activity of any kind. Please raise your hand if you have a medical excuse."

Ten hands go up.

"That means that of the fifty-nine soldiers in this platoon, thirty-three—more than half—cannot move, work, or fight. So my question is this: who are you? Are you a platoon of Israel Defense Forces combat soldiers? Or is this Platoon Two, Company B of the One Hundred Eighty-eighth Crybaby Brigade?"

Lately, I've been asking myself the same question. I joined up thinking I'd be the runt in a platoon of Israeli he-men. Instead, I'm one of the rare warriors in a platoon of wimps.

As platoon scribe, I'm on top of every one of my platoon mates' ailments. And I'm astounded by how far they'll go to get out of guard duty, punishments, and physical labor.

Some of my comrades' injuries are legit, but most are exaggerated or outright fakes. It's the same guys over and over who are supposedly hurt; only the injuries change. On any given Wednesday—the night we hike into the desert for a grueling forced march—there's a sudden uptick in the number of bum knees, twisted ankles, and other waist-down ailments. Monday, the day we send guys to the kitchen, everybody suddenly has cuts on his fingers and hands—grounds for immediate disqualification for handling food.

My platoon mates' favorite ailment is diarrhea. Diarrhea is the Israeli Army Get Out of Jail Free card. A soldier with diarrhea can't do kitchen work because he could contaminate the entire base. He can't be punished with wind sprints or push-ups because he might dehydrate. He can't stand guard because if he has an emergency, he'd have to abandon his post for the latrine. Diarrhea is also impossible to verify. No thermometers, no need for a fake limp. Short of following a guy into the john, there's no way to know if he's really got the runs or just pulling a fast one. But here's how I know they're faking it. One morning, right before morning inspection, I dash into the bathroom to make sure it's been mopped. There, on the supply shelf, is the same package of twelve rolls of toilet paper, still in the plastic wrap, just as it was three days ago. Which means we're not using more TP than usual.

Slackers.

It's to the point where our platoon now consists of two subplatoons—the *Bri'im,* or Healthy Guys, and the *P'tornikim,* the Medical Excuse Guys. Now, when Ro'ee Shemesh needs someone to guard or work in the kitchen, the first question he asks is, *"Ata bari oh p'tornik?"* Are you a Healthy Guy or a Medical Excuse Guy?

My friend Liran, whose twin brother is a paratrooper, assures me this kind of kvetching isn't unique to Armored. "The difference," Liran explains, "is that when you bitch and whine in the Paratroopers, they kick you out, because you're useless, and there are too many other guys eager to take your place." Here in Armored, meanwhile, we can cry all we want and we still get to stay, because it's unlikely that our injuries would stop us from doing our job. As Liran puts it, "My ninety-year-old grandmother could ride around in a tank."

What Lieutenant Yaron doesn't understand is that we Healthy Guys despise the Medical Excuse Guys as much as he does. With half the platoon disabled, the rest of us guard twice as much, sleep half as much, and do twice the amount of kitchen work. At night, when we're punished with wind sprints, the Medical Excuse Guys stand to the side and root us on like cheerleaders. What's worse is that after every hike, our commanders give us some kind of token that we "earned" by hiking—after our first hike, we received the brigade shoulder tag, the next week it was the Armored Corps medallion for our berets—and the Medical Excuse Guys have the gall to take these tokens and wear them as if they'd earned them like the rest of us.

This medical excuse nonsense disturbs me on another level: it contradicts the image I grew up with of the valiant Israeli soldier. Where did those hero soldiers go? And what happened to the army I idolized as a kid?

Actually, I know what happened to that army. That story started on February 4, 1997, in a tragedy known in Israel as *Ason Ha-masokim*—the Helicopter Disaster.

Around 8 P.M. two Israeli Army transport helicopters collided over Lebanon, killing all seventy-three soldiers on board. The ensuing investigation revealed disturbing details. The two pilots, it turned out, had shut off their lights prior to landing—a common practice, to avoid being seen by Hezbollah, but in this case, the cause of the crash. Investigators also found that the pilots hadn't trained on this kind of helicopter for several months, nor had they performed a maintenance check or filed the proper preflight paperwork.

For the first time in its storied history, the Israeli Army had been knocked off its pedestal. Until then, the army was untouchable. The media and civilians alike gave the military a free pass, assuming that whatever the army had to do to keep the country safe, it should do. Now, suddenly, journalists demanded access to classified information. Families of soldiers—which, since everyone in Israel serves, means just about everybody—demanded accountability. Parents wanted a promise that if they were going to hand over their sons and daughters for three years, in return the army would not be careless with their lives. And it didn't stop with safer helicopter rides. These weren't just mothers making demands, these were Jewish mothers—they wanted to know that their children were sleeping enough, eating well, and could see a doctor if they got injured or sick.

So the Israeli Army did what anyone faced with an onslaught of Jewish mothers would do: they caved. They had no choice, really—without parents' support, the army couldn't draft the soldiers it needed and the military would fall apart.

To appease parents and boost morale among current and future soldiers, the army adopted a series of new policies that formed what I like to call Operation Friendly Army. Some of these new regulations were logical and long overdue—for example, the rule requiring that soldiers have access to military psychologists on demand, and that soldiers get seven hours of sleep the night before a Sabbath leave, so they'll be awake enough to drive when they go out on Friday night. Other rules backfired when soldiers began to take advantage of them—such as the rule stating that soldiers with injuries are issued a medical exemption from physical activities. It's a good idea, but here in Platoon Two, Company B, my comrades abuse it.

And then there are the policies that are so downright embarrassing that I shake my head in shame—like the 10/4 Snack Rule. Twice a day, every day, at 10 A.M. and 4 P.M., we stop what we're doing, sit in a big circle, and eat a snack. Some days snack is bananas. Most days it's white bread and chocolate spread. A couple weeks ago, during survival training, we were practicing the Indian crawl, panting and sweating as we slithered on our bellies in the sand, when, suddenly, Lieutenant Yaron stopped the exercise so we could eat snack. We sat in a circle, in full combat gear, and munched chocolate sandwiches. Just like kindergarten.

But Operation Friendly Army is about more than just policy. Underlying the change is a fundamental divide in the way different generations of Israelis view the army.

I got my first taste of this generational divide the day I landed in Israel. I was in a taxi on my way to Dorit's parents' apartment when I passed a giant billboard with a picture of two smiling soldiers with their arms around each other. The soldiers looked fresh from the fight—helmets on heads, faces painted in camouflage. Across the top of the billboard, in giant Hebrew letters, was the phrase, *"Kravi—zeh ha-chi, Achi!"*—a cute rhyming slogan that means "Combat—it's like no other, brother!"

I was miffed. Why had the mighty Israeli Army taken to advertising?

I asked the taxi driver, an older man with weathered skin, about the sign. He wrinkled his face into a scowl. "Spoiled brats," he rasped. "Nobody wants to serve."

"But don't they have to?" I asked.

"Of course they have to. But they want desk jobs so they can sleep at home with their mommies. So the army put up these signs to convince them to go combat."

I was stunned. Having been raised on the narrative of the gung-ho Israeli soldier, I wondered what had happened to Israeli teenagers that so many of them didn't want combat. As it turns out, I didn't have to look any further than Dorit's family.

During those early weeks in Israel, when I lived with Dorit's parents and twenty-year-old brother in their apartment, I got a close-up look at this new anti-army phenomenon. Dorit's family was like a microcosm of the argument playing out in Israeli society. On the one side, there was Dorit's father, Menashe. He's sixty years old and a veteran of every Israeli war since the Sinai Campaign of '56, which he fought in when he was nineteen. On the other side was Dorit's brother Alon, a punky-looking twenty-year-old with an eyebrow ring, black fingernail polish, and a ponytail. On his first trip to the IDF Induction Center, Alon brought along a dove. "I believe in peace," he told the draft officer. The officer didn't buy it. On his next visit, Alon declared that if the army gave him a rifle, he'd shoot himself in the head. He never heard from the army again.

Menashe and Alon begin to argue at the same time each day—4:20 in the afternoon, the moment Menashe comes home from work and finds Alon camped out in front of the television, a Fender guitar across his lap and a cigarette in his hand. The trouble starts when Menashe picks up the remote and flicks off the TV.

"What's your problem?" Alon gripes.

"My problem?" Menashe shrieks. "You mean, *your* problem! You do nothing!"

"I had rehearsal!" Alon shouts.

"For what?" shouts Menashe. "Your band?" Then he turns to his wife, Tzionah, who's dicing cucumbers in the kitchen. "Your son thinks he's goddamn Aviv Geffen."

"God forbid," Tzionah cries.

Aviv Geffen is an Israeli rock star who refused to serve in the army—the first Israeli celebrity to do so. With lyrics like "It's time we bury the guns / Instead of our boys," he's an outspoken critic of the military. Depending on who you ask, Geffen is either the icon for a new generation of young, open-minded Israelis or the poster child for a new wave of self-centered brats who put themselves ahead of their country.

Menashe picks up Alon's ashtray, overflowing with butts. "This is what happens when you don't go to the army."

"My dick on the army," Alon says, and storms off to his room.

"God forbid," Tzionah wails.

"When I was your age, I'd already fought in a war!" Menashe calls after him.

"I'll serve when the Black Hats serve," Alon cries and slams his door.

The Black Hats, as Alon calls them, are Israeli Ultra-Orthodox Jews who dress all in black and are excused from military service by virtue of religious exemptions negotiated by the small, but disproportionately powerful, religious minority in Israeli government. These religious exemptions are a huge point of contention among secular Israelis.

"The Black Hats serve God!" Menashe shouts.

"My ass," says Alon through his door.

"They serve Torah!" Menashe shouts, shaking his fist.

"My dick on the Torah!" Alon screams.

"God forbid!" Tzionah wails, clutching a chair and close to fainting.

"I fought in four wars!" Menashe shouts.

"Good for you!"

"With no army, there's no Israel!"

Alon flings open the door and steps into the living room. His shirt's off, and he's smoking a cigarette. "What do you want, old man?" he says. "That I kill kids?"

"God forbid!" Tzionah cries from the kitchen.

"Or maybe you want a dead son?" shouts Alon.

I sat quietly in the kitchen and observed these dramas day after day—and I quickly realized the issue wasn't the army. Instead, it was an issue of two Israels.

In Menashe's Israel, the army is the only thing stopping the Arabs from driving the country into the sea. Menashe's Israel is black-and-white: the Arabs always have and always will hate us, and the intifada is just the latest incarnation of the same war Menashe began fighting when he was nineteen.

In Alon's Israel, the Israeli Army isn't the solution, it's the problem. The only war Alon knows is the intifada—a war that in no way threatens to wipe Israel off the map. Alon sees Israeli soldiers not as protectors of Israel, but as policemen who chase Palestinian teenagers armed with nothing but rocks. To Alon, the Palestinian-Israeli conflict is a political problem that requires a political solution and most certainly isn't a war worth sacrificing your life for.

One evening, after I'd been in Israel about a week, I walked with Alon to the grocery store. Along the way, we passed a bus stop crowded with soldiers. I looked at the soldiers, then at Alon. "You ever have regrets?" I asked.

"Not one," he replied.

"Never?" I said. "Be honest, Alon—don't you ever look at soldiers and feel guilty?"

Alon took a long drag on his cigarette. "This country doesn't need another soldier," he said. "We've got too many as it is. Our prime ministers are all ex-generals—"

"But that's good!" I cut in. "It means they know how to keep Israel safe."

"It means every problem they see, they try to solve it like a general." For a few minutes, we walked in silence. Then Alon said, "You know when Israel will finally have peace?"

I shook my head.

"When we elect a prime minister who never served in the army."

Sometimes, when I'm sitting out in the sun, enjoying my chocolate sandwich, I think about the old Groucho Marx expression, the one where he says he wouldn't want to join any club that would have him as a member. I feel the same way about armies—I wouldn't want to join any military where I was one of the strongest soldiers in the platoon. Yet that's exactly what's happened. With so many Medical Excuse Guys crying their way out of exercises and drills, I'm left as one of the strong ones. This worries me. Because if the skinny, lactose-intolerant Jew from the suburbs is the strongest soldier in your platoon, how safe can Israel be?

SONS

The first time I heard about Lebanon I was nine. I was in Israel on a two-week trip with my father. He'd been invited to speak at a medical conference in Jerusalem, and he somehow convinced my mother to let me tag along. I don't remember much from that trip. I recall my mother bawling in the airport, and that once I got to Israel I wore my yarmulke everywhere, because to me, that's what Israel was—one big synagogue.

What I remember most was my first Sabbath dinner in Jerusalem. My dad's friend, who was also a doctor, had invited us to her apartment outside the Old City. My dad and I walked from our hotel. It was a quiet walk. My dad and I held hands the whole time. We strolled past apartment buildings made of tan stone and cars parked on the sidewalk. As we walked, my dad explained that his friend and her husband had two sons but that one of them was a soldier who recently died in a war. Her other son, who was also a soldier, might join us for dinner if he could get permission to leave the army.

My dad's friend was named Hannah. She had curly brown hair and big glasses. Her husband, Sol, had gray hair and a yarmulke and looked like a rabbi. Their apartment was filled with books. On one of the bookshelves was a picture of a soldier. He was smiling. I stared at the picture for a long time.

That's my son, said Hannah.

I asked her if it was her son who was dead or the son who was alive. Hannah shook her head and didn't answer.

During dinner, Hannah told my dad that her son had died in a place called Lebanon. She said sometimes she woke up in the middle of the night and walked to her dead son's bedroom to see if maybe he was in bed and she'd just been dreaming. The whole time they talked, I pushed my food around with my fork. I'd been hungry when we came, but when Hannah talked about her dead son it made my stomach hurt.

While the grown-ups drank tea, a soldier walked into the apartment.

He had a gun. It was Hannah's other son. He had red hair, a red beard, and a yarmulke. The son hugged his parents and shook my dad's hand. I felt scared. I'd never been in a room with someone who had a gun. The son put his gun on the couch and then sat at the table. He asked me my name and told me his, but I didn't hear him because I was frightened of his gun.

When my dad and I got up to leave, my dad asked if he could take a picture of the woman's son and me.

It's the Sabbath, said the woman.

Come on, Mom, said her son. She shrugged her shoulders and said, Why not? My father laughed.

The son picked up his gun and crouched next to the sofa. I stood next to him. He put his arm around me. I held part of his gun. Even though my stomach hurt, I made myself smile.

At the front door, Hannah knelt down and hugged me very tight. When she let go, I could see she was crying.

As we walked back to our hotel, I asked my dad why Hannah cried when she hugged me.

My dad said, I think it's because you remind her of her son.

THE ARMORED CORPS
SING-ALONG JAMBOREE

Week Seven is Education Week. Instead of the usual drills at the Armored School, we deploy to an Education Corps base in the Galilee called Camp Yigal Alon. As Lieutenant Yaron explains it, Education Week has two purposes. First, to give us a relaxing, laid-back week after a tough month and a half of basic training. And second—to teach us about Hezbollah, Islamic Jihad, Hamas, the Syrians, and other Arabs who hate us, which makes me think this week might not be all that relaxing.

We begin with a walking tour of the Israeli-Syrian border in the Golan Heights.

I'm standing on a windy hilltop overlooking Syria. Lieutenant Yaron is pointing out the names of Syrian mountains when suddenly I notice a series of long, parallel trenches dug into the Syrian terrain. I walk up to Platoon Sergeant Guy and ask, in English, what they are.

"Antitank trenches," he says. "The Syrians dug those ditches to stop our tanks."

This makes me chuckle. "Wait a sec. You're telling me we've got the best tank in the world, and all it takes to stop it is a ditch?"

"Yep." Then the platoon sergeant turns me around and points at the Israeli landscape. Everywhere, through the entire Golan Heights, are the same long, parallel ditches I saw on the Syrian side. "We've got them, too."

"Let me get this straight," I say. "Syria has trenches to stop our tanks. And we have trenches to stop their tanks?"

"Exactly."

"Do they know about our ditches?"

"Of course. And they know we know about theirs, and they know we know they know about ours."

I mull that over. "So what's the point?" I say.

Platoon Sergeant Guy laughs. "It's a game. If there's a war, our tanks advance into Syria and their tanks advance into Israel. But the trenches slow everyone down. So to advance our tanks, we send combat engineers to build bridges across their trenches. Meanwhile, they send their combat engineers to build bridges across our trenches. So then we bomb their tanks and combat engineers with our artillery, and they bomb ours with their artillery. Which is why . . ."

He stops mid-sentence.

"Why what?" I say.

"I'm not sure you want to know this, Yoel."

"Tell me."

"It's why tank soldiers have the shortest life expectancy of any soldier in the army."

"How long?"

"Seventeen minutes."

"What?" I shriek.

The platoon sergeant nods.

"So if there's a war, from the moment that war starts I can expect to live seventeen minutes?"

"On average," he says.

"But I could live longer."

"Sure. Maybe you'll get lucky. You could live twice as long."

"Thirty-four minutes."

"Or, if you're *really* lucky, you might last an hour."

I let the information sink in. Then I have a thought. "How about Infantry? They've gotta be less than us. They're exposed."

Platoon Sergeant Guy shakes his head. "Infantry are always the last ones in. So they live longer."

"How long?"

"Eighty-six minutes."

"Graybeards," I say.

"Think of it this way," the platoon sergeant says. "If there's a war, we'll win that war with our air force. But the air force needs an hour to mobilize. We tank soldiers give them that hour."

"So we're tripwire."

"Basically. And on average, that tripwire lasts seventeen minutes."

Huh.

• • •

After lunch at a kibbutz, we return to Camp Yigal Alon for an afternoon of lectures and films about Lebanon.

Unlike the situation with Syria, which is precarious but probably won't lead to war, it's a pretty safe bet my platoon mates and I will at some point deploy to Lebanon. Because the fighting in Gaza and the West Bank takes place in urban areas and residential neighborhoods, infantry soldiers are ideal for those conflicts. Lebanon, meanwhile, with its wide-open spaces and hilly terrain, is better suited to a combination of foot soldiers and tanks.

As for when we'll deploy—that's still up in the air. Every four months, the 188th Armored Brigade rotates a fresh battalion into the Security Zone. The next scheduled rotation is in two months, in early November. If our battalion, the 71st, is next to deploy, my platoon will miss the entire tour because we'll still be in training. After that, we wouldn't deploy for another year, by which time I'll be out of the army. But if the 74th Battalion deploys next, then ours will deploy in March, at the exact time my platoon mates and I finish advanced warfare training in the Golan Heights—in which case we could go straight into combat against Hezbollah.

As for why we're in Lebanon in the first place, that's the point of today's lecture.

Our classroom looks like the kind in a typical high school—rows of wooden desks, a chalkboard, a TV/VCR cart in the back corner. The one difference is the weapons: on a table next to the blackboard is a handsomely curated collection of Kalashnikov rifles, magazines, rocket-propelled grenades, and shoulder-launched antitank missiles confiscated from Hezbollah, Hamas, Islamic Jihad, and their various factions.

Our guest lecturer is an intelligence officer named Captain Aryeh. He's scrawny, with wire-framed glasses and a pointy Adam's apple. He looks like the kind of officer who knows every date, fact, and dirty detail of every Israeli war. As it turns out, he is. I can barely keep up as he dances through the twenty years of Lebanese history that explain how Israel wound up there. According to Captain Aryeh, it all goes back to the 1975 Lebanese Civil War. At that point, the situation in Lebanon was this:

The Shiites hated the Maronites. The Maronites hated the Nasserites and Amalites. The Sunnis joined the Shiites, Nasserites, and Amalites against the Maronites, because the one thing Sunnis hated more than Shiites were Christians.

In '78, the Palestine Liberation Organization, who'd been attacking Israel from Jordan, tried, but failed, to overthrow Jordan's King Hussein. The PLO fled to Lebanon, and since they're Sunni, they joined the Shiites, Nasserites, and Amalites against the Maronites and proceeded to terrorize Israel from Lebanon. To stop the PLO, Israel invaded Lebanon in June 1982 in Operation Peace to the Galilee and teamed up with the Maronites, who were Christians, against the PLO and the Sunnis, Shiites, Nasserites, and Amalites. Israel marched all the way to Beirut, seven hundred Israeli soldiers died, the PLO fled to Tunis, no more PLO in Lebanon—end of story.

Except that while Israel was busy chasing the PLO, a new Iranian-funded, Syrian-backed, Soviet-armed Shiite resistance militia called Hezbollah was born. Their goal was to oust Israel from Lebanon and—as stated in their charter—wipe Israel off the map, which they attempted to do with attacks on Israeli soldiers in Lebanon and suicide bombers and Katyusha rocket attacks across the border in northern Israel. So even though the PLO was gone, Israel was stuck in Lebanon fighting its new enemy, Hezbollah.

"In other words," says Captain Aryeh, "Israel came to the dance with one date and went to bed with another."

In '85, Israel withdrew from Lebanon, staying only in a six- to fifteen-mile-deep buffer area called the Security Zone, which Israel occupied to keep Hezbollah rockets beyond firing range and stop Hezbollah guerrillas from crossing into Israel. The northern border of the Security Zone is called the Blue Line and the southern border is the Red Line, neither of which is to be confused with the Purple Line (the Israeli border with Syria), the Green Line (the original pre-1967 Israeli border with Jordan), or the other Green Line (the dividing line between Muslim and Christian Beirut in the 1975 civil war that began this whole mess). Currently, Israel maintains a force of several hundred soldiers in the Security Zone to fight its war of attrition against Hezbollah. It is this war that awaits Tomer, Doni, Dror Boy Genius, and the rest of my Platoon Two, Company B comrades—and myself.

The longer I listen to Captain Aryeh, the more difficult it gets to keep track of the warring factions. So to simplify it, I draw a diagram:

BACKGROUND: ISRAELI INVOLVEMENT IN LEBANON

Captain Aryeh follows his history lesson with a lecture on the current state of Hezbollah. Over the course of an hour, he debunks everything I'd previously thought about our enemy in Lebanon, from the weapons they carry to the clothes on their backs.

"Tell me what you know about Hezbollah," Captain Aryeh calls out.

They're guerrillas, we say. Ragtag freedom fighters who wear T-shirts and jeans.

"And how does Hezbollah stack up against the Merkava tank?" he asks.

No match, we say. The Merkava's armor is impenetrable. Weighs sixty-five tons and hits speeds of sixty kilometers an hour. Hezbollah has nothing on us.

"And how much does each Merkava tank cost to manufacture?" he asks.

None of us knows.

"Five million dollars," says Captain Aryeh. "Each."

Next, Captain Aryeh walks to the blackboard and picks up a piece of chalk. On one side of the board, he writes the Hebrew word *mytos*—"myth." On the other side, he writes *u'vda*—"fact."

"Myth number one," says Captain Aryeh. "Hezbollah is nothing but a bunch of ragtag freedom fighters who wear T-shirts and jeans. Fact: man for man, Hezbollah has better uniforms and equipment than the average Israeli soldier. Anyone know why?"

We're too shocked to raise our hands.

"One reason," Captain Aryeh says. He rubs his thumb and fingers together. "Cash. There is no limit to Hezbollah's coffers. Iran and Syria are all too happy to pay Hezbollah to do their dirty work against Israel, and the Russians are happy to sell off old armaments cheap."

We sit quietly while Captain Aryeh writes the word MERKAVA on the chalkboard. "Myth number two," he says. "The Merkava battle tank is impenetrable. Fact: Hezbollah's number one priority is to destroy a Merkava. It would be the ultimate symbol of victory against Israel and the West. To achieve their goal, Hezbollah has taken an academic approach to the Merkava. They study photographs and film of the tank, and they've discovered a few tiny but potent weak spots in the tank's structure. To put it bluntly—Hezbollah knows more about the Merkava than the average Israeli tank soldier."

By this point in the lecture, I feel sick.

"I've got one last question for you," says Captain Aryeh. "Who started Hezbollah?"

Iran, we say. Syria. The Iraqis, the Jordanians, the Lebanese.

"You're all correct," Captain Aryeh cuts us off. "But you left one out. Israel."

We stare at him in quiet disbelief.

"In the early eighties, the Israeli government supported the idea of a homegrown, Shiite militia in Lebanon that would rival the PLO. That guerrilla militia turned into the enemy we're fighting today—Hezbollah."

We sit in silence. I wonder to myself if there's a word for what happens when insanity becomes more insane.

"Now, if anyone has questions," says Captain Aryeh, "I'll try to—"

"When do we find out if we're going?" someone shouts.

"How long will we go for?"

"What will we do there?"

"What's it like?"

And on and on, our questions come gushing out like water through a busted dam.

"Do you think we'll deploy?"

"Do you think we'll be safe?"

"In the last year, how many tank soldiers died?"

"Platoon Two!" shouts a voice from the back. We hush. From his seat in the corner, our officer, Lieutenant Yaron, stands and walks to the head of the class. He takes off his rifle and places it on the table beside him. Then he looks at us with an expression of genuine compassion.

"Platoon Two," he says in a voice just above a whisper. "I understand you're nervous. And maybe scared. But Captain Aryeh is not God and neither am I. We can't promise you'll be safe, and we can't promise you'll come back alive. But I will promise you this: if you do go to Lebanon, you will go only after you've been thoroughly trained. The Israeli Army doesn't play dice with your lives."

The classroom is quiet. A bird chirps outside. Then, all of a sudden, Lieutenant Yaron breaks into a smile. "Captain Aryeh just delivered some difficult news," he says. "But now I'll share some good news. I recently spoke to a friend of mine who's a tank commander in Lebanon. He tells me that the way things are now, seven infantry soldiers die for every tank soldier."

You know it's a shitty place when this is considered good news.

• • •

After our Lebanon briefing, I sit outside on the grass. It's evening, chilly, and I feel ill. It's starting to hit me that there are men in the world who want to kill me. These men don't know a thing about me. They don't care that I grew up in Chicago or that I've lived in Israel for less than three months. All they know is that because of the uniform I wear, I am on the other side— and for that, they're eager to end my life.

One thing that nags at me about Lebanon is that I can't picture it. I've witnessed traffic accidents and house fires, but I've never been in an ambush or seen a firefight. I can picture the consequences of a firefight. That's easy, and I do it often: I see myself in a wheelchair like my mother's, and I wear baggy blue jeans and perfectly clean white sneakers—clean because I never walk. But what I can't picture is the firefight itself.

Now, sitting underneath this tree less than fifty miles from the Lebanese border, I imagine what a Hezbollah guerrilla looks like. When I hear the word *guerrilla,* I think of the word *gorilla*—so that's how I picture him: like a gorilla, tall and hairy, with a black beard, gnashing white teeth, and bloodshot eyes. But he's a person. A man. With a nose, lips, eyelashes, ears.

I wonder if I'm going to kill one. I wonder where he is now. I mean, right now, this very moment—where is he? What are you doing, Hezbollah guerrilla that I'm going to kill? Are you eating supper? Taking a piss? Do you know that I'm out there, and that one day I will end your life?

Or he could just as well kill me.

How very strange, that the person who might end my life is out there, right now, engaged in some activity that will lead to another activity, and all those activities will eventually lead to the activity of killing me. How odd that for the past twenty years, we've been living these parallel lives, but that soon our lives will cross and one of us will end the other's for good.

After dinner, the entire company, Platoons One, Two, and Three, gathers in the base auditorium for a lighthearted evening activity called the Armored Corps Sing-Along Jamboree.

It's your typical summer camp–style sing-along. Our commanders pass out song sheets. Our company commander, a tall, beady-eyed officer named Captain Lior, teaches the words. We learn half a dozen songs, each extolling the glory of the Armored Corps, and each with incredibly cheesy lyrics, such as

> *Joyous is the tank crew*
> *We are brothers, one and all*
> *In our chariot, the Merkava,*
> *We heed the battle's call.*

(FROM *ARMORED LEADS THE WAY*)

and

> *We conquer every hilltop*
> *We triumph in the valley*
> *The Hundred Eighty-eighth Brigade is like no other.*
> *We are fearless, full of might*
> *We are not afraid to fight*
> *But we never shoot at children or their mothers.*

(FROM *THE 188TH ARMORED BRIGADE ANTHEM*)

Tim and I are certain the evening will be a flop. We're Israeli combat soldiers. We carry assault rifles. We throw grenades. We're way too cool for some hokey sing-along.

But our eighteen-year-old comrades eat it up. They clap their hands, stomp their feet, and sing at the top of their lungs. When Captain Lior shouts, "I can't hear you, Company B!" my company mates scream louder. From the way my comrades belt it out, you'd think they were trying to defeat Hezbollah by frightening them away with really loud singing.

In fact, the only two soldiers who don't sing like a bunch of loudmouth lunatics are Tim and me. Instead, we sit in the back row with our mouths open, flabbergasted, that this is the legendary Israeli Army—the baddest, cleverest, toughest army in the world—and we're having a sing-along.

"My friends back home think I'm hunting terrorists," Tim says.

"Just be glad they can't see you now," I say.

To get us to sing even louder, Captain Lior announces a three-way contest, Platoon One versus Platoon Two versus Platoon Three, where he'll award points for volume and bonus points for spirit. When they hear this, my company mates erupt in an earsplitting round of clapping and singing. When Captain Lior proclaims Platoon Three the winner, the soldiers of the victorious platoon cheer and scream, "Three! Three! Three!"

"Booo!" The rest of us drown them out. Then, spontaneously, we break into the infamous Israeli soccer chant:

> *Ha-shofet ben-zonah!*
> *Ha-shofet ben-zonah!*

Which means

> *The referee is a son of a whore!*

"Quiet!" roars a voice from the back of the room.

We swivel our heads. Standing in the rear of the auditorium is the meanest, most barbaric commander in the company: the company master sergeant.

He stands with his arms crossed, a look of pure menace on his face. His blond hair is perfectly clipped. His blue eyes cut into us like daggers. He struts down the center aisle like a sheriff. The auditorium is silent except for the *clack . . . clack* of his boots on the tile floor.

At the front of the auditorium, he pivots, faces us.

"Did you enjoy your singing, Company B?"

We don't say a word.

"Did you! Enjoy! Your Singing!"

"Yes, Company Master Sergeant!" we shout.

He paces the front of the room. "In the Armored Corps, we have two traditions during Education Week. The first is the Company Sing-Along. The second is what happens next." He checks his watch. "In exactly three minutes, you will meet me on the parade ground, in formation by platoon. May God have mercy on your souls if even one of you is late. Move!"

We stand in three separate formations at the edge of the parade ground: Platoon One on our right, Platoon Three on our left. It's cold, and foggy. A mist hovers over the field. Our officers and commanders are nowhere in sight. I feel like a little boy who's been left alone with his mean older brother.

Fifty yards ahead, shrouded in fog, stands the Executioner—our company master sergeant.

"Good evening, Company B!"

"Good evening, Company Master Sergeant!"

He ambles toward us through the haze. "I gave you three minutes to line up in formation. It took you ten. That's unacceptable. And it's time to pay." He points behind him. "There's a telephone pole at the other end of this field. You have thirty seconds to run to that pole and back. Go."

We burst out of formation and sprint across the field. The parade ground is enormous—as long as a football field and just as wide, covered with sand, rocks, and dead grass. The sound of us trampling across the field is like a horse race. As we run, we kick up a cloud of dust that mixes with the fog.

This kind of punishment, called *kader*, is our commanders' favorite way to torture us. The word *kader* is derived from the Hebrew word *kadoor*, which means "ball"—the idea being that a soldier running back and forth between two points is like a bouncing ball. The rules of *kader* are simple. Our commanders point to some landmark, such as a pole or bush; they then give us an insanely small amount of time to run there and back. When we don't make it, they call us lazy shits and order us to run some more. It's tremendous fun.

Panting, heaving, we line up in formation as fast as we can. "I gave you thirty seconds, Company B. You took"—the Executioner checks his watch—"two minutes, forty seconds. Let's try again."

"Company Master Sergeant!" shouts a soldier in Platoon One. "I have a medical excuse!"

"Me too!" shouts someone else.

"Quiet!" roars the Executioner. "If you have a medical excuse, take it out and hold it above your head."

About forty soldiers wave white papers in the air. The company master sergeant walks row by row and collects them. He then holds the medical excuses above his head. "Any more?" he shouts.

No one says a word.

He tears the papers in half. The Medical Excuse Guys gasp. My jaw drops. I'm shocked—and thrilled—that someone's finally got the balls to tell the Medical Excuse Guys to shove it. The Executioner is one crazy mother. But in a sick way, I like him.

"You have thirty seconds to touch that pole and make it back. If you do it in thirty seconds, we'll stop. If not, we'll stay here all night. Go."

We sprint to the pole, sprint back, Medical Excuse Guys chugging right along with us, which just goes to show they're completely full of it. We don't make it back in thirty seconds, so we do it again. And again. To the pole and back, over and over, for an hour. We never come close to making it in thirty seconds—that would be impossible. The company master sergeant knows this, of course. But his point isn't to be fair. His point is to screw with us.

"How do you feel, Company B?"

We don't answer. We're spent. Bent over at the waist, panting. I feel like I'm about to pass out.

"I hope you're not too tired, because the fun is just beginning," the Executioner says. "Everyone—Position Two!"

We let out a weak groan. Having dispensed with our legs and lungs, the evil Executioner will now demolish our backs, arms, and necks.

We lower ourselves down into push-up position.

"I'm going to tell you a bedtime story, Company B. Would you like to hear a bedtime story?"

"Yes, Company Master Sergeant," we moan.

"Once upon a time—actually, it was yesterday, the Sabbath, when you were home on leave—a soldier in Platoon Three, Company B, forgot what time the platoon bus was departing the next morning from Tel Aviv. So the soldier called his platoon commander, Lieutenant Gadi, on his cell phone and asked what time he was supposed to meet the bus."

My comrades' stupidity never ceases to amaze me.

"Did you hear that, Company B? A soldier from this company called his officer on his cell phone. Like they were buddies. Pals. Old friends. Well I've got news for you, Company B. *Your officers are not your friends!* Clear?"

"Yes, Company Master Sergeant!" we shout from the ground.

"You will never, ever call your officers on their cell phones. And now we're going to make sure this never happens again. Who's the soldier who called his officer yesterday?"

A soldier in Platoon Three stands.

"Soldier—do you remember your officer's phone number?"

"No, Company Master Sergeant."

"I do. The area code is zero-five-four. Everyone—fifty-four push-ups. Together."

"One, Company Master Sergeant," we count them off. "Two . . ."

I hate to say it, but we deserve this one. Calling your officer on his cell phone? I can't imagine what the idiot was thinking.

When we reach fifty-four, I'm in so much pain I actually fantasize about running back and forth to the pole. I have also decided that I don't like the Executioner after all.

"I believe the next two digits of his phone number are three and six. That means thirty-six push-ups. Together."

And we push-up our way through Lieutenant Gadi's entire ten-digit cell phone number.

When we finally stand, my face and teeth are coated with dirt. I feel like a rag doll. A rag doll that was doused in gasoline, set afire, and pounded with nails.

"I have a question for you, Company B. *Ech holech barvaz?*"

I'm certain I misheard. I thought I heard him say, "How does a duck walk?" But that makes no sense. Unless he's asking a crazy riddle. Or maybe he's just being a schmuck.

"Come on, Company B. I'm sure somebody knows. How does a duck walk?"

He's being a schmuck.

"Platoon Two," he barks. "Who's your platoon scribe?"

Shit.

I slowly raise my hand.

"What's your name, soldier?"

"Yoel, Company Master Sergeant."

"I hear an accent. Where you from?"

"Chicago, Company Master Sergeant."

"Chicago? *Pshhh.* Do they do the duck walk in Chicago?"

I stare at him blankly. I have no idea what he's talking about.

"Step forward."

I hobble toward him.

"Hold your rifle out front, arms straight."

I stretch out my arms.

"Squat," he orders.

I crouch down, like a catcher behind home plate.

"Now walk."

Is he insane?

"Walk!"

I waddle forward on my haunches, bounce up and down. A fool.

"That, my friends, is the duck walk. You have two minutes to duck walk to the pole and back. Do it in two minutes, and we stop. Longer than two minutes, we'll duck walk all night. Go."

With that command, three platoons of Israel Defense Forces combat soldiers squat to the ground and waddle like ducks to a telephone pole a hundred yards away.

> *May He who blessed our forefathers Abraham, Isaac, and Jacob bless the soldiers of Israel who valiantly stand guard on our country and the cities of our God . . .*

"Hey, Chasnoff." Tim greets me as he wobbles by on my right.

"Think they do this in the Marines?" I grumble.

> *From Lebanon to the deserts of Egypt, from the Mediterranean Sea to the Plains of Jordan, on land, in the air and sea may God afflict the enemies that rise against them . . .*

As we totter along, we kick up dust clouds that follow us like shadows. The dust fills my eyes, my mouth. I turn my head and spit, but then my knee hits the barrel of my rifle and the muzzle jerks up and smacks me in the chin—*wham!*

"Goddammit!" I yelp.

> *May the Holy One, Blessed be He, protect and save our valiant soldiers from any misfortune or calamity, from any sickness or disease . . .*

I keep kicking my own ass, over and over, with the heels of my boots. As I wobble around the pole, I curse many things. I curse this army. I curse the company master sergeant. I curse Theodore Herzl, whose idea it was to start this country in the first place. And I curse myself for leaving America and putting my life on hold for this—for an idiotic, godforsaken duck walk.

May the Lord send blessing and success in all their courageous handiwork, destroy their enemies before them and anoint them with the crown of redemption and the crown of victory . . .

When I was a boy, I stood in synagogue every Saturday morning and recited the Prayer for the Israeli Soldier. I poured my heart into the prayer. As the congregation read the words aloud, I closed my eyes and pictured the valiant men who kept the Jewish people free. I imagined them storming up a mountain in the heat. I imagined them perched in a watchtower, standing guard over the border under cover of night. I imagined these brave heroes of the Jews doing many things. But not once did I imagine them walking like a motherfucking duck.

May it be your will, O our Rock and Redeemer, that the verse, "For God walks among you, to wage war for you with your enemies, to save you," should be fulfilled . . .

When they lower my casket into the ground, will they tell my mother the truth? Will they tell her I was unprepared for combat because instead of training for war, I was walking like a duck?

And let us say . . .

"Company B, you are the most pathetic combat soldiers I have ever seen!"

Amen.

"Sit!" the company master sergeant orders.

We collapse to the ground. We are dead. Our shirts hang out untucked. Bootlaces untied. Soaked with sweat. Guys are wheezing. Choking. A couple feet away, a soldier vomits. I'm too exhausted to give a damn.

"Company B. Does anyone know why we're here?"

We don't know. Don't care. And even if we did, we're too tired to talk.

"For the past six weeks, I've watched you fight over the guard duty list and whine like children when you're sent to the kitchen. Tonight, I watched you run back and forth, and not once did one of you turn to another soldier and ask if he's okay. You're selfish. You care nothing about the other soldiers in the company. Am I wrong?"

We don't answer.

"So now you're going to work together," he continues. "Everyone stand up. Find a partner. One of you hop on your partner's back. You're going to take turns carrying each other to the pole. I'm giving you one minute. If you do it in a minute, we say good night. If not—I promise you we'll stay here until you do it in a minute. Go."

I scramble up, grab Clemente the tiny Russian, throw him over my shoulder, and sprint away. He's the lightest guy in the platoon, but I feel like I'm carrying a giant. When we reach the pole, Clemente hops down, I climb onto his back, and he carries me piggyback to the formation.

"Try again!" the company master sergeant barks.

But before we dash off a second time, a bunch of us repartner into teams of strong man/little man. This way, the light, slow, and weak can ride on the backs of the heavy, fast, and able.

Since I'm one of the featherweights, my buddy Shai picks me up and drapes me over his shoulder like I'm a rolled-up Persian rug. Then he sprints across the field much faster than Clemente ran. My head jerks up and down and the whole world shakes as Shai charges toward the pole. I'm certain he'll trip and I'll come crashing down, smashing my head on a rock.

"Careful!" I shriek.

"Hang on, *Achi*!" he shouts.

It takes ten round-trips, but we finally make it. At midnight, the Executioner sets us free. We stumble back to the bunk like marionettes with tangled strings.

Education Week ends with a discussion not about the Arabs who want to kill us, but about the Arabs we might kill and how to kill them. The session is called *Tohar Ha-neshek*—the Purity of Arms.

To start things off, Lieutenant Yaron presents us with a scenario.

"This is a true story," he says. "It happened in the West Bank during the first intifada. During a skirmish in Ramallah, a colonel in the Paratroopers ordered his platoon to open fire on Palestinian civilians. His soldiers refused the order. The officer then repeated his order a second time and threatened to court-martial any soldier who didn't obey.

"My question for you, Platoon Two, is this: If you were a soldier in that platoon, what would you do?"

First, we toss out a bunch of hypothetical questions. Like good Jews, we answer each other's questions with other questions:

"Were there terrorists mixed in with the civilians?"

"Does it matter?"

"Do you really want an army where each soldier thinks for himself?"

"Do you want an army where soldiers follow orders blindly?"

"If you don't fire, and your fellow soldier dies because you didn't, could you live with yourself?"

"Could you live with yourself if you killed a child?"

After twenty minutes of spirited debate, it's clear we fall into two camps. About half of us think the soldiers should fire because an order is an order, the army's not a democracy, and the minute soldiers start deciding for themselves which orders to follow and which to ignore, that's the end of your army.

The rest of us think the soldiers should refuse to fire, because once soldiers start following orders blindly, you're left with an army of Nazis.

As for me—I know exactly what I feel:

Relief.

Relief that as a tank soldier, I'll most likely deploy to Lebanon, not the West Bank and Gaza. I want my war to be clear-cut and unambiguous, where the bad guys look like bad guys and there are no women and children complicating the fighting. That's what I like about Lebanon—the lines are drawn. There's an enemy who wants to kill us, he's dressed like a soldier, he's armed with a Kalashnikov rifle, and, best of all, he wants to wipe us off the map. There's nothing ambiguous about killing an enemy like that.

In the West Bank and Gaza, though, everything's mixed up. Your enemy could be a masked gunman or a ten-year-old boy armed with a Coke bottle filled with gasoline and a match. Your battlefield is street corners and cafés. You're taking cover in bakeries, behind pita carts. Too many lines are blurred. Next thing you know, you're wondering if you should refuse your officer's order to shoot. Lebanon's like a boxing match, where you're in the ring with one enemy, you can see who he is, and you do your best to knock him out. But fighting in the West Bank and Gaza is like being in the ring with Muhammad Ali. Only, you're blindfolded, and you don't know which Muhammad Ali you're fighting—the twenty-year-old Cassius Clay, or the sixty-year-old Muhammad Ali with Parkinson's.

How hard do you punch?

When the shouting gets too loud, the insults too personal, and the Nazi-calling out of hand, Lieutenant Yaron cuts short the debate and reveals the answer.

"After the colonel repeated his order a second time, his soldiers obeyed and opened fire as commanded. For violating Israeli military law, the colonel was stripped of his rank and sentenced to prison. The soldiers who fired were sent to jail. They were supposed to refuse the order."

We're an army of kids. But as soldiers, we could face dilemmas more extraordinary than we'll ever see as adults.

FUNERAL DREAMS

Most nights, I read the newspaper before bed. Lately, the news out of Lebanon isn't good. On Wednesday, six Israeli infantrymen stumbled upon a Hezbollah ambush. The ensuing firefight lasted nine hours. Three of the Israeli soldiers were killed and two others sustained burns on 90 percent of their bodies when a nearby oil tank exploded. Thirty-six hours later, a platoon of elite Navy SEALS entered Lebanon by boat. They had intelligence on a Hezbollah operation. But the tip was a Hezbollah ploy, and all seven Israelis died, including the platoon commander, a thirty-eight-year-old officer with an infant son.

What frightens me most is the randomness of it all. Just the idea that I could be walking along and then the ground explodes, or a missile comes flying at me out of nowhere, scares me. I've always lived my life as if it were a game of chess—if I had a decision to make, I knew that if I thought about it long enough, carefully enough, I'd make the right move. That's why I didn't join the army straight out of college—I began to doubt, and I could only go once I was sure.

The more I learn about Lebanon, though, the more I realize that I won't be able to think my way out of trouble. For the first time in my life, I won't be playing chess. I'll be playing Russian roulette with someone else's gun.

When I was a child, I turned to God for protection. Every night, before bed, I said the same prayer:

> *Please, God, don't let me be blind, deaf, throw up, or die. Please don't let me fall out of a window. Please don't let me choke. Please don't let me drown. Please don't let me be kidnapped. Please don't let me get in a car accident. Please don't let me be attacked by an animal. Please don't let me catch fire. Please don't let me run out of oxygen. Amen.*

I felt certain God was listening. I wonder if He is now.

• • •

Sometimes, for fun, my platoon mates and I talk about our funerals. We don't do this often, but it comes up more frequently than you might think. The first time we do it, we're out in the field, sitting around after lunch, when our social worker, Dassi, shows up with a stack of newspapers. On the front page is a photo of an infantry officer killed the day before in Lebanon.

Moshe Rosenbaum takes one look at the photo and cries, "Hey, wait a minute! I know this guy!" He reads the details aloud. "First Lieutenant Yitzhak Klein . . . Twenty years old . . . Killed yesterday morning at 7 A.M. on his way back from an ambush . . . Buried yesterday afternoon on Mount Herzl, Jerusalem."

Moshe folds up the paper. "Yitzi Klein. I can't believe it. He was at my Yeshiva."

"His poor mother," says Tomer. "She woke up in the morning, and by the time she went to bed, her son was in the ground."

For some reason, this makes us chuckle.

"You ever think about it?" says Nitzan.

"About what?" I say.

"Your funeral. You ever watch it in your head?"

At first, no one says a word. Then Nitzan says, "I think about it all the time," at which point the rest of us admit it.

"I imagine the newspaper the morning after," says Tomer. "My picture on the front page. My teachers in high school would all see it. There'd be a paragraph underneath. 'He played piano. He hoped to one day become a doctor.' "

"Eighteen years and all you get is a paragraph," says Etai.

"I think about the eulogy," says Itamar. "I wonder what my dad would say. I wonder if he'd make it through or just break down at the grave."

"My cousin died in Gaza," says Ro'ee. "At his funeral, there was no eulogy. My uncle and his brother and sister tried. They couldn't get it out."

"I think about my girlfriend," says Shai.

"I think about her too," says Gerber.

"Fuck your mother," says Shai.

"He's just jealous," says Ronen. "No babes in Motzkin."

"You want a slap?"

"*Nu?*" says Tomer. "Your girlfriend?"

"Donna," says Shai. "We've been together since ninth grade. You know those pictures on TV of dead soldiers' girlfriends, holding on to the coffin so tight that people have to pry her off?"

"Oh, why, God, *why*?" Gerber does a perfect imitation of the bereaving girlfriend.

"That'd be Donna," says Shai. "Except she's strong. They wouldn't be able to pull her away."

"I think about my sister," says Assaf, a Yeshiva Boy from Be'er Sheva. "She's eight. Adores me. When I come from the army, she grabs my leg and I swear she doesn't let go until Sunday morning. We have this tradition. Friday night, after dinner, I tuck her into bed and sing her 'Hatikvah.'"

"You sing her the national anthem?" says Etai.

Assaf shrugs. "She likes it. I started doing it when she was four and she doesn't want me to stop."

"It's sweet," says Shai.

"She likes it. But if I die, I wonder who'll sing her 'Hatikvah.'"

Nitzan, who kicked off this conversation, jumps in. "I picture my mother's face the moment she sees the bereavement officer."

"God forbid," says Moshe.

"I think she'd faint," says Nitzan.

"My friend's brother died in the Helicopter Disaster," says Shai. "When the bereavement officer showed up at their apartment, it took two hours before his mother let him in the door."

"Two hours?" I say.

"Swear to God. To this day, his bedroom's exactly the way it was the day he died. His sneakers are still in the corner. The book on his desk is open to the same page it was when he left home after his last leave. The only things that get touched are his bedsheets. My friend says that sometimes, his mother goes into his brother's bedroom and smells his sheets."

"Disgusting," says Gerber.

"Why disgusting?" says Shai.

"It's disgusting, smelling your dead son's sheets."

"He didn't die in those sheets, you schmuck."

"You guys want to hear a great bereavement officer story?" asks Etai.

We pull our kit bags into a tight circle.

"This story's a hundred percent true," says Etai. "My mother's best friend is married to a bereavement officer, and he swears by it. This happened in the first month of the Lebanon War, in '82. So one morning, the bereavement officer pulls up in his white van outside the apartment building at 62 Hillel Street in Givatayim, my mom's old neighborhood. He walks up to apartment 3. Rings the bell. A woman answers the door. The officer says, 'Are you the mother of Corporal Tal Lavi?' She says yes. He tells her he's very sorry, but her son Tal was killed the night before in Lebanon.

"The woman screams. She starts beating her chest and wailing. The neighbors come over. The news spreads, and within fifteen minutes, half the neighborhood's in her living room. Everyone's crying. The family's crushed. They hang posters all over town announcing the death and the funeral and the address for the shiva. Total mayhem.

"So a few hours later, the bereavement officer shows up again. It turns out the army made a mistake. There's another Tal Lavi who lives at 26 Hillel Street, two blocks away. He's the one who died. Not this woman's son."

"No way!" we shriek.

"So the bereavement officer tells the first family there's been a mix-up, that it's a different Tal Lavi who died and that their son is alive."

"Oh, my God!" I say.

"How'd she react?" says Tomer.

"How do you think? It was the happiest moment of her life! It's like her son had come back from the dead. Meanwhile, the bereavement officer drives down the street to tell the other family that their son was killed in Lebanon. So they start screaming and wailing, and the neighbors go over, and the whole neighborhood moves from the first apartment to the one down the street. They hang up new signs, announcing a new time and location for the new funeral and a new address for the shiva."

"Unbelievable," says Shai.

"It gets better," says Etai. "So that night, the first family walks down the street to pay their condolences to the second family. About an hour later, they walk back to their apartment. And who's waiting for them at the front door?"

"Their son," I say.

"Nope," says Etai. "The bereavement officer. Turns out it wasn't a mix-up after all. Both Tal Lavis were killed on the same day, one at 62 Hillel Street, the other at 26 Hillel Street."

We crack up laughing like it's the funniest goddamn joke in the world.

THE MARCH FOR THE BLACK BERET

On the last night of basic training, we line up behind the bunk in full gear in preparation for the thirty-kilometer March for the Black Beret. It will be our eighth hike of basic; we've hiked once a week, beginning with a two-kilometer trek over flat land and ending with tonight's, which Lieutenant Yaron promises will be hilly. After each hike, we receive a token of accomplishment. The first time, we received our rifles. Next came our 188th Armored Brigade shoulder tags and the silver tank medallions for our berets. Tonight, we are hiking for the most prestigious prize of all—the black beret of the Armored Corps.

After an hour-long roll call and equipment check, we prepare to march.

KILOMETER 0

Midnight. We assemble in full battle gear, plus three twenty-liter jerry cans, one twenty-five-pound field radio, and one canvas field stretcher per platoon. We're excited and nervous. We hop up and down in place and rub one another's shoulders like boxers before a fight. Just before we set off, Lieutenant Yaron tells me he's chosen me to be his radioman. This means I'll carry the gargantuan field radio on my back for the duration of the hike. It's an honor, so of course I accept. Lieutenant Yaron explains that I'm to shadow him step for step. When he runs, I run. When he stops to drink, I stop to drink. When he sticks out his hand, I'm to hand him the receiver. And if I hear his name uttered over the radio, I'm to whisper, "Lieutenant!" and see to it that he gets the call. In other words, I'm Lieutenant Yaron's bitch.

KILOMETER 2

We march in absolute silence. Night discipline is in effect. We're forbidden to talk. Dog tags and watches have been covered with cloth so they don't reflect in the moonlight. Under our fatigues, we wear dark undershirts instead of white. Canteens are filled to the rim so water can't be heard sloshing.

I love these hikes. The desert is dark and beautiful. Tonight there's a quarter moon and many stars. The rocks smell dusty and ancient, like an attic. The mountains look like silhouettes of castles.

KILOMETER 4
We stop for our first pee break. The entire company stands in a long line and pees into the sand. I attempt to piss, but with Lieutenant Yaron standing next to me, I get shy pee and nothing comes out.

KILOMETER 15
Pain. My knees and ankles ache. The field radio, which sits on my back in a canvas backpack, digs into my neck like a ferocious Spock nerve pinch. My arms feel tingly. This is probably due to the shoulder straps of the field radio cutting off the circulation in my arms, but I can't help but think what I think anytime my body feels tingly: that I might be coming down with MS.

KILOMETER 22
Lieutenant Yaron breaks into a jog. I scurry to keep up, but I stumble. I'm drenched in sweat and it hurts to breathe. I hate these goddamn hikes.

KILOMETER 25
4 A.M. I'm standing at the foot of a mountain. The mountain is enormous—a skyscraper of rock and sand. Lieutenant Yaron says, "We're going to sprint up this mountain." I shake my head no. My legs feel like sponges. I have no plans to sprint up the mountain. Instead, I plan to curl up in the sand and take a nap.

"Ready?" says Lieutenant Yaron. And just like that, the son of a bitch charges up the mountain.

"Wait," I moan. But of course he doesn't hear. So I trudge after him, slowly. I trip over rocks, stumbling like a drunk. The higher I get, the more the surface turns from rock to sand. I begin to sink. I feel like I'm climbing a mountain of sugar. I'm not one to think things are impossible, but this mountain is different. The mountain is a dinosaur, gurgling sand. He will swallow me. Finally, I quit walking and refuse to move.

Up ahead a hundred meters, Lieutenant Yaron stops. "Yoel—what's the story? Let's move!" he shouts down at me.

"I can't!" I groan back.

"There's no such thing as can't! There's only I don't want to!"

"Then I don't want to!"

He skips down the mountain until he's standing next to me. "You're going to climb this mountain," Lieutenant Yaron says.

I shake my head, no. I'm actually crying at this point—a few sniffles at first, then sobbing like a child.

He puts his hand on my shoulder. "So what's it gonna be, Yoel?" he says.

I don't say anything. I'm too tired, in too much pain.

"Fine," he says. Then he grabs my collar, faces forward, and tugs me up the mountain.

I stumble along behind, my legs splaying this way and that, like I'm the Scarecrow in *The Wizard of Oz*.

"Faster!" he shouts, and starts to run.

Since he's still got me by the collar, I start running too. And then my stomach feels hot, and I gag, and for a quick second I think this might be good, because now Lieutenant Yaron will let me go. Only he doesn't let go, he just clutches my collar tighter.

And that's when I throw up on his shirt.

"Keep moving," says Lieutenant Yaron.

I groan, gag again. But the bastard never lets go for a minute. Instead, he keeps dragging me up the mountain while I retch and heave and make disgusting croaking sounds. Then I throw up a second time, this one to the side, splattering on my boots.

When we reach the peak, I collapse. Lieutenant Yaron sits next to me. It appears he didn't even break a sweat. He looks immaculate, except of course for the vomit covering his back. The sky is purple-blue. Below, the rest of the company begins the slow climb up the mountain.

Lieutenant Yaron offers me a sip from his canteen. "But I just . . ." I point to my mouth.

He shrugs. I take the canteen, gurgle, spit. "Sorry about your shirt, Lieutenant," I say.

"Call me Yaron," he says. "Basic training's over."

KILOMETER 28

Daybreak. Yaron stops the hike and orders, "Stretchers open." We open our canvas field stretcher and strap in our lightest man, Clemente, the tiny Russian. Then we hoist him to our shoulders and take turns carrying him, four at a time, while Clemente bounces up and down and holds on for dear life.

KILOMETER 29

Yaron shouts, "End of night discipline!" We respond with a raucous cheer that doesn't stop until we reach the Armored School.

KILOMETER 29¾

With 250 meters to go, the Medical Excuse Guys meet us at the rear entrance to the base. They join the hike, run alongside us, shout and yell, as if they'd been marching with us from the beginning. Assholes.

KILOMETER 30

Behind the bunk, at the exact spot we started, Yaron leads us in a post-hike cheer. The atmosphere is euphoric. We heave the stretcher in the air, with poor Clemente still strapped in, and sing the 188th Armored Brigade Song. Gerber and Uri do a silly dance where they face each other, hop in a circle, and chant, *"Achim! Achim!"*—"Brothers! Brothers!" The rest of us join in, throw our arms around one another, and sing.

While we celebrate, our commanders set up a table and lay out sixty new black berets. We stand in formation while our sergeants walk through the ranks and place berets on our heads.

Then Lieutenant Yaron asks me to step forward. "How was the hike, Yoel?" he says.

"Hard," I say.

"You puked on my shirt," he says, and gives me a wink. My platoon mates chuckle.

"Do you know why I asked you to step forward?" Lieutenant Yaron says. I shake my head.

"You've been chosen Outstanding Soldier of the Platoon. Tonight, at your graduation ceremony, you'll be called out to receive your award."

I'm speechless. It's a dream come true. My platoon mates applaud and whistle while I stand there stupidly with my head bowed and hope to God

I don't begin to cry. A second later, Platoon Sergeant Guy faces me and salutes. I salute back. Then he yanks off my beret and places his own, beat-up black beret on my head. Without thinking, I wrap my arms around the platoon sergeant in a giant bear hug while my platoon mates crack up laughing.

Basic training ends with a graduation ceremony at the Latrun Armored Corps Museum and Memorial outside Jerusalem.

During the 1948 War of Independence, Israel's fledgling Armored Corps lost a series of bloody tank battles at Latrun, a strategically located hilltop just west of the Tel Aviv-Jerusalem Highway. Nineteen years later, Israel finally gained control of Latrun in the Six-Day War. Ever since, Latrun is the spot where Armored soldiers take the Military Oath of Allegiance upon completion of basic training.

After the six-hour bus ride from the Armored School, we spill out into the museum parking lot. In two hours, our families and girlfriends will arrive, the IDF marching band will begin to play, and the festivities will officially begin. But first, Colonel Avi, the commanding officer of the 188th Armored Brigade, issues a bizarre order:

"Shower."

I'm confused. We're at an outdoor tank museum on a hilltop overlooking the highway. Where in God's name are we supposed to shower? But, alas, even as Colonel Avi speaks, an Arab construction crew is hard at work installing three portable showers, one per platoon, in the museum parking lot. The showers look like porta-potties but somehow they're hooked up to the museum's water tank.

We line up single file while the construction workers test the connection. *"Halas!"* says one of the Arabs. *"Ein mayim!"*—there's not much water. So to cut down on the time between showers, Colonel Avi orders us to strip. Thus, anyone lucky, or unlucky, enough to be driving south on Highway 1 this sunny late September afternoon could look up and see a most unusual sight: two hundred buck-naked Armored Corps basic trainees standing in a line on a hilltop, dressed in nothing but assault rifles, which they wear across their backs, diagonally, nozzles just below their butt cracks.

• • •

By 5 P.M. a long line of cars idles on the entrance ramp to Latrun. The soldier guarding the front gate, an infantryman with an M-16, reminds them that gates don't open until six. But even though he's the one with the assault rifle, the soldier is no match for the inhabitants of these cars. The Israeli drivers are armed with something more powerful than an M-16: Israeli chutzpah. They blare their horns and curse the soldier until the poor kid has no choice but to open the gate thirty minutes early.

Our families arrive in droves. They show up in boxy, early-model cars that they drove caravan-style so there'd be enough room for the grandparents, the siblings, the girlfriends, the uncles, aunts, and cousins, and even a few nieces and nephews. Immediately, they stalk the parking lot looking for their boys. When they find them, they shriek, hug, snap photos, and cry. Then they drop their blankets and picnic on the spot.

During basic training, I didn't have time to miss my family. Now I wish they were here. I can imagine my parents insisting on meeting every one of my platoon mates, embarrassing me with their rudimentary Hebrew while my comrades answer back in English. My brothers and I would pose for pictures in front of a tank, and they'd be proud to be related to me. During the ceremony, my parents would wave from their seats while I'd pretend to not know them. We'd have a blast.

As I watch my buddies celebrate with their own families, I begin to understand why some of them never had a bar mitzvah. It's because they don't need it. In America, we need a hokey ceremony and a party at a swanky hotel to come of age. In Israel, the rite of passage is real. When an Israeli takes the oath to defend his country, he's responsible for the lives of his fellow citizens. After my bar mitzvah, I was responsible for thank-you notes.

A little before six, Dorit shows up in her father's antique Subaru. She wears a black T-shirt, jeans, and sandals. She looks terrific. And even though I'd love her no matter what, I'm relieved she looks beautiful. A big part of tonight's graduation ceremony is the sizing up of one another's girlfriends.

The graduation ceremony is a dream. The outdoor amphitheater is packed. We march in to live music, courtesy of the Israel Defense Forces band, while two thousand Israelis cheer. Against a background of popping flashbulbs, Lieutenant Yaron presents us with a rifle in one hand and a Bible in the other. When the sergeant at arms announces my name as the Outstanding Soldier of Platoon Two, Company B, the stadium erupts in a deafening roar. And then the crowd hushes silent as the sergeant at arms recites the Oath of the Israeli Soldier—

> *I swear my allegiance to the State of Israel and take it upon myself, without reservation, to adhere to the laws of conduct of the Israel Defense Forces, to obey all orders given by authorized command-ers, and to devote my strength, and even sacrifice my life, to the defense of my country and the freedom of the State of Israel.*

—after which we soldiers shout, en masse, *"Ani nishbah! Ani nishbah! Ani nishbah!"*—"I swear! I swear! I swear!"

Except I never recite the oath. At the last second, I decide to fake it. When it comes time for my comrades and me to shout *"Ani nishbah!"* I instead shout *"Aki rishpah!"*—a silly nonsense phrase that means nothing and, therefore, obligates me to nothing. I want to leave myself an out because I suddenly remember the story Lieutenant Yaron told us about the paratroop-ers who opened fire on civilians and went to jail. In a moment of panic, I decide I want to be sure I can refuse an immoral order without breaking my oath. So I jumble the words on purpose and continue to serve Israel without having sworn myself to anything.

After the ceremony, I feel drunk with happiness. My buddies and their fam-ilies congratulate me on my award. Then Dorit and I walk hand in hand through the museum grounds, alone.

"My outstanding soldier," she purrs. Then she stands on her tiptoes and kisses my cheek.

I don't know if it's the euphoria pumping through my blood or how beautiful she looks in the floodlights, but quite suddenly I'm seized with a spectacular idea. I whisper it in Dorit's ear.

"What?" she giggles.

I face her, take her hands in mine, and say it out loud. "Marry me?"

BEAUTIFUL CHILDREN

We will have beautiful children: a pair of olive-skinned Semites with curly black hair, Dorit's chin dimple, and my perfectly smooth Scotch-Irish nose. The boy we'll name Jonathan, the girl Daniel. People will marvel at our choice of such a hip, ironic name for a girl. Our children will be geniuses, of course, equally adept at reading Talmud and hitting a curveball. Dorit will be a wonderful mother. She will cook every night, large Sephardic meals, complete with chicken, lamb, Persian rice, hummus, diced salad, and Yemenite spices such as *hilbeh* and *ambah*. Friday nights, we will recite the Sabbath blessings and discuss the Torah portion, which, because they are geniuses, our beautiful children will know by heart. After dinner, I will wash the dishes by hand. On either side of me, our children will dry the dishes with a hand towel. While we do this, we will sing Sabbath songs if it's the Sabbath. If it's not the Sabbath, we'll sing Broadway show tunes and Simon & Garfunkel.

I will of course be an amazing father. I will teach our beautiful children the names of constellations and the difference between stratus and cumulus clouds. At baseball games, I will teach them to keep score. During playdates, I will entertain their friends with magic tricks. When our beautiful children are old enough, I will speak to them frankly about condoms and reassure them that their mother and I will love them even if they are gay.

I've got a week off from the army between basic training and Tank School. I'd wanted to drive to Eilat with Dorit, lie on the beach, drown myself in Coca-Cola, and enjoy the benefits of a rejuvenated libido that, with proper sleep and mental nourishment, would magically spring back to life.

But no.

Because of the unique nature of our soldier-civilian relationship, I have once again been forced to improvise. It's similar to what happened with the ring. I'd always fantasized that I'd propose to Dorit, or some other lucky girl, with flair. I'd get down on my knee, read a poem, and present an immaculate diamond ring I'd designed, and paid for, myself. But since I'm an active-duty soldier who earns eighty bucks a month and comes home once every fourteen days, I have neither the time nor money to purchase a ring. So instead, we've agreed that Dorit will pick out the ring, pay for it herself, and submit a receipt. I will then reimburse her for the cost of the ring, most likely over the course of many months, until the ring is paid off and, finally, mine, which is to say, hers.

So instead of a week on the beach, Dorit decided—I mean, we decided—to get a jump on the wedding planning, because Dorit believes the wedding will take place next summer, right after my discharge from the army. I believe it will take place sometime between next summer and the year or three immediately after. For the past four nights, Dorit and I have been crisscrossing the country in Menashe's blue '88 Subaru, visiting five or six potential wedding venues a night.

"So what do you think," says Dorit. "DJ or a band?"

"Band," I say.

"But a DJ would get the young people dancing."

"Then a DJ," I say.

"Or we could do both."

"No way. We're not paying for both."

There's suddenly so much to decide. The wedding hall, of course, and whether to hire an outside caterer or stay in house, and then waiter service or buffet, and whether we need to order a special (very expensive) *glatt* kosher meal for Dorit's cousin Yitzhak, who became ultra-Orthodox a month ago (the bastard couldn't wait until after the wedding?). I still don't know how we'll pay for all this. I don't expect Dorit's father, who's sixty and valet parks cars to keep food on the table, to pay for everything. But that means I have to go to my parents, and I hate asking my parents for money— especially when 95 percent of the guests aren't mine.

Most of my family and friends will not attend. My parents and brothers will of course be there. My best friend, Dan, who's studying Arabic in Cairo, will try to make it. My dad's parents, Zayde Daniel and Bubbie Rose, will attend. Gramma Ruth and her husband, Stan, will not attend because Gramma Ruth is afraid of a terrorist attack.

"You shouldn't worry about the money," says Dorit. "The wedding will pay for itself."

"How?" I say.

"In Israel, wedding guests always give money."

"No blenders? Toasters?"

"Never. And they always give enough money to cover their meal."

"No way."

"I'm serious. The fancier the place, the bigger the check. And if a guest doesn't like his meal, he'll ask for his envelope back and write a new check for a smaller amount."

"Wow," I say. "That's so goddamn Israeli."

We applied for the marriage license this morning. We took a cab to the Rabbinical Authority headquarters in Tel Aviv City Hall, filled out the application, and submitted copies of our national ID cards, birth certificates, and our parents' wedding contracts, called *ketubah*s, to prove we're both Jewish. We still need to find someone to design our own *ketubah*, although personally, I'd prefer Dorit design it herself. Dorit's an incredible artist, and if she designed our *ketubah* it would be so much more personal, and intimate. And cheap. It's not that I'm obsessed with money. But with no income, no job on the horizon, and a soon-to-be-wife who can't wait to have babies, I strive to be frugal. Dorit, on the other hand, thinks I'm a pennypinching tightwad.

In other words, American.

I love Dorit, and Dorit loves me. But we have many differences, the main one being that Dorit is so incredibly Israeli and I'm not nearly as Israeli as I thought.

I'd always known Israelis were hotheaded, stubborn, and painfully blunt. But I assumed that after a couple of weeks in the Israeli Army, I'd not only get used to it, but also take on those characteristics myself, as if Israeliness were a foreign language I could pick up simply by exposing myself to it. But the longer I'm here—and the longer I'm with Dorit—the more I realize how different Israelis are from the American Jews I grew up with.

For example—the way Dorit and I fight. Like all couples, we argue plenty. What makes our arguments unbearable, however, is that Dorit, like any good Israeli, will never admit to being wrong. Nor will she apologize, because saying she's sorry would imply she'd been wrong in the first place.

As for why Israelis hate the idea of being wrong—I've thought about it, and I've concluded that it has to do with a deep-rooted psychological fear of looking weak, which itself is a result of living in such a tiny country so close to their enemies. In Israel, the fear is that even the tiniest insinuation of weakness will send a message to the Arabs that we're vulnerable to attack—which explains why Israel can't simply withdraw from Gaza and the West Bank (if we do, that will show the Arabs that terrorism works) and why many Israelis oppose a peace treaty with Syria (only weak countries sign treaties; strong countries don't need them).

In a region as volatile as the Middle East, this kind of logic might make sense. But somehow, this way of thinking has embedded itself into the Israeli psyche—and now I'm the one who has to suffer. Because when Dorit and I argue, she will say anything, dredge up any long-forgotten episode, and bad-mouth anyone, living or dead, if it means she'll get the last word and, consequently, avoid looking weak. In the two years I've been with her, Dorit has called me names I never dreamed a loved one might call me, including *holerah* (diseased), *kartziyah* (lice), and *hatichat kahka al ha-na'al sheli* (piece of excrement on the sole of my shoe)—all of which I try very hard to take with a grain of salt.

In a sense, Dorit's and my relationship is like a microcosm of the Middle East. Whether it's two people or two countries, there's no such thing as a skirmish in this part of the world—there are only all-out wars. So when I toss a rock, Dorit has no choice but to hit back with a twenty-two-ton cluster bomb.

It's ironic, I suppose. Growing up an American Jew, all I heard was that Israelis are our brothers, our kindred people, that they're Jews and we're Jews and together we're one big happy Jewish family.

Show me an American Jew who believes that, and I'll show you someone who never had to argue with an Israeli.

• • •

We park in a gravel lot. I take Dorit's hand, and we walk beneath a canopy of palm trees, to the kibbutz office. Inside, a tall man with a ponytail greets us. His name is Shmulik.

"We're getting married," says Dorit, beaming.

"Mazel tov!" says Shmulik. "Do you have a date?"

"Not yet," I say.

"August," says Dorit.

TANK SCHOOL

FALL

Merkava 3 Baz Battle Tank—Side View

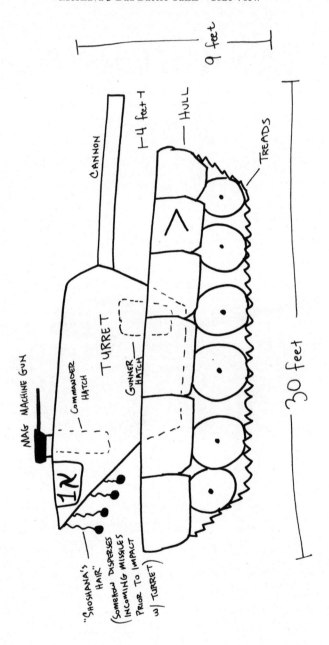

Merkava 3 Baz Battle Tank—Bird's-Eye View

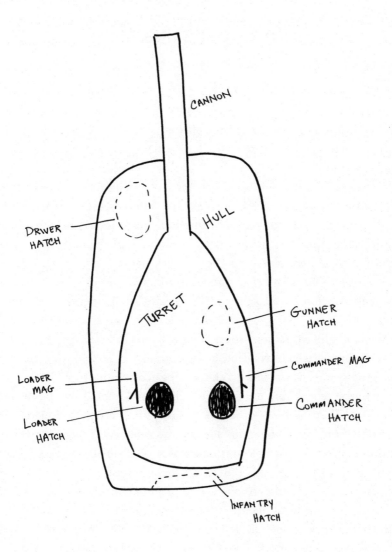

I! LOVE! TANKS!

We're down to fifty-one guys in the platoon. On the first morning of Tank School, Lieutenant Yaron, in his final act as our platoon commander, kicks eight guys out of the unit. All eight are lazy Medical Excuse Guys who didn't belong in Armored in the first place. For this reason, we're neither surprised nor unhappy to see them go. Nor are they unhappy to be leaving. For most of the booted guys, this is a dream come true. Instead of training, guarding, and deploying to Lebanon with the rest of us, they'll spend the next three years fixing jeeps, packing parachutes, and working other support jobs with Fridays and Saturdays off, evenings free, and the same pay as before, minus the measly hundred-dollar-per-month combat bonus.

The only guy who's not happy to go is Eytan Frankel. Eytan's an ugly kid with thick glasses, a nose like a boxer, and a face so badly pockmarked it looks like someone stabbed his cheeks repeatedly with a fork. When Lieutenant Yaron tells Eytan he's been kicked out of Armored, Eytan screams, "Nooooo!" Then he picks up a metal trash can and chucks it across the courtyard, sending Coke cans and candy wrappers flying everywhere. Within a second, Sergeant Eran scrambles up from behind and bodyslams Eytan to the ground. But Eytan kicks Sergeant Eran in the nuts, wiggles free, and embarks on a violent rampage in which he single-handedly tries to destroy the bunk. First, he flips over the picnic table. Next, he runs to the orange pay phone, picks up the receiver, and slams it into the wall, over and over, as he shouts, "No! No! No!" As this transpires, the rest of us watch with a mixture of horror and joy. On the one hand, he's liable to pop in a magazine and shoot us. On the other hand, this is the best entertainment we've had in weeks.

As Lieutenant Yaron sprints across the courtyard, Eytan takes off his rifle. For a second I think he's about to shoot. But instead, Eytan slams his rifle to the ground and shouts, "Goddamn this fucking army!" That's when Lieutenant Yaron grabs Eytan in a choke hold and drags him from the courtyard while Eytan kicks and screams like a four-year-old being removed from a toy store.

The rest of the morning, all we can talk about is Eytan's temper tantrum and how glad we are that a psychotic schmuck like him is finally off our hands. So imagine our surprise when, four hours later, Eytan saunters into lunch with his rifle over his shoulder and a huge grin on his face like he just scored a date with the head cheerleader.

"You're back?" I say.

"I told Lieutenant Yaron I didn't want to leave."

"And he let you stay?"

"Yep. He even apologized for kicking me out in the first place. He's such an ass."

I'm shocked. And yet, I'm not surprised. I adore Lieutenant Yaron because he's so compassionate. The problem is, he's too compassionate. Someday, Lieutenant Yaron will make a great father. But as a combat officer, he's just too damn soft.

Tank School is like college, except there's no partying, our professors are jaw-droppingly gorgeous female soldiers, and instead of letter grades, it's pass/fail, where pass means you're more likely to live, fail means there's a good chance you'll die.

The purpose of Tank School is to teach each of us soldiers one of three jobs in the tank: drivers will learn to drive; loaders to load missiles into the cannon; and gunners will learn to blow shit up.

Most of us want to be gunners.

To determine our jobs, we take an intelligence test that reminds me of the SATs, play a Space Invaders-style video game that gauges our hand-eye coordination, and endure an hour-long interview in which a girl soldier asks us tricky questions such as "If you walk into a shop, and sitting on the shelf are three bottles labeled Leadership, Intellect, and Courage, which bottle would you choose?" In the end, however, our assignments appear to come down to one thing: our socioeconomic backgrounds. With few exceptions, white guys from good neighborhoods, including Tomer, Dror Boy Genius, and myself, are all gunners; dark-skinned guys and white guys from so-so neighborhoods are loaders; and Russians, dark-skinned guys from working-class neighborhoods, and misfits like Tim Bailey, who doesn't speak a word of Hebrew, are drivers.

Every morning, we scramble from one classroom to the next for lectures on the following topics:

TANK MECHANICS

We learn how the Merkava battle tank works, with a focus on the gunner's best friend, the laser-guided lock-on firing system. Subjects include optics, ballistics, and Ohm's Law—none of which I'd understand in English, much less in Hebrew. My attitude is, as long as the tank works, I don't care how.

FIRING SKILLS

A hands-on course in which we gunners learn the art of blowing shit up. First, we practice manipulating the two-pronged rubber joystick that controls the cannon. Then we learn how to line up the crosshairs on stationary and moving targets. Speed is key: from the moment he spots a target, a gunner has thirty seconds to fire. Precision is a must—just half a millimeter of error on the periscope translates to ten meters on a target one kilometer away.

BATTLE COMMANDS

We learn the language of a tank crew, including how to verbally respond to, and execute, orders. Of all my classes, this one's the easiest—I just do what my tank commander tells me. If he says, "Antitank," I press the button for a *Chetz* antitank missile. If he says, "Distance," I fire a laser at the target; the in-tank computer then calculates how long it takes for the laser to reach the target and multiplies this number by the speed of light to determine how far away the target is. If my tank commander says, "Fire," I press the red button on my joystick and try not to think about the human being I'm about to annihilate. It's kind of like a high-stakes game of Simon Says.

KNOW YOUR ENEMY

In this class, we learn to identify enemy tanks, planes, helicopters, armored personnel carriers, and soldiers by their physical characteristics. Usually, it comes down to the subtlest of details, such as the number of wheels in a tank track or the location of the antennae on an armored command car.

Once a week, we take a field trip to the sand dune behind the bunk, where tiny toy soldiers and military vehicles are set up in the sand. We take turns looking through binoculars and identifying which of the toy soldiers and vehicles are friendly (Israeli or American made) and which are enemy (Russian made, Arab used). The idea, I suppose, is that in a war, we'll be able to identify which tanks, trucks, and aircraft are ours and which belong to the enemy. Personally, I prefer the alternate method of identifying the enemy, namely, if there's a tank, plane, or soldier firing missiles at me, it's a safe bet that's the guy I should shoot.

CHEMICAL WAR

Our most disturbing class of the lot. We learn about mustard gas, sarin, 3-quinuclidinyl benzilate, and other frightening nerve and biological agents with which our Arab neighbors plan to literally melt our faces and rot our brains. We also learn the symptoms and side effects we can expect to suffer if exposed (common side effects include nausea, vomiting, and hydrophobia), and recommended antidotes (everything from digesting bromide pills to sniffing an onion). Since I have little faith I'd actually remember what to do in the event of a chemical attack, I compile my notes into a handy pocket-sized chemical war flowchart (see next page).

Ever since Israeli intelligence figured out that in the Syrian Army, every Tuesday is Chemical War Day, our officers decided to take our own chem-war training more seriously.

On day three of Tank School, we visit the gas tent, which is pretty much exactly what it sounds like—a large, olive-green canvas tent filled with odorless teargas. Outside the gas tent, my comrades and I strap on our gas masks and check one another for leaks. Then, one by one, we step inside the tent and are duly greeted by a pair of Chemical War Brigade officers, themselves in gas masks, sitting behind a table.

"State your name," says the first officer through her mask.

"Chasnoff, Yoel," I reply. I sound like a muffled Darth Vader.

"You have any siblings?" the second officer asks.

"Two brothers," I say.

"Take off your gas mask and tell me their names."

I loosen the rubber strap, lift the mask over my head, and feel absolutely

Chemical-War Flowchart

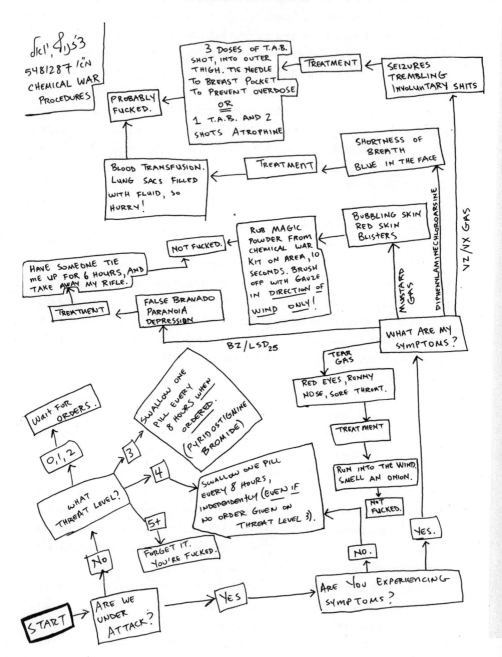

nothing. They told us the tent was full of gas so we'd take the drill seriously. But now I realize that it was a hoax.

"My middle brother is Ari," I say. "And the youngest is—"

And then it hits me. A sting in the eyes, like a thousand needles thrust into my retina. My esophagus on fire, doused in gasoline and lit with a match—

"State your other brother's name," the officer orders.

"Gabriel!" I croak. Then I beeline through the door and collapse on the pavement, terrified and gasping for air, like an asthmatic with his head in a plastic bag.

And then there are the tanks themselves.

The Merkava battle tank is a sixty-five-ton behemoth consisting of two sections, the turret and the hull. The circular turret sits inside the rectangular hull—picture a can of soda (the turret) standing upright in a shoebox (the hull). The driver, using a gas pedal, brake, and steering wheel, drives the hull forward and backward, left and right, like a car, while, simultaneously, the gunner rotates the turret 360 degrees both clockwise and counterclockwise with a joystick. The driver sits in the upper-left corner of the hull; the loader, gunner, and tank commander sit in the turret, in the following positions, assuming the standard forward-pointing cannon position of twelve o'clock: loader at nine o'clock, gunner at two o'clock, and tank commander at five o'clock on an elevated seat, so he can navigate with his head outside the tank. The loader, gunner, and tank commander enter and exit the turret through one of two portals in the top of the turret, each about the size of a manhole on a city street. The turret's most noticeable feature is the lack of space: the entire inside is roughly the size of two side-by-side bathtubs beneath a five-foot ceiling. The cannon, missile cache, and our control panels take up a third of the turret space. This leaves barely any room for the tank's most important piece of equipment of all: the crew.

Along with the tanks, we get a list of new *Hora'ot B'tichut*, or safety rules—thirty-four new safety rules, to be exact. These safety rules are designed to keep us soldiers from getting injured or killed in, on, and near the tanks. The rules govern our every interaction with the tank, from how we enter and exit the tank to how we clean it, drive it, and park it. Some rules are obvious, such as "Rule Two: No lying down in front of a tank" and "Rule Twenty-six: If your tank starts to tip over, yell 'Tank tipping over!' "

Other rules are less intuitive, such as "Rule Nine: When parked in the tank lot, rotate turret by hand only" and "Rule Twelve: Do not rotate turret electrically or by hand when the driver's hatch is open."

What these rules all have in common is that each is the result of a gruesome accident that in turn led to the establishment of the rule. In other words, the reason we're not allowed to lie down in front of a tank is because, once upon a time, some idiot soldier chose to lie down in front of a tank and was summarily crushed. Likewise, at some point in Israel's illustrious military history, a tank driver lost control of his tank, tipped it over, and injured his crew—an accident that, the army believes, would have been less severe had the driver yelled, "Tank tipping over!" This makes me think our list of safety rules should be called "The 34 Dumbest Things Tank Soldiers Have Ever Done."

To keep us safe inside our tanks, we receive new equipment, including: one pair of Nomex fireproof gloves, three one-piece fireproof jumpsuits, and one fireproof intratank communication helmet—all of which make me realize that one of the major challenges of being a tank soldier is not catching fire. The easiest way to catch fire is for the tank to get hit by a Russian-made Sagger II antitank missile, but there are plenty of other ways, namely: the electrical system can short-circuit, the air-conditioning coolant can spontaneously combust, the engine can overheat, the gas tank can rupture, and the tank can roll over a land mine. What makes each of these situations all the more treacherous is that each tank is packed with no less than one ton of explosives in the form of depleted-uranium 120-millimeter missiles, hand grenades, two MAG machine guns, a crate of .5-caliber shells, and five hundred 35-millimeter bullets. Thus is the great irony of the Armored Corps: the tank's greatest asset is also its greatest liability. In battle, there's no better place to be than sealed up, safe and sound, inside an armored metal box with a ton of ammunition. But God forbid your tank is hit, and suddenly you're trapped in a sealed-up metal box with two thousand pounds of explosives. This makes me wonder, if my tank is hit, just how useful my fireproof gloves, helmet, and jumpsuit would actually be.

About the same time as I realize that riding in a tank is akin to wearing a bulletproof vest made of dynamite, I discover yet another downside of our sixty-five-ton metal machine: the maintenance.

For all its speed and firepower, the Merkava tank requires more pampering than a newborn baby. We spend hours each day greasing, tightening, and lubricating every inch of the tank. Thursdays we take the tank apart, top to bottom, and fine-tune the engine, wax the treads with Vaseline, and dunk every knob, switch, lever, and bolt in a barrel of benzene. And if we drive the tank forward or back even a single meter, we're required to do the whole procedure all over again.

Our tanks are spoiled bitches.

Our new platoon tank commander is a twenty-one-year-old schlemiel named Captain Pinchas Fluman, or, as we call him, Captain Pinny. From the moment we lay eyes on him, we can tell Captain Pinny is a dork. He's skinny and pale with a pockmarked face and buzz-cut hair the color of rust. "I named my tank after my girlfriend, Rikki!" he exclaims in his introductory speech. "You know why? Because I! Love! Tanks!"

Serving under Captain Pinny is a team of eight sergeants, all of them tank commanders, and a new disciplinarian called Platoon Sergeant Yoav.

We spend afternoons inside the tanks with our commanders, reviewing hands-on what we learned in class that morning. Our sergeants' teaching methods contradict every known theory of pedagogy. Our tank commanders never praise us, and when we make a mistake, they encourage us with curses and swift kicks to the head.

"We're on a mountain," says my tank commander, Sergeant Hezzi. "Below us, in a valley, are two enemy tanks. Our mission is to take out both in sixty seconds. Clear?"

"Got it," I say. I'm inside the tank, sitting in the gunner's hatch. I'm wearing my helmet and Nomex gloves. Above me, in the commander's chair, is Sergeant Hezzi.

"So when I say, 'Antitank,' what do you do?"

"I say, 'Missile select,' and push the orange button."

"When I say, 'Distance,' what do you do?"

"I put the crosshairs on the tank on the right, fire a laser, and state the distance."

"When I say, 'Fire!' what do you do?"

"I fire."

Wham!—Sergeant Hezzi kicks me in the back of my head.

"Ow!" I say.

"When I say 'Fire!' what do you do?"

"Uhm . . . I fire another laser in case the distance changed?"

Wham!

"Ow, fuck!"

"One more time, retard. When I say, 'Fire!' what do you do?"

"Uhm . . . I . . . Oh, I know! I readjust the crosshairs so they're in the exact middle of the tank!"

Wham!

"What?"

"You wait for the loader to shout, 'Loaded!' you schmuck. Otherwise, the kickback could puncture his lungs."

Oh.

Within a week, it's evident that we gunners have the most important job in the tank. Unlike previous generations of tanks, the Merkava 3 Baz has a lock-on firing system that allows a gunner to hit moving targets. So instead of trying to guess where a moving target is headed, a gunner places the crosshairs on the target, locks on, and the tank's internal computer continually recalibrates for changes in velocity, distance, and wind. Over and over, our commanders drill it into our heads that the Merkava is only as good as its gunner and that a gunner's skill—or lack of it—will make or break the success of the entire crew.

Not surprisingly, this leads to resentment within the platoon. Loaders and drivers hate hearing that they're not as important as we are (even though—let's be honest—they're not). We gunners, meanwhile, think it's unfair that we're forced to spend hours each day learning aerodynamics, meteorology, and ballistics while loaders and drivers do nothing but shove missiles into cannons and turn steering wheels. Before long, loaders and drivers despise us gunners because they think we're nothing but a bunch of stuck-up pricks who think we're God's gift to the Merkava tank (which—let's face it—we are), and we gunners despise the loaders and drivers because to us they're nothing but a bunch of lazy shits who get three-hour siestas after lunch and who at night, when the gunners sit in study groups cramming for our upcoming exam, sit around in their underwear playing backgammon.

Compounding the tension is that our split perfectly mirrors stereotypes already alive and breathing in Israeli society (that is, Ashkenazi white guys are latte-sipping elitists, Russians are lazy parasites, dark-skinned Sephardim are the nonupwardly mobile working class). This makes the rivalry more intense and adds subconscious fuel to an already raging fire. For the first time since basic training began, the platoon begins to fall apart. We've always had our cliques, but now it's official: we are no longer one platoon, but three.

FUCK SHEETS

Of the twenty gunners, I'm the dunce. The coursework is more difficult than anything I studied in college, made worse by the fact that it's all in high-level, academic Hebrew. This role—dunce—is a new one for me. In high school, I was the guy who rolled my eyes when others didn't get it. Now I'm the kid with his hand in the air while my eighteen-year-old Israeli platoon mates shout, "Yoel—how do you not *get* this?"

One night, I'm visiting Tim in his room when he pulls out an English tank manual. It's enormous—the size of a phone book. "Where'd you get that?" I say.

"Captain Pinny gave it to me," Tim says. "You didn't get one?"

The next day, I ask permission to speak to Captain Pinny.

"I was wondering if maybe I could get an English tank manual, too," I say.

Captain Pinny glares at me as if I'm crazy. "Why?" he says.

"Because I'm American," I reply.

"You are?" he says in disbelief. "I thought you were Israeli. I figured you ran away from home and grew up on the streets, and that's why your grammar's so bad."

Tank School is every bit as haphazard as basic training. Every night, our commanders punish us with an hour of push-ups and wind sprints—an hour we should be using to study. The morning we learn to fire the MAG, Captain Pinny yanks me out of class so I can pull weeds. I can't believe this is the same military that pulled off such legendary feats as the Raid on Entebbe and the Six-Day War. And I get this sick feeling in my stomach that I'm not getting the training I need—and that if I do deploy to Lebanon, I won't be ready.

After three weeks of tedious coursework, brutal punishments, and excruciating physical labor, the obvious happens: our morale plummets, we begin to not care, and our test scores drop.

Captain Pinny is furious.

"What in God's name is wrong with you?" he roars in our weekly Thursday night platoon meeting. "You are tank soldiers in the Israel Defense Forces! These exams"—he picks up the stack of papers from the lectern—"are shit!" He slams the pile down with a whack. "Do you realize that in four months, you might be going to Lebanon?"

I feel like I'm living in some bizarre, twilight zone-like alternate universe that's ruled by aliens who tell me to do one thing, make me do the opposite, and wonder why I didn't do what they told me to do in the first place. It's a frightening thought. Because it isn't just test scores that are at stake, but something bigger and more important: my life.

Once again, I can't help but think about what I'd do if I were the officer in charge of this platoon. For starters, I'd implement a one-hour study hall every night, in which teachers and tank commanders would be available to answer questions. I'd declare a moratorium on punishments, since all they do is waste time and kill morale. And I'd add an extra hour of sleep each night so my soldiers would be well rested for class.

Instead, Captain Pinny comes up with an idea more brilliant than anything I ever could've dreamed up on my own:

Fuck Sheets.

The idea is simple. From now on, we'll keep track of our *fuckim*—army slang for "mistakes"—on Captain Pinny's *Dapei Fuckim*, or Fuck Sheets. This, supposedly, will increase discipline, boost morale, and salvage the platoon.

"In my hand are two hundred Fuck Sheets!" Captain Pinny announces as he proudly waves a stack of pink papers in his hand. "Each night, every soldier in this platoon will fill out at least three Fuck Sheets. On each Fuck Sheet, you will list your name, military ID number, and one fuck you made that day. You will also write what you learned from your fuck and what steps you'll take to prevent this fuck in the future. The next day, I'll punish each soldier based on the severity of his fucks. Right now, I want each of you to fill out three Fuck Sheets. When you're finished, you can go to bed. Questions?"

The minute he's out the door, we burst out laughing.

"Fuck One," shouts Gerber. "Joining the Armored Corps."

"Fuck Two—getting stuck with a schmuck like Pinny Fluman," I chime in.

"Fuck Three is your Sabbath leave if you don't shut your mouths!" roars Platoon Sergeant Yoav, who we didn't realize was sitting in the back.

I take out a pen and get to work on my first Fuck Sheet. I try to remember a mistake I made in the past twenty-four hours—but nothing so bad that I'd be severely punished for it.

I start with a mistake I've made at least once a day since Tank School began:

FUCK SHEET: PLATOON TWO, COMPANY B, 188TH ARMORED
NAME   *Chasnoff, Yoel*
MILITARY ID   *5481287*
FUCK   *This morning, I hit my head on the cannon of the tank during guard duty.*
WHAT I LEARNED FROM THIS FUCK   *Hitting my head on the cannon hurts so bad I can feel it in my balls.*
HOW I'LL PREVENT THIS FUCK IN THE FUTURE   *Next time I guard the tank, I'll watch where I'm going so I don't hurt my head/balls.*

For fuck number two, I write:

FUCK SHEET: PLATOON TWO, COMPANY B, 188TH ARMORED
NAME   *Chasnoff, Yoel*
MILITARY ID   *5481287*
FUCK   *This afternoon, I nearly fell off the tank because I climbed onto the hull with only one hand.*
WHAT I LEARNED FROM THIS FUCK   *Tanks are dangerous machines! They should be mounted with care!*
HOW I'LL PREVENT THIS FUCK IN THE FUTURE   *I'll climb onto the tank with two hands.*

I can't think of a third mistake. But I need to write something, or else I can't go to bed.

Suddenly, I remember a fuck I made last week:

FUCK SHEET: PLATOON TWO, COMPANY B, 188TH ARMORED
NAME   *Chasnoff, Yoel*
MILITARY ID   *5481287*
FUCK   *When I put on my tank suit, my penis got caught in the zipper.*
WHAT I LEARNED FROM THIS FUCK   *I learned that zipping my tank suit too quickly can lead to genital mutilation.*
HOW I'LL PREVENT THIS FUCK IN THE FUTURE   *Next time I put on my tank suit, I'll pay close attention to the whereabouts of my penis.*

Permeating all of this madness is the ever-present riddle of Lebanon. There's still no word on whether we'll go. And from what I read in the papers, I'm no longer sure I want to. It seems like every day, I find myself staring at another front-page photo of somebody's dead son. The deaths are at once tragic and sick. For example: a paratrooper steps on a land mine and is instantly killed. That part is tragic. It turns out that three days earlier, on his last Sabbath leave, he proposed to his longtime girlfriend and they got engaged.

Sick.

I tell myself I should stop reading the paper, but I'm addicted. As long as there's a chance I might go to Lebanon, I can't put these newspapers down.

For as many stories as there are about Israeli soldiers lost in battle, there is an equal number about civilian protests against the Israeli presence in Lebanon. One group in particular—the Four Mothers Movement—attracts an enormous amount of attention. The Four Mothers is thousands strong and includes women, men, university students, teenagers about to be drafted, and former soldiers. The group was started by four women who lived on a kibbutz up north. Each had a son serving in a combat unit in Lebanon. The Four Mothers utilize the usual protest group tactics, writing letters to the editor and picketing at major intersections on Friday afternoons. But they're best known for their demonstrations: When an Israeli soldier dies in Lebanon, the next morning the Four Mothers rally outside the Ministry of Defense, where they unfurl a banner with a running tally of soldiers killed in the Security Zone. The Four Mothers' central claims are, first, that the Israeli presence in Lebanon is pointless, as evidenced by the Katyusha rockets that continue to fall on the north despite our presence in the Security Zone; and second, that soldiers' lives matter just as much as civilians' lives, so the idea that soldiers dying in Lebanon instead of civilians dying in Israel is somehow a success is ludicrous. The more I read about the Four Mothers, the more I think their arguments make sense. And I'm not the only one who's paying attention. It gets so bad that Colonel Avi, the head of the 188th Armored Brigade, calls a company-wide meeting on the Thursday night before our upcoming Sabbath leave.

"How many of you have heard of the Four Mothers?" he asks in a gravelly voice.

Nearly all 150 of us raise our hands.

"So it seems that four housewives on a kibbutz suddenly know more about Israel's security than the officers of the Israel Defense Forces. By show of hands: How many of you would go into battle with your mother in command of the platoon?"

We chuckle.

"Let me be clear, Company B: The Four Mothers are traitors. When they march, they endanger the lives of Israeli soldiers and encourage Hezbollah to fight harder. Soon, the war in Lebanon will be your war. You will lie in ambush in the cold, protecting Israel, while the Four Mothers march against you. They say they care about you, but don't believe it. They care about getting themselves on television. And the only time they do that is when soldiers die."

As he speaks, my platoon mates nod their heads and pump their fists. I lean forward and tap Tim Bailey on the shoulder. "Do you believe this chump?" I whisper.

"I don't understand a word," says Tim.

"Basically, he says that anyone who protests the war in Lebanon is a traitor."

"He's right," says Tim.

"You kidding me?" I nearly jump out of my seat. "He's like fucking Nixon and Vietnam!"

"Soldier!" the colonel barks. I look up with a start. He glares at me, his eyes like granite. "Something you'd like to share?"

"No, sir," I say.

"Stand up when you're speaking to me," he orders.

I stand.

"What's your name, soldier?"

"Yoel."

"Have you ever heard of the Four Mothers, Yoel?"

"Yes, sir," I say.

"And what do you think?"

I open my mouth—but my voice catches in my throat. I feel frozen. I'm not sure what to say. So I utter the first thing that comes to mind. "Bullshit, sir," I say in English.

The guys in my company snicker. Colonel Avi smiles.

"Sit," he says.

I sit down, my face boiling. I can't decide if I should feel proud for thinking so quickly on my feet or ashamed for being such a cop-out.

Meanwhile, on the Dorit front, the situation is quickly deteriorating. We see each other only once every twenty-one days. As a result, our entire relationship is reduced to a series of twice-a-week, three-minute phone calls in which, for all the obvious reasons, we find it increasingly difficult to relate to each other's lives. I try to tell her about Tank School. But where to start? She tells me about her job at the Vita Soup company—but why should I care?

On the rare Friday when I'm allowed home, the visit never lives up to the anticipation. By the time I reach Tel Aviv, I'm beat. What could be a wonderful reunion turns into a forty-eight-hour slugfest in which we bicker like angry dogs.

Mostly we fight about plans. In anticipation of my visit, Dorit makes plans for restaurants, day trips to Tiberias, a Saturday night outing with friends, and a host of activities to make up for all the plans we haven't had in the past three weeks. The problem with her plans is that they require effort by me, for example, to bathe, towel off, dress, descend a flight of stairs, open a car door, and, most importantly, peel myself off the couch onto which I've comfortably planted myself in front of MTV and Eurosport.

"But I made plans," says Dorit.

"But I don't want plans," I say.

"You no fun," Dorit says in her broken English. She has a point. But for the sake of pride, I argue back.

"I'm loads of fun!" I say.

"Look at you," she says.

I look at myself. I see a skinny white guy in tattered boxer shorts, sprawled on a ratty sofa watching British soccer, an island of marinara sauce crusting on his chest.

Worse, there are complaints about my performance—or lack thereof—in the bedroom. These complaints concern, in no particular order, my tendency to doze off during foreplay, her need to nudge me awake even as we approach the most exciting parts, and my inability to, shall we say, "maintain" (on the off chance we get that far in the first place). I explain it's not her, it's me, and that actually it's not me, it's the army—this goddamn army that's destroying in a matter of weeks what Dorit and I built over the course of two years.

Looking for a way to ruin a perfectly good relationship? Join the Israeli Army.

ADVANCED WARFARE TRAINING

WINTER

WORK MAKES FREE

We're down to forty-four.

December 1, we deploy north to the Golan Heights for fourteen weeks of advanced warfare training. But first, Captain Pinny gives seven more guys the boot. Two Yeshiva Boys, a kibbutz kid named D'vir, three Medical Excuse Guys, and Gil Weitzman, who we still think might be gay, are sent to a munitions factory, where they'll spend the next thirty months assembling missiles Monday through Friday, nine to five, weekends off.

Bastards.

The rest of us climb aboard the rickety Platoon Two, Company B school bus for the eight-hour drive to our new base, a tiny outpost in the Golan Heights called Sindiana.

We drive north, past the Dead Sea and the red-rock mountains of Jordan. In Ein Gedi, we stop for a pee break. Then north on Highway 90, past Jericho and Beit She'an, and into the Galilee. Somewhere around here, I fall asleep. An hour later, I awake to a sound I haven't heard in half a year:

Rain.

There are two seasons in Israel: winter, when it rains, and summer, when it doesn't. At the Armored School, we experienced violent winds and a sandstorm that canceled training for a day. But the rain that pummels our school bus is the first I've seen since I arrived in Israel nearly half a year ago.

The downpour is torrential, the sound deafening, like someone dumping an endless bucket of nails on the roof of our bus.

At Mahanayim Junction, we turn right, cross the Jordan River, and begin the slow, winding climb into the Golan Heights. We pass a fenced-off meadow that Platoon Sergeant Yoav tells us is a holding cemetery for dead Palestinian suicide bombers. Farther up, we come to an old minefield marked with a yellow DANGER! sign in Hebrew, English, and Arabic and a skull and crossbones for people who only read pictures.

The bus creaks to a stop at the foot of a grassy mountain. "Everybody off!" shouts Captain Pinny.

We scramble off the bus into the pouring rain. After a quick head count, Captain Pinny leads us up a muddy path. We march with our heads bowed. The raindrops prick my cheeks like tiny darts. High up, on top of the mountain, a tattered Israeli flag snaps in the breeze. As we near the peak, I get my first view of our new home: barbed-wire fence; a cluster of white, aluminum-sided trailers; a row of Merkava tanks.

"Formation!" barks Captain Pinny when we reach the top. We line up next to a black iron gate. The gate is tall, with thick wrought iron rails that run bottom to top, like jail bars. The gate looks ominous, impenetrable—the type of gate that once you enter, you never leave. It reminds me of the gate at the entrance to Auschwitz, the one marked ARBEIT MACHT FREI—Work Makes Free.

I turn to Tim. "You ever visit Auschwitz?"

Tim shakes his head.

"I did," says Etai. "We went in high school." He follows my gaze to the heavy iron gate and chuckles. *"Sha'ar Auschvitz,"* he says.

The name sticks. For the next fourteen weeks, my platoon mates and I will refer to the entrance to our base as the Auschwitz Gate.

The goal of advanced warfare training is to learn to fight a war. Every combat platoon in the Israeli Army completes a similar war games-style course. But ours has a reputation for being the most difficult because of its location: the sparse, hilltop bivouac called Sindiana.

Whereas the Armored School was a city unto itself, complete with a barbershop and canteen, Sindiana is like an abandoned ghost town. The entire base is the size of a soccer field. At one end are the tiny white trailers where we live eight to a room. Behind the trailers, near the Auschwitz Gate, is a phone booth, and behind that a latrine with two toilets, a sink, and one shower. On the opposite end of the base is the tank lot—a concrete slab that serves as the parking lot for our eleven Merkava tanks. Our tanks sit with cannons pointing northeast, toward Syria. Between the tanks and our trailers is the dining hall. Under the dining hall, dug into the mountain, is an ammunition bunker with enough ordnance to last us through six months of war.

Here at Sindiana, we're required to post four guards at all times: one to guard the tanks, a second in the ammunition bunker, a third who patrols the fence, and the fourth to stand watch at the Auschwitz Gate. Soldiers guarding the first three are allowed to guard in snowsuits, ski caps, and gloves. The Auschwitz Gate is a different story. Captain Pinny declares that for the sake of Armored Corps pride, whoever guards the front gate must wear his dress uniform and black beret no matter how biting the wind or torrential the rain.

Because of our proximity to Syria—we're less than two miles from the border—we're on a constant state of high alert. This means that we sleep in our tank suits, boots on, and that no more than nine of us—three tank crews—shower at a time. The old Operation Friendly Army rules such as six hours of sleep per night and chocolate sandwiches no longer apply.

I'm assigned to Tank 2B. My tank commander is Sergeant Adi, an ox of a twenty-year-old with a crooked nose and a missing front tooth. My loader is Uzi Zamoosh, the stuttering Yeshiva Boy. We have two drivers—Pasha, the perpetually limping Russian, and a loudmouth nitwit named Yair Lavi. This isn't the crew I'd hoped for. On the last night of Tank School, Captain Pinny passed out tank crew request sheets and asked that we list the soldiers we wanted to serve with in a tank crew. I requested Tim for my driver and Ronen Peretz for my loader. But as Captain Pinny reads off our new tank teams, it becomes apparent that not a single request was honored.

Along with my own crew, I'm rooming with the guys from Tank 2C: Kobi, Moti Sasson, Itamar, and a Russian named Nikolayev. Our tiny trailer has a space heater in the middle. The walls, light blue, are covered with graffiti. The trailer is freezing.

"P-p-p-p-put on the heater!" says Uzi Zamoosh.

"Are you stuttering or shivering?" snaps Yair.

I flick on the space heater. The coils glow orange.

Waiting for me on my top bunk is a pile of winter clothing. Most of my new gear is ripped. Anything big enough to write on has been vandalized. My equipment includes a one-piece snowsuit; plastic rain pants and parka; a blue knit ski cap that falls over my eyes because there's no elastic; green cotton gloves, each with a finger missing; two pair of white long johns, one with holes in the knees and the other with a hole in the crotch; and one sleeping bag decorated with a sketch of a naked woman with no head.

As I unpack my kit bag, Sergeant Adi comes by the trailer so I can sign for my equipment. I hold up a glove with three missing fingers. "How's this supposed to keep me warm?" I ask.

"You want my advice?" he grumbles. "Next time you're home, buy your own gear. This crap won't do you any good."

I climb on my top bunk and unroll my sleeping bag. On the wall, just above my head, is a poem scrawled in black magic marker:

> *There's a place on earth*
> *Far worse than hell*
> *Where the sun never shines*
> *The wind is a spear*
> *The cold is an ax*
> *And the rain falls*
> *Like it fell on Noah.*
> *There's a place on earth*
> *Far worse than hell*
> *A place called*
> *Sindiana.*

We start with a week of emergency drills. In these drills, we practice the step-by-step procedures for rescuing the tank, and each other, from harrowing situations.

In the drill "Incoming Missile," the driver throws the tank into reverse while the commander and loader duck inside the turret and the gunner fires a blind shot that, ideally, will disrupt the enemy's ability to navigate his antitank missile by remote control. In "Turret on Fire," we practice putting out an imaginary fire with our assigned fire extinguishers before the two thousand pounds of ordnance blow us to bits. In "Ruptured Tracks," we jump out and remove the heavy metal treads using mallets and wrenches while simultaneously fighting off enemy foot soldiers with the MAG. As far as I'm concerned, each of these drills could just as well be called "Holy Shit—We're Screwed," because I simply cannot see myself coming out of these horrific scenarios alive.

My least favorite drill is "Commander Killed." In this exercise, the tank commander's been shot dead, leaving the gunner, loader, and driver to fight the battle alone. First, the loader drags the commander's body into the infantry hatch while the driver backs the tank to a secure location, like the downward slope of a mountain or behind a thicket of trees. Once the commander's been evacuated, the gunner—in this case, me—climbs into the commander's chair and takes charge of the operation. I'm then supposed to fire the MAG machine gun at enemy infantrymen and radio headquarters for an artillery strike and medical backup.

The problem is, I don't know how to do any of these things. I never learned to fire the MAG—the day we did that in Tank School, Captain Pinny ordered me to pull weeds. As for radioing headquarters, I never learn to do that because the guy who's supposed to teach me how—my tank commander, Sergeant Adi—is pretending to be dead.

The first time we run the drill, I simply flip a bunch of random switches on the radio and shout, "Help! Help! My commander's dead!" into the microphone and make "Pow! Pow!" sound effects as I pretend to fire the MAG. After a couple of times doing it this way, and feeling very much like a jackass every time, I ask Sergeant Adi if he'd please demonstrate these procedures so I'll know exactly what to do in case he dies.

"But how can I show you if I'm dead?" he asks.

"I realize you're dead," I say. "But after, when you're back alive, you could show me. Possible?"

Sergeant Adi shakes his head. "The point of these drills is to teach you to use your instincts in an emergency. If your commander dies in Lebanon, there won't be anyone around to walk you through it."

I take a deep breath, remind myself he's only twenty, and try again.

"I understand that you're dead." I say slowly. "But maybe—just once— you could show me what to do, so that next time I can do it instinctively."

"But if I show you, then it's not instinctive."

Another deep breath. "Then how am I supposed to know how to command a tank if you never teach me?"

"Did you pay attention in Tank School?" Sergeant Adi asks.

"Yes," I say.

"Then you should know exactly what to do."

True to the poem on my trailer wall, the rain pummels us nonstop. Most days, the rain is accompanied by a piercing wind that slashes our faces like a whip.

Within a week, our base is transformed into a thick, soupy mud. The mud smothers us. When we walk, the mud gurgles and burps like boiling fudge. At the tanks, where the ground is soft, we sink in the mud to our knees. Getting from our trailers to the tanks necessitates the placing of our hands beneath our knees and pulling our boots, one at a time, up and out of the mud, which makes a sucking sound—*th-wop!*—as if we're wearing suction cups on the soles of our feet. We try to escape the mud, but it follows us into our sleeping bags, gets stuck beneath our fingernails and on our teeth. When I shower—about once every three nights—I scrub viciously, like a man afflicted with body lice. But the mud stays, and I go to sleep brown.

Were it simply the weather, Sindiana would be hell on earth. What makes life here truly unbearable is the fatigue. We're allotted four hours of sleep a night, but every other night we lose one of those hours to guard duty. Soon, I'm overwhelmed by a sense of exhaustion the likes of which I've never known. The fatigue invades every bone in my body. I feel like I'm made of wet paper, my muscles of applesauce. It reaches the point where I can no longer hold in my gas. Instead, my farts slip out at will without the slightest resistance. I am a zombie, and I cannot function.

One night, I stand in line outside the phone booth for twenty minutes. When my turn finally comes, I step inside, pick up the receiver, lift my index finger to dial—and freeze. I cannot for the life of me remember Dorit's phone number. I hover my finger over the keypad to trigger a memory. I recite numbers out loud, hoping to stumble on the correct combination. No dice. I couldn't be more blank if I'd never dialed her number in my life. Other nights, I hallucinate during guard duty and carry on long conversations with a bush that I swear is my best childhood friend, Dan.

The weather and exhaustion break us down. But there's only one explanation for why the platoon disintegrates as quickly as we do: the absolute lack of leadership from our officer—the arrogant, impudent, and thoroughly incompetent Captain Pinchas Fluman.

To command a military platoon, an officer needs to be equal parts Mussolini, Mister Rogers, and Martin Luther King, Jr. Lieutenant Yaron, our platoon commander in basic training, had the right mix; if anything, he was too much "won't you be my neighbor?" Captain Pinny, on the other hand, is all Mussolini, but without the charisma to back it up. Ever since we moved north to Sindiana, Captain Pinny's gone from annoying misfit to world-class, A-1 prick.

Nobody knows the reason for his sudden transformation. There's a rumor floating around that his beloved girlfriend, Rikki, dumped him, leaving him suddenly single and in command of a tank named for his ex. We're not sure if the rumor's true or simply hearsay. What we do know is that since advanced warfare training began, Captain Pinny Fluman is a monster.

The first I saw of the new evil Captain Pinny was last Thursday, the day designated for us to disassemble and clean the tanks. I was on my back, under the hull, scraping mud off the belly of the tank with a giant spatula when Captain Pinny knelt behind the tank and said, "How's it coming, Yoel?"

I scooted out and sat up. "Fine, Captain Pinny," I said.

"And how's your new tank team?"

"Good, Captain."

"And you have a girlfriend, right?"

"Yes, Captain."

"How's she?"

"We don't get to talk much. But she's fine."

"Good to hear," he said. "By the way—since you didn't salute me, I'm taking your next Sabbath." Then he stood up and walked away while I sat there, frozen, with my mouth open. I hadn't saluted an officer since basic training. And he wanted me to start now?

A couple of nights later, at around 2 A.M., I'm guarding the Auschwitz Gate when Captain Pinny orders me to wake up my buddy Idan Oren. "It's urgent," Captain Pinny says. "Bring him to my trailer. Quick."

I hustle into Idan's trailer and shake him awake. "It's urgent," I say.

Idan flies out of bed, dresses. Together, we run to Captain Pinny's trailer. "You wanted to see me, sir?"

Captain Pinny gives Idan a quick once-over. "Look at you, Idan," he sneers. "Your boot's untied. Snowsuit's unzipped. You're not wearing a beret. You look like a schmuck. Is that the proper way to greet your officer?" He slams the door in Idan's face.

Idan runs back to his trailer, gets his beret. I make sure he's all zipped and laced. Then he knocks a second time.

"That's more like it," says Captain Pinny.

"You needed to tell me something, sir?" says Idan.

"Yes. Your father called. Your grandmother's dead. Take the first bus home in the morning."

Captain Pinny implements a training regimen whose sole purpose appears to be ensuring that we'll be unprepared for combat. We spend the majority of our time cleaning—cleaning the tanks, the kitchen, the latrine, our trailers—the result of Captain Pinny's maniacal obsession with cleanliness. When we deploy to the field, we spend hours straightening and re-straightening the flagpole, for the sake of what Captain Pinny calls "Armored Corps pride."

Most atrocious of all are the rules that actually put us in jeopardy. There's an epidemic of head hitting throughout not just our platoon, but the entire Armored Corps. It's a fact of life when you're a tank soldier; you're going to whack your head on the cannon at least once every few days. But to Captain Pinny, hitting one's head is a sign of poor discipline. Hence, the Head Rule:

"From now on," he declares, "any soldier who hits his head on the cannon will lose his next Sabbath leave."

The Head Rule has dire consequences. One day, my driver, Pasha, is greasing the treads when he stands up and *wham!*—smacks his head into the cannon so hard that he passes out. We crowd around him, and Tim, who was a volunteer EMT in college, douses Pasha's face with water and checks his pulse.

"You alive?" Tim says in English.

Pasha's eyes flutter open.

Just then, Captain Pinny ambles over. "What's the story here?" he asks.

We look at one another, not sure of what to say. On the one hand, his injury could be serious. On the other, we don't want to out Pasha.

"My knee!" Pasha moans. He grabs his right knee and winces. "I slipped and hurt my knee."

"You should be more careful," says Captain Pinny. Then he walks away.

Twenty minutes later, we're walking to the trailers when Pasha suddenly keels over and pukes. "You've got a concussion," says Tim. "Tell the medic."

But Pasha refuses. He doesn't want to jeopardize his Sabbath leave. So instead he jeopardizes his life.

Taking their cue from Captain Pinny, our sergeants torture us with push-ups in the rain and nightly crawls through the mud. Meanest of all is Platoon Sergeant Yoav. He's the devil incarnate and, I'm convinced, psychotic to boot. Not content with abusing our bodies, he attacks us psychologically. He gets pretty racist, calling the Sephardic kids *kooshim*—"darkies"—and addressing the Russian kids with a mock Russian accent. One night, when we drop for push-ups, he whips out a disposable camera and snaps pictures of our faces covered with mud. His favorite target is Uzi Zamoosh, the chubby Yeshiva Boy with the stutter. Night after night, at evening formation, Yoav orders Uzi to step forward and recite the Nine Rules of Guard Duty.

"N-n-n-o . . . s-s-s-s—"

"Spit it out, Uzi!"

"S-s-s—"

"Sitting, you stuttering shit, sitting! *Ata mefager?* Are you retarded?"

The first time Yoav did this, we chuckled. Now we just stare at the mud.

As the weeks fly by, it becomes increasingly clear that if we do deploy to Lebanon, we won't be ready. Between the mopping, mud scraping, and wind sprints in the rain, there's no time left to train for war.

Faced with this grim prospect—i.e., the possibility of our imminent death—Tim and I do the one thing you'd expect a couple of college-educated, twenty-four-year-old Americans to do:

We begin a haircut contest.

It's Tim's idea. I take out my notebook and we draw up the rules.

"It's simple," says Tim. "Whoever goes longest without being forced to cut his hair, wins."

I think it over. "How about, first one to cut his hair, loses?"

"What's the difference?" he says.

"Let's say your commander orders you to cut your hair, but you're sneaky, and you find a way to put it off. That way, you're still in the contest."

Tim nods. "I like it. Put it in."

"What's the prize?" I say.

"Fifty shekels?"

I click my tongue. "Too much. Especially if you just had to pay for a haircut."

"Dinner at Burger King?"

"How about ice cream?" I say. As long as I take my lactose pills, it'd be a fine prize.

Tim agrees.

It's not about the ice cream, of course. Even though we're poor, both Tim and I can afford an ice cream bar. No, the Platoon Two, Company B Lone Soldier Haircut Contest is about something bigger than ice cream. It's about an idea. An idea that is at once grand and beautiful: the chance to fuck over the goddamn Israeli Army.

SPOILED AMERICAN

By week six of advanced warfare training, we have dissolved into forty platoons of one.

We bicker nonstop. It is any night at all that two of us come close to blows. Much of it is the usual bitching over guard duty, but there's a twist: In the old days, we whined about our guard duty slots but still guarded. Now many of my platoon mates simply refuse to get out of bed. When it's their turn to guard, they stay cuddled up in their sleeping bags and force whoever's guarding to pick up an extra shift.

We steal. If we see a pair of gloves with no fingers missing, we swipe it. We don't care if our comrade freezes. We are animals and we'll do what it takes to survive.

I turn into a person I don't recognize. I hate everyone, everything—my officer, my tank, my sergeants. I'm sick of the noxious stink inside my trailer—the damp, cheeselike stench of sweat, gas, and dirty flesh that happens when you live eight to a room. I'm sick of Pasha, my Russian driver, sitting naked on his bed, picking mud out of his pubic hair and flicking it on the floor. And Uzi Zamoosh, who screams at me to get out of the shower and then, when I don't, jumps into the stall with me, resulting in his penis accidentally brushing my thigh.

With no outlet for my frustration, I'm forced to express my anger in other ways.

I become violent. Standing in line for dinner, I ram my rifle, hard as I can, into Gerber's back. "Ohhh!" he moans, and I feel fantastic. During our morning jog, I sneak up behind Itamar, pretend to trip, and then tackle him to the ground. When he wails and groans, I feel an exhilarating sense of power. Since I can't create, I destroy, and when I destroy, I feel alive.

In my heart, I know this isn't me. I've never been violent, for the simple reason that I've always been the smallest guy in the group and I didn't want to get my ass kicked. But this army brings out the devil inside me. Hatred gurgles in my gut like lava.

One night, it comes to a head.

It's midnight. I'm in line for the pay phone. Inside the phone booth, Erez Talmor chats with his girlfriend. Talmor is a puny twerp with acne and beady eyes. He's a Medical Excuse Guy. This week, he stayed in bed with a sore back.

I pound the glass. "Hurry up!" I shout.

Talmor slides opens the door. "Relax," he says, and slides the door shut.

I open the door. "You've got all day to make your phone calls, you lazy fuck, so get off the goddamn phone."

"Spoiled American," he says.

I grab Talmor by the collar and shove him into the glass. "The fuck you call me?" I shout in English.

"Let go!" he screams in Hebrew.

He pushes. I stumble back, into the mud, but I'm clutching his collar and he tumbles down with me.

"I'll kill you!" I shout as he falls on top of me.

"P'tuh!" he spits in my face.

I grab his neck, punch—

"Ow!"

"You're dead, you little fuck!"

We roll, flail, fingernails, fists, while in the background my platoon-mates scream, "Get him!"

"Yallah!"

Suddenly, someone grabs me from behind, hauls me off, while I continue to shout, "Fuck you, you little shit!" in English. I'm seething. I will kill Talmor. I try to charge at him, but Tim restrains me, holds my arms like I'm under arrest. He walks me a couple of steps away, next to a trailer.

I'm panting. Sweating and freezing. A few feet away, Talmor squirms while Doni and Tomer hold him back.

"What's the story?" barks Captain Pinny, who appears seemingly out of nowhere.

That night, as punishment, I sleep in a pup tent with Talmor. As the rain patters down and the little schmuck snores next to me in his sleeping bag, I finally admit what I've suspected for some time: I'm not one of them.

The next night, after everyone else is asleep, I sneak into the phone booth and dial.

My dad answers.

"It's me," I say.

"Joel—are you all right?"

I open my mouth, but I can't talk around the lump in my throat.

"Son?" he says.

"Yes."

"What's wrong?"

I take a deep breath. "I want out," I whisper.

From the silence on the other end, it's clear my father has no idea what to say. This is a first. My dad's always been the man with the answers. But he has no template for this. No clue how to help a son through the army.

The third time I almost die it's a Wednesday. I'm on my knee, in the mud, shooting at cardboard Arabs in the rain. All of a sudden, Lior Tanenbaum, who's next to me, yells, "Shit!"

I turn my head to look. A couple of feet away, Tanenbaum flips over his rifle and starts pounding the magazine, with the nozzle pointing straight at my face.

"Tanenbaum!" I shout. But he doesn't hear.

I lean back, away from the nozzle, but no matter where I move the nozzle seems to follow me. Finally I just get up, grab Tanenbaum's rifle by the barrel, and push it away from my face and out toward the targets.

"You trying to kill me?" I say.

Tanenbaum stares at me in shock. "I'm sorry. I don't know where my head was," he says. As if on cue, a bullet shoots out into the range.

Two days after I almost die, Tim almost dies. Except instead of being almost killed by a fellow soldier, Tim is almost killed by his tank commander, Sergeant Amir.

I'm next to my tank, smearing Vaseline onto the axles, when for no reason in particular I look at the tank next to mine and see Tim pop his head out of the driver's hatch. About a millisecond after my brain processes this image, I watch Sergeant Amir climb into the commander's hatch of Tim's tank and begin to rotate the turret. As soon as I see this, I know it's a disaster in the making: in approximately two seconds, Sergeant Amir will slice off Tim's head with the cannon.

I open my mouth—but I'm so shocked that nothing comes out. I watch in horror as the cannon swoops toward Tim's head like a giant razor blade.

"Tim! Down!" shouts Sergeant Adi from atop my tank. Tim turns, looks, ducks—*Whoosh!*—as the cannon swings over his head.

Strike three happens the next Monday. I'm in my trailer, changing into my tank suit after a stint of guard duty at the Auschwitz Gate, when I hear a muffled explosion, followed by a scream. I zip up, grab my rifle, and hustle to the tanks. Everyone's crowded around Tank 1B, about a hundred yards out in the field. All around me, my platoon mates jabber away excitedly.

"Blind!"

"Appelbaum!"

"Dead!"

"Grenade!"

I still haven't heard the story when a military ambulance shows up at the Auschwitz Gate and a team of medics rush the tank.

"Everyone back!" shouts Captain Pinny. "Into your trailers! Now!"

In my trailer, Doni fills me in. According to him, Appelbaum and the other loaders were learning how to throw grenades from inside the turret of the tank. Standing next to Appelbaum, in the commander's hatch, was Sergeant Hezzi. Each loader threw three grenades—two dummies, then one live. On Appelbaum's third throw, he pulled the pin but then accidentally dropped his grenade onto the hull. Thinking fast, Sergeant Hezzi reached across and pushed Appelbaum's head down into the turret, like a kid stuffing the puppet into a jack-in-the-box, while the live grenade lay on the hull like a ticking time bomb. Then Sergeant Hezzi tried to duck inside himself, but it was too late. The grenade exploded, riddling his face with shrapnel. Sergeant Hezzi was alive and conscious. But as for whether he'll see again, nobody knows.

With no officer to inspire us, a team of sergeants intent on breaking us, and a devastating winter that freezes our sentences halfway out of our mouths, it's simply a matter of time before somebody crumbles. The only question now is, who will go first?

Yossi Barzel is the first to crack.

I'm on top of the tank, squirting oil onto the MAG, when the rumor crashes into me like a tidal wave.

"Yossi Barzel!"

"The trailer!"

"His rifle!"

"Suicide!"

I scoot off the tank and double-time it to Barzel's trailer. When I arrive, there's already a crowd. I burrow my way through. My platoon mates whisper nervously among themselves. Only then do I look up and see what all the fuss is about.

Over in the corner Yossi Barzel sits on the top bunk in his underwear. He sits Indian style with a bag of potato chips in his lap. With one hand, he feeds himself chips. With the other, he balances his assault rifle on the mattress so that the nozzle points straight at his head. He's a chubby kid, with a shaved head and huge blue eyes that protrude out of his face like giant marbles. His tits sag like droopy pears. A ring of flab hangs over his skin-tight turquoise briefs. He looks like a hungry suicidal Buddha.

We gawk at him like he's the Mona Lisa.

"Say something," Ronen Peretz whispers in my ear.

"Me?" I say.

"You studied psychology, right?"

He has a point. Of all of us, I'm probably the best qualified to handle this. As an RA, I once talked a kid out of suicide until the paramedics came. Then again, all the kid had was a Bic razor. Yossi Barzel's got a loaded gun.

I step forward. I try to think of something eloquent to say.

"Hey."

Barzel smiles. Munches a chip.

"You don't really want to do this, Yossi." I say.

"Yes I do," he says.

This is going to be harder than I thought.

"Look. *Achi*. No matter how bad you feel now, it will pass."

"Fuck yourself," he says. He bites a chip.

Suddenly, Captain Pinny bursts through the door. He elbows his way through, straight to Yossi's bed. He holds out his hand. "Gun," he says.

Yossi hands him his rifle.

"All right, people. It's over. Everybody out."

We don't move.

"Out!" he roars.

That night, Captain Pinny orders us to sleep with our rifles strapped to our chests. He commands Yossi's roommates to sleep with the light on. And in addition to our four regular guard duty posts, Captain Pinny establishes a fifth: we are now to stand guard over Yossi Barzel twenty-four hours a day, lest the boy hurt himself. For one week, we take turns standing watch over Yossi while he sits on his bed in his underwear, reading magazines and munching pound cake. Eventually the mental health officer arrives and whisks Yossi away in a jeep. And we're down to forty-three.

After that, it's a free-for-all.

During dinner, Nitzan Siman-Tov starts to bawl. He cries like a baby, right there in the dining trailer, while the rest of us stare. Gerber pats his back, asks what's the matter. Nitzan bawls louder. Finally, when Nitzan starts to hyperventilate, Captain Pinny slams down his fork, picks up Nitzan by the hood of his jacket, and walks him outside into the rain. By bedtime, Nitzan's gone. Forty-two.

The next morning, after breakfast, Yair storms out of the dining trailer, strips off his assault rifle, shouts, *"Koos emok!"* and throws his gun at Captain Pinny, just barely missing his knees.

Captain Pinny, furious, picks up Yair's rifle and shouts, "What in God's name is the matter with you? You want me to kick you out of this platoon?"

Forty-one.

But it's Eldad Azulay, the runaway who hasn't seen his parents since he was fifteen, who pulls the biggest coup of all.

Two months into the course, we awake at three in the morning to the blare of a siren. This happens twice a week—it's an emergency drill where we simulate being attacked by Syria. We zip up our tank suits, throw on our helmets and flak jackets, grab our rifles, and sprint to the tanks. Except for Eldad, who shows up wearing his helmet, rifle, and combat boots but, otherwise, is completely in the nude.

The sight of Eldad with his helmet crooked on his head and rainwater dripping off his shriveled shlong is just too much. Everyone, soldier and sergeant alike, does what he can to not burst out laughing.

Everyone, that is, except Captain Pinny. Livid, he stares Eldad in the eye and growls, "I've half a mind to kick you out of the Armored Corps."

Eldad smiles. Forty.

• • •

On the verge of a nervous breakdown, I turn to the one sane voice in the platoon: Tim Bailey.

In the real world, we'd never be friends. But in this jungle of Israeli teens, Tim and I have a bond. We are bonded, first and foremost, by our disgust with our bratty eighteen-year-old platoon mates, whom Tim and I now refer to as The Kids. And we are bonded by the insanity of being twenty-four-year-old, college-educated Americans in an army run by children. Like me, Tim sees the lunacy in our orders and backwardness in how our platoon is run. Better yet, he sympathizes with my suffering. In this way, Tim is not only my new best friend, he's my new therapist. Every night, before bed, we swap stories and get the bad vibes off our chests. "So this morning," I say to Tim, "I'm standing on the turret when all of a sudden, I trip and drop the MAG near Platoon Sergeant Yoav's foot."

"Oh, no," Tim says.

"Oh, yes. So he calls me down with his finger. You know . . ." I wiggle my finger ominously, in the manner of our evil platoon sergeant. "Then he stands with his face an inch from mine and shouts, 'Chasnoff, *ata bizayon*! You're a waste!' "

"So what'd you do?"

"I bit my lip. Then I climbed into the tank, sat in the gunner's chair, and cried."

Tim nods. "I hear you."

Those three words—"I hear you"—are like gold. An Israeli would call me weak for breaking down. But Tim gets it. Talking to Tim makes me feel like me again, even if it's only for five minutes at the end of the day.

SNOW

And then there are moments when the world is right again. In these moments, the fighting stops, the hate subsides, and once again we are boys.

It happens the first night of Hanukkah, when we light the menorah in the dining trailer and Captain Pinny leads us in a round of songs. It happens again on December 15, when, during a twenty-kilometer hike through the Golan Heights, Tim blurts out that it's my birthday, even though I'd asked him not to tell. When it comes time to open the stretcher, my platoon mates strap me in, hoist me in the air, and sing "Happy Birthday," in Hebrew and distorted English, all the way back to the base.

And then there's the frigid January morning when we step outside our trailers and see a most incredible sight:

Snow.

For most of my comrades, this is their first snowfall. We dash into our trailers, change into our snowsuits, and hurry back outside to play. We pelt one another with snowballs and shout, "Grenade!" We wrestle and mash snow into one another's faces while we shriek and giggle like children. Tim teaches the platoon to make snow angels. Platoon Sergeant Yoav and I build a snowman. We name him Yoram. We use bullets for eyes, a pipe cleaner for a nose, and an empty magazine for a mouth. When we finish, Platoon Sergeant Yoav leans his assault rifle against Yoram's round torso. Then he takes off his dog tags and wedges them beneath Yoram's chin.

"I'll get my beret," I say. Platoon Sergeant Yoav digs up an extra set of sergeant stripes, which he sticks on Yoram's torso.

"Now he's a sergeant," says Platoon Sergeant Yoav. I take a step back and salute.

By dinnertime, the snow is gone. Our snow angels turn to puddles and Sergeant Yoram goes AWOL into the mud. But for those two hours when hell froze over, the world was actually beautiful.

GAME OVER

On the haircut front, Tim jumps out to an early lead when, ten weeks into advanced warfare training, Sergeant Adi asks me how long it's been since I cut my hair.

I pat my head, survey the growth. "Maybe a week?" I lie.

Sergeant Adi clicks his tongue. "Find someone with clippers and cut it."

When I tell Tim, he's ecstatic. "Mmm . . . ice cream." He rubs his tummy.

That night, I check my hair in the mirror. The problem isn't what's on top. It's my sideburns. They grow wild and unruly, like stalks of wheat.

I need a plan.

The next day, at morning inspection, I tuck my sideburns behind my ears and wear a beret. Sergeant Adi eyes me suspiciously. I'm the only one in the trailer wearing a beret. I'm certain my gig is up. He must know I'm only trying to hide my hair.

"What's with the beret?" he asks.

"Respect for the Armored Corps!" I say without thinking.

He nods. "Now that's what I want to see!" he says. "Tomorrow morning, you're all in berets!"

But at lunch, my luck runs out. On his way out of the dining trailer, Sergeant Adi puts his enormous hand on my shoulder and says, "Bee dulls."

I look up. He's smiling—a wide, gap-toothed grin, like a happy hockey player.

"Huh?" I say.

He starts to play air guitar. "She love you, yeh, yeh, yeh," he sings in horribly accented English.

"I don't get it," I say.

"Bee dulls," he says.

I smile. "Oh! The Beatles!" I say.

"Yes. Beatles." Sergeant Adi grabs my hair. "You look like the Beatles. Cut your hair tonight or you lose your next Sabbath."

Across the table, Tim grins. "Ice cream," he hums.

Game over. Stupid American.

THE GAYEST TANK ON EARTH

It's official. In eighteen days, on the first Monday in March, Platoon Two, Company B will disband. Ten of us will be sent back to the Armored School for the twelve-week tank commander course. The rest of us will deploy to Lebanon, where we'll team up with a brigade of Golani infantrymen for a three-month tour in the eastern sector of the Security Zone.

When Captain Pinny Fluman delivers the news, I immediately feel sick. It's not that I don't want to serve in Lebanon. Despite the horror stories, I do. My year in the army would be incomplete without a tour. I'd feel like I'd climbed Everest only to quit twenty meters from the peak.

What gnaws at me is the sickening knowledge that we're completely unprepared. In the past eleven weeks of advanced warfare training, I've fired a grand total of three missiles. On two of those shots, I missed. Nor have we practiced a single ambush of the kind we'll employ against Hezbollah. I get the sense Captain Pinny couldn't care less if I live or die.

"Beginning Sunday," Captain Pinny continues, "we'll deploy to Area Sixteen in the Golan Heights for ten days of intense pre-Lebanon training. We'll sleep in the tanks. We'll eat combat rations and wear helmets and flak jackets at all times, just like you will in Lebanon. During the day, you'll learn first aid, hand-to-hand combat, and how to call in artillery strikes. At night, we'll run ambushes exactly like the ones you'll carry out in the Security Zone. Trust me: you'll see more action these next ten days than in your entire three months in Lebanon."

Outside in the rain, I put my arm around Tim and say, "Well, looks like you and I are about to die."

"No one's going to die," he says.

I stop walking. I look him in the eye. "Seriously, Tim. They're going to kill us."

"What, Hezbollah?"

"Hezbollah? Ha! No, not Hezbollah. Captain Pinny, man. This army. This army's going to *fucking kill us!*"

"Chasnoff, relax," Tim says.

"Relax? How am I supposed to relax when I'm about to die?"

Around me, my platoon mates gather in a clump.

"What's your problem?" says Gerber.

"My problem? My problem is that we're about to fucking die!"

"Chazzy," Tim says and grabs my arm.

"No!" I shout and shake loose. "They need to know, Tim. They need to know this army doesn't give a shit about their lives."

"You're crazy," says Gerber.

"I'm crazy?" I lunge at Gerber, throw a punch, miss. I stumble, and then the next thing I know Tim's got me in a headlock and then I'm down, on my back, in the mud, with Tim straddling me and pinning my arms to the sides. "We're going to die!" I shout. I want the whole world to hear me. *"We! Are going! To—"*

Whap!

Tim slaps me upside the face. Suddenly, it's quiet. Rain patters down on my forehead. Above me, my platoon mates stand in a huddle and stare down at me like I'm a madman. Which I am.

"The hell's wrong with you?" says Tim.

"Get off," I say.

"You cool?"

"Yes. Get off."

Tim stands and pulls me up. He grabs the back of my coat, like he's the cop and I'm the hoodlum, and walks me to my trailer. "You guarding?" he says.

I nod. "Three til four, at Auschwitz."

"I'll cover you," he says. "You sleep."

I strip off my coat and slide into bed. Right before he leaves, I say, "Tim. Tell the truth. Do you really think they're not sending us to die?"

He doesn't answer.

Sunday morning, we transfer to Area 16 for ten days of maneuvers, drills, and intense pre-deployment training. The short version of the story is that none of it happens. The longer version is that most of our instructors can't be bothered to show up. In our *Krav Maga*, hand-to-hand combat class, scheduled for all of one hour, my comrades and I kick sleeping bags. Our class is cut short when our instructor, Miri, gets a call on her cell phone that requires her to leave, a family emergency. She promises to return but never does. Our first aid class is canceled when Zev, the battalion medic, leaves a message on Captain Pinny's voice mail that his jeep got stuck in the mud near Katzrin Junction. Nor can he make it out later in the week, because tomorrow morning he leaves for his ten-day, once-every-four-months military vacation and he's already got a hotel room booked in Eilat.

The artillery class happens at 1 A.M. in a freezing field tent. Shivering and exhausted, we can barely keep our eyes open, much less remember a single detail about how/why/when to call in artillery.

And as for the whole point of this ten-day pre-Lebanon training camp—our preparation for combat against Hezbollah—we don't do a single practice ambush.

Not one.

Instead, we spend these ten days the same way we spent the previous twelve weeks at Sindiana: scraping mud off the tanks, greasing the treads, straightening and restraightening the flagpole to display our Armored Corps pride, and a thousand other pointless activities in which we do everything but train for war.

Tim and I are horrified. But we're the only ones who seem to care. Our seven sergeants don't seem the least bit disturbed by their complacency in this fiasco. It obviously doesn't occur to them that if one of us dies, it's not just Captain Pinny who'll have blood on his hands, but them. Nor do my eighteen-year-old platoon mates appear the least bit concerned that with just days until we do battle with the fiercest guerrilla army on the planet, we're still cleaning per usual. Not even the smart guys get it. When I tell Dror Boy Genius that there's something fishy going on, he doesn't say, "You're right. We should protest." Instead, Dror shrugs his shoulders and says, *"Mah ta'rotzeh? Tzavah!"* ("What do you want? It's the army!") As if the sheer fact that we're in the army excuses it, and that the same crazy ol' military bureaucracy that explains why last week's shipment of chocolate milk didn't arrive until Thursday and why Moshe Schwartz received one pair of long johns instead of two, is the reason we'll ship off to a war zone unprepared.

Captain Pinny says, "You'll learn more in your first twenty-four hours in Lebanon than I could teach you in a year."

"But what if I don't survive twenty-four hours?" I ask Tim.

As deployment day nears, I experience an odd, but not surprising, return of every OCD tendency I've ever had. When I shave, I declare that if even a single stubble of hair remains on my face, I'll die in Lebanon. During breakfast, I must eat every last morsel of cottage cheese, or I won't live. I invent games to test my fate. We'll be walking to the black field tent when I'll suddenly think, *If I reach the tent first, I'll live through Lebanon.* I then sprint, fast as I can, while my platoon mates look on as if I'm some sort of freak. In another game, I pair thoughts with actions and repeat the action as many times as necessary until it matches a positive thought. For example, I'll bend over to pick up, say, a wrench, but at the exact moment I touch the wrench I'll think, *Die in Lebanon.* According to the rules of the game, I must then drop the wrench and pick it up again and again until I can do it without thinking, *Die in Lebanon.* Sometimes it takes thirty times before my thoughts are pure. It's torture, but these rituals are my security blanket. Without them, I'd feel like my life was out of my hands.

On three separate occasions, I tell three different sergeants that I don't feel we're training as we should. On each occasion, Sergeants Adi, Omri, and Amir say the same thing: "You'll learn more in your first twenty-four hours in Lebanon than I could teach you in a year."

In other words, Lebanon is so dangerous and unpredictable that it'd be a waste of time to prepare.

On the final night of pre-Lebanon training, Colonel Avi, the commanding officer of the 188th Armored Brigade, shows up for a pre-Lebanon briefing and pep talk. We gather in the field tent and sit Indian style in the mud as he addresses us.

His speech is the standard fare: he congratulates us on completing the course and commends Captain Pinny for his leadership. He reminds us that we Armored soldiers are the backbone of the operation in Lebanon. Without us, northern Israel would be dangerously exposed—"naked as a bride on her honeymoon," are his exact words. Regarding Hezbollah, he offers this advice: "Trust your training and stay alert. The real enemy in Lebanon isn't Hezbollah. It's surprises."

Before he leaves, Colonel Avi asks if we have questions. A few guys ask the usual moronic questions about more sleep, better furloughs, and not enough food. Colonel Avi brushes aside their questions as if they're mosquitoes buzzing near his shoulder. He then addresses us with these final words:

"Stay safe. Be smart. Good luck." Then he stacks his papers and heads to the door.

Before I can think about what I'm doing, I throw up my hand. "Colonel!" I shout.

He turns. "Question?" he says.

"No. Something to say."

"What's your name?" he snaps.

I stand up. Suddenly my heart is pounding. "Yoel, Colonel."

"Nu?" he says.

I look at my platoon mates.

"We're not ready," I say.

He glares at me as if I'm insane. "What?"

I begin to tremble. I look at my comrades for backup. Nobody moves.

"We didn't train," I say, my voice quivering. "This platoon isn't ready for Lebanon."

The colonel stares at me. Then he turns to our platoon commander. "Pinny," he says. "Are your boys prepared for Lebanon?"

"Absolutely," says Captain Pinny.

"It's not true!" I say.

"Quiet!" the colonel shouts. "Platoon Two—does anyone agree with Yoel that you're unprepared?"

Silence.

"Sit," he orders.

I sit. The colonel's eyes stay glued to my face. "I understand that with four days to go, you're scared. But don't confuse fear with lack of preparation. Understood?"

I nod.

"Second: most of what you need to learn about Lebanon you can only learn in Lebanon. Captain Pinny trained you the best he could. The rest you'll learn on the battlefield. That's not negligence. That's war."

• • •

Advanced warfare training ends with a ceremony. On the first Sunday in March, our families trek up to our hellhole, Sindiana. By now, though, the rain's stopped, the mud's caked, and the sky's a cloudless blue. In a way, it's disappointing. Now they'll never know the hell we've been through.

I recognize many of the families, though some things have changed. Little brothers are taller. Hayim's dad, who has cancer, is in a wheelchair, bald and covered with a blanket, cheeks sagging like wet bread. Fewer girlfriends show up this time.

Dorit drives up in her new company car. I give her the quick tour. I explain how the Auschwitz Gate got its name. She isn't amused.

After lunch, Captain Pinny Fluman gives a speech. He tells our parents we've trained hard and promises we're prepared for our fight against Hezbollah.

Lies.

The highlight of our ceremony is the Presentation of the Tank. At first, I thought the whole idea of presenting a tank was crazy. After all, it's one thing to present a soldier with an assault rifle; it's another to present him with a sixty-five-ton battle tank. But Captain Pinny and our commanders, geniuses that they are, manage to pull it off.

"Ladies and gentlemen," Captain Pinny shouts like a ringmaster. "I now present to you . . . the Merkava Three Baz battle tank!"

Far ahead, in the green field, our tank appears like a brown dot on the horizon. The tank drives toward us, growing bigger as it nears. As it gets closer, I see five of our sergeants walking in a triangle, in front of the tank, as if they're an arrowhead. They walk slowly, like robots, with their rifles held flush against their torsos, perpendicular to the ground. Another commander sits inside the driver hatch, driving. The seventh—I think it's Sergeant Adi—stands in the commander hatch with both hands raised high over his head. He's holding something. Something gray and rectangular. It looks like a block of cement. I can't figure out what it is.

And then I hear the music. Sergeant Adi holds a giant boom box over his head, the way John Cusack did in *Say Anything*. Except instead of "In Your Eyes," it's the theme from *Chariots of Fire*.

Our sergeants march in rhythm to the beat. As the tank gets closer, I see it's decorated with streamers and balloons. The tank looks like a birthday party.

"Oh. My. God," says Tim.

"Our tank," I say. "It looks so—"

"Gay?" says Tim.

"Precisely," I say.

"Our tank is homosexual," Tim says.

"It's the gayest tank on earth," I say.

When they're fifty yards away, the tank fires a smoke screen: *Poof!*

My platoon mates and their families break into wild applause. Our sergeants scurry forward and bow, actors taking a curtain call.

"Bravo!" someone shouts.

"That was incredible!" Dorit exclaims.

Tim stares straight ahead with his mouth open. "You okay?" I ask.

He looks at me. "Kids," he manages.

At dusk, we march en masse through the Auschwitz Gate, down the hill to the minefield, where our families parked their cars. Dorit and I walk in silence. I clutch her hand tight. It occurs to me this could be the last time I ever see her. I banish the thought from my mind, but it shoves its way back in like a battering ram.

"What are you thinking about?" Dorit says.

Out of the corner of my eye, I see the yellow skull-and-crossbones sign next to the minefield. "Tomorrow," I say. "How about you?"

"I'm thinking about your Gramma Ruth," she says.

I pull away. "What?"

Dorit nods. "I could worry about the bad things that might happen to you in Lebanon. But then I think about your grandmother. If she were here, she'd remind me about hundreds of other ways we could die. We can get hit by cars, drown in our bathtubs—"

"Choke on our bedsheets," I say.

"It makes me feel better," says Dorit. "It means there's nothing all that different about Lebanon."

When we get to Dorit's car, I tear up. I want so badly to say something poignant. Something she'll remember me by forever. Last night, a couple of us stayed up late and wrote farewell notes, in case we didn't make it back alive. This morning, I reread my note, saw how corny it was, and tore it up. Now I wish I had something to give her. The only thing I can think to give her is my dog tags. But I need those, in case . . .

I hug her. Tight. Many times. "Stay safe, love," she whispers.

"Uh-huh," I mumble.

I watch her car until it disappears behind a bend. Then I sit in the grass, next to the minefield, and cry.

At seven o'clock on the first Monday morning in March, we line up in two formations. In one stand the ten soldiers headed to the Armored School to become tank commanders, including Tomer, Idan, Doni, Dror Boy Genius, and six other Ashkenazi White Guys from good neighborhoods and laudable schools. I could have been one of them—I was given an invite to tank commander's course. But it would've meant signing up for two more years, so I declined.

In the other formation stand the rest of us, who, in a matter of minutes, will board the rickety Platoon Two, Company B school bus and head north to the border with Lebanon.

"Take two minutes to say good-bye," orders Captain Pinny.

From that point on, it's pretty much like the last morning of summer camp: the handshakes that turn into hugs, the promises to stay in touch, and the realization, like a kick in the stomach, that it's actually over. For the past fourteen weeks, we've hated each other's guts. Now, with most of us shipping off to war, we're brothers once more.

Dror Boy Genius throws his arms around me. "Who am I going to share a tent with?" he asks.

My buddy Doni, six foot four with hands like Samson's, smothers me in a giant hug. "Promise me you'll stay safe," he says.

"Okay," I say, my voice cracking. For some reason, hearing this eighteen-year-old kid say this like he's my father makes me cry. But no need to be embarrassed, because it's not just me. It's all of us. It's odd. For the past three months, we've done nothing but argue and stab one another in the back. Now that it's time to say goodbye, our hearts are breaking.

Someone touches my arm. I turn.

It's Tomer.

"Oh, no," I say. I throw my arms around my friend and sob quietly on his shoulder.

"Stay safe," he croaks.

I nod. If I speak, I'll go to pieces.

"Let's go!" yells Captain Pinny. "On the bus!"

But we ignore him. Instead, we embrace one another and weep. So picture that, too, if you can: forty Israeli combat soldiers, in olive-green uniforms and assault rifles, bawling their eyes out like little boys who just buried their puppies.

LEBANON

SPRING

STARBUCKS OF LEBANON

I'd heard Lebanon was beautiful, but I never would have believed it if I hadn't seen it myself. I mean, dear God, have you seen the sky in Lebanon?

The sky is an ocean, smooth and aquamarine. The clouds, gooey and white, stretch across the heavens like melted marshmallows pulled at either end. Have you ever seen a sky so luscious, so rich, you actually wanted to drink it?

And the hills—the hills are marble, swirls of brown and green rolled together like undulating layers of mint and fudge. Below, in the valley, a forest grows thick and bright green, the trees like stalks of neon broccoli. Boulders, gray and metallic, dot the hilltops. The sun, low over a mountain, drips orange into the hills.

"You should sit," says the soldier on the bench.

I'm in the rear of an armored truck. The truck is olive green and fortified with steel plates. The back, where I sit, is covered by a heavy brown tarp that arches over us like a bulletproof rainbow. We're last in a convoy of two Humvees, one jeep, and two other armored transport trucks. With me in the truck are fifteen other soldiers, none of whom I know. We range in age from eighteen to about forty. Per orders, we wear helmets and flak jackets. We hold our rifles with magazines in, a bullet in the chamber, safety switch on. We sit on two wooden benches that run the length of the truck bed. We bump up and down over a dusty, one-lane road that snakes through South Lebanon like an interstate highway through Eden.

The soldier next to me takes out a cigarette. He offers me the box.

"No thanks," I say. He is a reserve soldier, middle aged, with short gray hair. His suntanned face is wrinkled and cracked, like a tire.

"First time here?" he asks.

"Yes," I say. "You?"

He takes a drag. "Too many times," he replies.

I stand and walk to the back. Through the rear portal, I watch hills that look like coffee urns melt into the summer sun.

"Beautiful, right?" says the old soldier.

I nod.

"Don't be fooled," he says.

"What do you mean?"

He takes a puff. Exhales. "This war is Hezbollah's wet dream."

I stare at the countryside. "How?"

The soldier stands and joins me at the back. "You see these mountains?" he says, and sweeps his hand, cigarette between his fingers, at the passing landscape.

"Yes," I say.

"When you were a kid, did you ever play hide-and-seek?"

"Of course."

"Remember how, when you played at your friend's house, you could never find him because he knew all the good spots?"

I nod.

"Lebanon is like hide-and-seek," the soldier says. "And this is Hezbollah's backyard."

After an hour of rolling hills, the convoy stops on the outskirts of a village. The village is sparse—a row of cinder-block storefronts, an auto parts shop, and, behind it, up in the hills, a cluster of squat, flat-roofed homes. We drive through at low speed. We pass a tiny restaurant marked with a rusty white sign that says, in English, "Najaf's Café." Outside Najaf's, a pair of old men dressed in kaffiyehs and robes sit on plastic chairs next to a plastic table and play backgammon. Between turns, the men take hits off a nargileh. A little girl on a tricycle waves. I wave back and her grandmother yanks her arm.

Back in the countryside, we speed up, but not for very long. Within minutes, we come to a second village—though in comparison to the first, this one is a bustling metropolis. The street is paved and split in two by a grassy median. Red lampposts sprout up from the median, each adorned with a giant, globe-shaped bulb. Boxy Subarus, white and light blue, blare their horns and jostle their way into a cul-de-sac. On the sidewalk, women in headscarves carry vegetables in pink shopping bags. Above a bakery, a blue and red Pepsi sign squeaks in the breeze. Two teenage boys in oddly patterned sweaters and dark slacks sit on a street corner, on a bench, eating pita.

A child peers into a toy store, the window packed with inflatable Mickey Mouse heads. Next to the toy store, another Najaf's Café.

Najaf's. The Starbucks of Lebanon.

It's strange. Whenever I imagined Lebanon, I pictured tall men with beards, dressed in camouflage. I pictured land mines and booby-trapped rocks. I never thought about shopping carts, coffee shops, or inflatable toys. Somehow, I forgot to imagine ordinary people.

As we rumble down the street, a boy, maybe eight years old, runs down the sidewalk, chasing us. He waves wildly and smiles. I wave to the boy, and when I do, he stops running and waves frantically with both hands high over his head. He has black hair and light brown skin. He wears sandals, blue pants, and a white T-shirt upon which he has scrawled, in childish handwriting in red Magic Marker, imitating a basketball jersey:

BULS
23

The South Lebanon Security Zone encompasses nine hundred square miles of Lebanese farmland, villages, and uninhabited countryside. At its narrowest point, in the southeast corner, the Security Zone encroaches a mere two miles into Lebanon, and at its deepest, ten. At any given time, about one thousand Israeli troops patrol the buffer zone, including soldiers from Infantry, Armored, Artillery, Air Force, Navy SEALs, Special Forces, Intelligence, and a handful of top-secret units whose names and missions I don't know. Israeli soldiers rotate into Lebanon for stints lasting anywhere from a few hours to four weeks. Army rules dictate that every soldier must be allowed one twenty-four-hour furlough at least once every twenty-eight days. The joke is that the only thing worse than a string of consecutive 1-in-28 leaves is a bunch of 1-in-28 leaves that match up perfectly with your girlfriend's menstrual cycle. A guy could go three years without getting laid.

The Security Zone is divided into two sectors, east and west. The eastern sector is known as the "hot" zone, with more Hezbollah strongholds, violent clashes, and Israeli soldiers killed than in the western, "cool" sector. For this reason, stronger Infantry and Armored units, like the 188th, serve in the east. There are ten to twenty Israeli bases spread through the buffer zone, almost all of them named for the closest Lebanese village—our bases all have Arabic names, not Hebrew. Bases range in size from tiny outposts manned by a squad of infantrymen to large, city-like compounds accommodating tanks, artillery, and a slew of armored trucks.

Aiding us in our mission are the soldiers of the South Lebanese Army, or SLA. The SLA joined sides with Israel not because they suddenly love Jews, but because they are Christians and, therefore, happy to help anyone fighting Muslims.

As for that mission I mentioned above—

The reason Israel established the Security Zone in the first place was to push Hezbollah back, away from the border, deep enough to keep their Katyusha rockets out of range of northern Israel. According to the army, without Israeli soldiers to patrol the Security Zone, Hezbollah would resume firing their rockets at will. According to the Four Mothers, the cost in Israeli soldiers' lives isn't worth the cost of preventing Hezbollah from firing rockets we're not even sure they'd launch if we left.

I'm stationed in the eastern sector of the Security Zone on a hilltop compound called Eshyeh. From the outside, Eshyeh looks like a hastily built sand castle, mashed together by a child using whatever sand, rocks, twigs, bottle caps, candy bar wrappers, and other junk he could scrounge up in his last twenty minutes at the beach. The base is fortified with four long concrete slabs aligned in a square. At each corner, a cement watchtower shoots up like a giant gray dandelion. Each watchtower is manned by an infantryman who stands watch with binoculars and a MAG.

The front gate of Eshyeh looks much too simple for a war zone. It's a basic aluminum swing gate, the kind that might prevent access to a boat ramp after hours. The back gate, next to the tank lot, is the same, except there's no soldier manning it. Instead, when we drive our tank to an ambush, my loader, Tal, opens the gate himself. After we drive through, Tal locks the gate and hops in the tank. It reminds me of that one long Chicago winter when our garage door opener didn't work so I had to open and close the garage by hand every morning before car pool.

At Eshyeh, amenities are sparse. The toilets—there are three for the entire base—overflow daily. There's hot water in the showers, but water pressure varies from a weak stream to a drip. My bunk is a low-ceilinged concrete dungeon, half underground and lit with a single lightbulb that we turn on and off with a string. In our bunker are four creaky bunk beds, just enough for the eight Armored soldiers at Eshyeh. On each bed is a thin rubber mattress that barely prevents the rusty coils of the bed frame from penetrating my back. There are no cubbies in our bunker. Instead, I hang my dress uniform and shaving kit on nails. The walls of the bunker are decorated with photos of our families and girlfriends that we've Scotch-taped next to our beds. Aside from these photos, every inch of wall space is covered with graffiti, most in Hebrew and some in English, including everything from names and dates to poems, Led Zeppelin lyrics, yin-yang signs, an assortment of breasts and hairy vaginas, and a tank whose cannon is a penis.

The view from our base is stunning: a patch of forest, green, rolling meadows, and, far ahead, layers of mountains unfolding to the horizon. Embedded in this pastoral landscape are the land mines, booby-trapped tree branches, and hollowed-out rocks that lie in wait, patiently, for the next Israeli soldier.

My new tank commander is a dark-skinned first lieutenant named Yaniv. He has closely cropped black hair, wire-rimmed glasses, and a navy blue yarmulke. He's the first brown-skinned tank officer I've seen since I joined up.

Tal, my new loader, is a loudmouth smart aleck. He has blond hair, crooked teeth, and a large hooknose like an ogre. He's easily one of the most disturbing, and disturbing-looking, persons I've ever met. From the moment we were introduced, he's been a prick.

"I hear you're twenty-four," Tal sneered as we shook hands. I confirmed that this was true.

"Pshhh," he said—Israeli slang for "Look who thinks he's hot shit."

Ever since, Tal calls me "Grandpa" and bosses me around nonstop. He orders me to fix him coffee, sweep the floor, take out the trash, and do a hundred other chores, while he watches with a sinister grin that betrays the pleasure he gets from ordering around a twenty-four-year-old American. I comply, because I have no choice. Although technically Tal doesn't outrank me, it's tradition that when a new soldier joins the battalion, the older vets kick him around as they please. More importantly, he's stronger than me. I prefer making Tal coffee than having him kick my ass.

My new driver isn't new at all; it's Pasha, the limping Russian whom I've known since basic training. I'd never liked Pasha much—he didn't pull his weight, always came up with a handy medical excuse to get out of guard duty and kitchen work. But here at Eshyeh, he's the closest thing I've got to a friend. His familiarity alone is enough to make me glad to have him in my crew.

Our tank is one of only two assigned to our tiny base. Serving with us is a squad of infantry soldiers from the rambunctious Golani Brigade, bringing to thirty the number of soldiers stationed on the base. From what I'm told, Eshyeh hasn't suffered a death in over six months—a trend I hope continues.

I'm still sorting out how I feel about being here. On the one hand, I'm afraid. I know that Hezbollah is out there and by virtue of the uniform on my back, they want to kill me. But at the same time, there's something wickedly exciting about all this. Sexy even. Before our nightly seek-and-destroy operations, I feel much the same way I did in high school before a date. There's the same sense of possibility, and danger, the harrowing but thrilling leap into the unknown. In high school, the vast majority of my dates ended with no action. In Lebanon, I should only be so lucky.

CAT AND MOUSE

To the extent that war has a schedule, our days go something like this:

5 P.M.—INTELLIGENCE BRIEFING
My tank commander, Yaniv, stands in front of a giant map of Lebanon. Using red pushpins for Hezbollah and blue for us, he identifies the locations of every Israeli ambush and suspected Hezbollah activity. Next, he reviews which areas are Closed Fire Zones, where we need permission to shoot, and Open Fire Zones, where we shoot anything that moves. Yaniv then provides each ambush with a code name for the night. Last night, our code name was Homer, Tank 1A was Lisa, and infantry was Bart. Tonight, we are John, Paul, and Ringo.

6 P.M.—DINNER
Cottage cheese, fried eggs, and hot tea on blue dairy-meal plates.

6:20 P.M.—SNACK RAID
I ransack the kitchen pantry for ambush munchies—usually some combination of chocolate bars, beef jerky, potato chips, and Luf. I then brew one thermos of Turkish coffee and a second of hot tea.

7 P.M.—TANK CHECK
In preparation for the ambush, we inspect the brakes, periscopes, and treads. We rotate the turret and wipe the cannon with a ten-foot-long pipe cleaner. Overall, an enormous pain in the ass.

7:30 P.M.—PRAYER AND CIGARETTES
Yaniv, who's a Yeshiva Boy, stands next to the back gate and prays the afternoon and evening services. Tal smokes. I goof around with Pasha and pretend I'm not the least bit nervous.

8 P.M.—ROLL OUT

At dusk, we set off for our nightly ambush. Depending on the location, we drive for between five and forty minutes. This drive to the ambush site is the second-most dangerous part of the mission; the only part more harrowing is the drive back: Hezbollah loves to trap Israeli soldiers on their way to and from ambushes, when we least expect it. Most nights, we take along a team of infantry grunts. They ride in back, in the infantry hatch. They're always very thankful when we drive them up the mountain, saving them the perilous walk. When we reach the ambush site, we open the infantry hatch and the infantry guys scurry out like kids getting dropped for soccer practice. For the rest of the night, they lie on their bellies in the grass, looking for Hezbollah with night-vision goggles, shivering and exposed. Watching them, I wonder why anyone would ever join infantry.

8:30 P.M.–5:00 A.M.—AMBUSH

We divide the ambush into four two-hour shifts. From 9 to 11 P.M. and again from 1 until 3 A.M., Yaniv and Pasha conduct the ambush while Tal sleeps in the driver's hatch and I sleep in the gunner's chair. From 11 to 1 and 3 to 5, Tal and I run the ambush while Pasha and Yaniv sleep. What's so absurd about this scenario is that at no time during the ambush are all four crew members awake. I see no point in sending soldiers into combat only to have half of them sleep. Even scarier is that when Yaniv sleeps, I'm in charge of the entire operation, including infantry. This despite the fact that I've never fired the MAG, can't operate the field radio, and don't know the first thing about calling in an artillery strike. I've mentioned this to Yaniv, many times. So far nothing's come of it.

The point of our nightly ambushes is to find Hezbollah, who themselves are camped out on hillsides looking for us. When Israel first began fighting Hezbollah fifteen years ago, our goal was to stop them from attacking Israel with rockets and suicide bombs. But now that we're here in Lebanon, Hezbollah doesn't have to bother attacking Israel. Instead, they just attack us soldiers. We have literally delivered their targets to them, and not just any targets, but the best kind: young, vibrant Israelis with their entire lives ahead of them. And anytime they kill one, we ship up a replacement.

To put it another way—the Israeli presence in Lebanon boils down to a lethal game of cat and mouse in which we go out looking for Hezbollah and Hezbollah goes out looking for us, and the only reason they're out looking for us in the first place is that they know we're out looking for them, which means if we didn't go out looking for them, Hezbollah would have no one to look for.

During our ambush, we stare at the countryside with night-vision goggles and a special night-vision television screen that's hooked up to the cannon of the tank. Our night-vision gear is heat sensitive—the warmer an object is, the darker it appears. Rocks and dirt show up white. Plants and trees, light gray. Human beings show up black. For all the excitement associated with the word *ambush,* when you get right down to it, I spend my nights in Lebanon looking for black on a yellow screen.

Most ambushes are dull. Therefore, we do what we must to keep things exciting.

One night, Yaniv kicks me awake to talk. "Yoel?" he whispers. "You ever go to summer camp?"

"Yes," I whisper back, groggy.

"Come up here a second."

I climb out of the gunner's hatch and sit on the turret.

"I heard that at Jewish summer camps in America, girls wear yarmulkes and bikinis."

"Maybe," I say. "Probably not at the same time."

"Yes they do!" Yaniv cries in a loud whisper. "My friend worked at a summer camp in Pennsylvania, and he said the kids prayed after breakfast and then went swimming, so they prayed in bikinis, and some of the girls wore yarmulkes."

I shrug. "Maybe. Anyway, can I sleep?"

"Hang on a second," he says. "How come they let the girls do that?"

"What bothers you? The yarmulkes or the bikinis?"

"Both! A girl in a yarmulke, it's a disgrace!"

"Where does it say in the Torah a girl can't wear a yarmulke?"

"Girls aren't commanded to wear yarmulkes," he says.

"That's not the same as a disgrace."

"Hang on," he says. He looks at his TV screen and checks for Hezbollah.

"And anyway, what's so bad about bikinis?" I say.

"They're immodest. They cause men to think about sex."

"And if girls didn't wear bikinis, men wouldn't think about sex?"

"They would. But they wouldn't masturbate."

"What's wrong with masturbation?" I protest.

"It kills Jewish souls," says Yaniv.

"Come on, Yaniv. You think Moses didn't masturbate? Forty days on Mount Sinai, by himself—"

"God forbid," says Yaniv, shaking his head.

"I'm going to sleep," I say. I climb into the turret, but Yaniv grabs my arm.

"Wait. One more thing. I want you to help me get a job at a summer camp. But only where the girls don't wear yarmulkes or bikinis."

"Okay," I say.

"Now sleep," Yaniv orders. "You're on in an hour."

5 A.M.—CLOSE SHOP

Just before sunrise, Pasha ignites the engine and we drive back to Eshyeh. During this ride back, the odor inside the tank is rancid—a pungent mix of four grown males' burps, gas, and rotten breath, all trapped inside the turret like sunlight in a greenhouse.

6 A.M.—BREAKFAST

Exactly the same as dinner, on the same plates. During the meal, soldiers stream in from their various ambushes. We eat quietly, unless one of us saw action, in which case we crowd around and get the story.

6:30 A.M.—SHIT, SHAVE, AND SHOWER

7 A.M.–12 NOON—SLEEP

12 NOON—LUNCH

Chicken, meatballs, or spaghetti with beef sauce on yellow meat-meal plates.

12:30 P.M.–5 P.M.—FREE TIME

If there's no line at the phone, I call Dorit. But because Hezbollah eavesdrops on our conversations, we're forced to speak in code.

"Where are you?" she says.

"Still here."

"In the place?"

"Yep."

"When will I see you?

"I'm not allowed to say."

"Try."

"Take your birth date. Double it. Take away four. That many days."

Behind the tank lot, just outside the back gate, there's an enormous boulder that's perfect for sitting. The view from the rock is magnificent: ahead, a mountain range; below, in the valley, the village of Eshyeh. Dorit once told me that Arab villages look so beautiful because unlike Israelis, Arabs build into the landscape, not on top of it. I think about this every time I look down at Eshyeh. During these long, hot Lebanese afternoons, I put a magazine in my rifle, cock in a bullet, and sit Indian style on the rock for hours, just staring at the view and losing myself. I watch schoolchildren walk with their backpacks and women hang laundry on lines. Sometimes I wonder what it feels like to be one of them. I imagine what it's like to look up at a mountain and see a soldier sitting on a rock.

The longer I'm here, the more I realize that Lebanon is a house of mirrors, a crazy backward land where up is down, right is left, and nothing is as it should be.

Time is backward. Because I sleep days and stay awake nights, night becomes day and day, night. The result is that I've lost all sense of time—instead of day and night, I experience only periods of more light and less light that bleed together in a never-ending haze.

Language is backward. Since we assume Hezbollah hears everything we say over the field radio, the officers at operation headquarters have issued code words for the most common and critical words we utter during missions. Sometimes these code words capture perfectly the essence of the word they're replacing: Hezbollah are "Uglies," civilians are "Cleans," Open Fire Zones are "Baskets," and Closed Fire Zones are "Cages." Other code words have no relation to the original word and in some cases are completely antithetical; the word for a dead Israeli soldier, for instance, is *perach*—flower.

Most backward of all is fear. Lebanon is full of frightening sounds. The war provides a continuous soundtrack of crackling gunfire, rockets whistling overhead, and the low, thunderlike rumble of artillery echoing off the hills. In the real world, these sounds would frighten me. But in this house of mirrors called Lebanon, these explosions and sonic booms are the soothing background music of our little war. It's only when the noises cease that my ears perk up and I panic. It's like when you're sitting in your kitchen, reading the newspaper, and the refrigerator shudders to a halt—and only then do you realize it'd been humming in the first place, and now that it's off, the house feels eerily quiet and you feel strangely alone.

One afternoon, I'm sitting on my rock when out of nowhere, Pasha walks up and sits on the ground beside me. For about a minute, neither of us says a word. We just stare down at the Arab village below. Then Pasha says, "When I was fifteen and still living in Russia, I got my girlfriend pregnant. She wanted to have the baby. But I convinced her to have an abortion."

I don't know what to say, so I just nod.

Pasha stares ahead hypnotically. "The baby would be three now. I wonder what he would have looked like." A minute later, Pasha stands up and walks away.

There's something about this place that makes a guy think.

THREE-PEAT

On my way back to the bunk, after an ambush, I see an Arab construction crew hard at work in the middle of the base. There are four of them, dark-skinned with black beards, dressed in button-down shirts and slacks. Two of them mix cement by hand while a third pushes iron rods into a square of fresh concrete and the fourth, on hands and knees, smoothes the wet concrete with a spade. They are constructing a new building right here in the middle of the base. Off to the side, an Israeli Army captain, in dress uniform and sunglasses, supervises the work.

For a couple of minutes, I just stand and watch. It's so bizarre: the occupied helping the occupiers to continue their occupation.

Welcome to the Middle East.

At one point, the Arabs sit on overturned buckets and drink from a green Israeli Army canteen. That's when I notice that one of the Arabs, the one who was smoothing cement with a spade, is wearing a Chicago Bulls hat. Only, it's no ordinary Bulls hat. It's the famous "Three-peat" hat, the one with bull's horns turned on its side, vertically, and twisted into a number 3, to commemorate the Bulls' third consecutive NBA championship. In Chicago, the Three-peat hat was a collector's item. Gramma Ruth promised she'd buy me one, but the stores were out of stock.

Time to see if those two years of college Arabic paid off.

I walk over to the construction workers. *"Sabah el-haire,"* I say, wishing good morning to the guy in the Bulls hat.

"Sabah el-nur," he replies.

I point to his hat. "Chicago Bulls," I say.

He shakes his head.

I point a second time. "Chicago Bulls," I say again. Then I motion for him to give me the hat.

He takes off his cap and holds it out. I point to the vertical bull's horns.

"Thelatheh!" I say, and hold up three fingers. I twist the cap on its side, so the 3 looks like antlers. "Chicago Bulls!"

His face lights up. "Bulls!" he says in a thick Arabic accent. "Michael Jordan!"

"Na'am, na'am!" I exclaim. "Michael Jordan!" I thump my chest. *"Ana a'ishun* Chicago!" I say.

"Lahn Isra'eel?" he says.

"Na'am, na'am, hona Isra'eel." I tell him that I live in Israel now. *"Weh'lakin ana . . ."*

I forget the Arabic word for "before," so instead I wave my hand over my shoulder, as if I'm fanning myself. "Chicago!"

He smiles. "Ah-hah," he grunts.

"Ana nur'in el-beit Michael Jordan!" I try to tell him I've seen Michael Jordan's house.

He stares at me blankly.

"El-beit Michael Jordan!" I try again. I point to my eyes.

He shakes his head. To him, it probably seems like I'm telling him Michael Jordan lives inside my cranium.

"Bulls," I say, and give him a thumbs-up.

"Bulls," he smiles and nods.

I go back to my flak jacket and he goes back to his cement. And thus concludes my attempt at Middle East peace.

HOUSE OF MIRRORS

In Lebanon, Israeli soldiers die for crazy reasons. They survive for even crazier ones. Three nights ago, a squad of Golani infantry guys is walking back to their base after an all-night ambush when they stumble upon a pair of Hezbollah guerrillas. There's a firefight, and one of the infantry kids gets shot in the chest—except that the bullet hits him square in his cigarette lighter, and he survives. Totally crazy. The twist: For the past year, he's been telling his mother, who's been begging him to stop smoking, that he quit. Now, here he is, alive, because of his stainless-steel cigarette lighter, which he'd been lying about to his mom. On the front page of the paper there's a photo of mother and son with their arms around each other, all smiles, while the kid holds up his cigarette lighter, the bullet still wedged inside. He should have died but didn't.

Another night, a different squad of Golani infantry guys heads out to an ambush after dark. There's no moon. The countryside is black. The soldiers walk single file behind their officer, a young second lieutenant. Before long, the officer discovers he's lost. Only he doesn't want to admit it, so he keeps walking. He turns left and right, then left again, leading his soldiers in a serpentine pattern until their single-file line looks more like an S. The officer stops to check his compass. As he does, he sees what he believes to be the silhouettes of armed Hezbollah guerrillas, facing him in the dark. The officer radios his first sergeant, who's standing at the back of the line. The first sergeant confirms that he, too, sees silhouettes of armed men in the dark. The officer radios back that in ten seconds he's going to open fire, and when he does the rest of the platoon should follow suit. Moments later, the officer opens fire, and then his soldiers open fire, and within seconds half the platoon is down, screaming and bleeding in the grass. The officer, who's one of the few that's not been hit, calls off the fire and races back to check on his men. It's only then that he realizes the silhouettes were not Hezbollah guerrillas. They were his own soldiers. Without knowing it, they were facing one another in the darkness. Six of his soldiers died. The twist: Three months earlier, these same soldiers had written a letter to the battalion commander, stating that their officer was a terrible navigator who often got them lost on hikes. They included a signed petition demanding that he be replaced. The battalion commander didn't respond. The soldiers shouldn't have died but did.

One of the most common ways to die is the Sabbath Switch. A soldier's grandfather is ill, or his sister's getting married, so he wants to go home this Sabbath instead of next. He asks his buddy, who's scheduled to go home this weekend, if he'd mind switching leaves. The buddy always agrees, because combat soldiers have a bond unlike any other, especially in Lebanon, and there's literally no limit to what one will do for a friend. That very weekend, while the first soldier's at home, the platoon gets hit. The soldier who stayed back dies. The one who went home spends the rest of his life tormented, because he knows he's supposed to be dead and his buddy is supposed to be alive.

The Sabbath Switch.

But of all the ways to die in this crazy house of mirrors, the most popular is the Final Tour.

In the Final Tour, a combat platoon spends two years on and off in Lebanon. In that time, they see some action, but mostly it's quiet. Then, on their final tour—usually with a week to go before they're out of the army altogether, at which point many of the soldiers already have their plane tickets to Thailand—Hezbollah ambushes the platoon, and the soldiers bite it. The army knows about this pattern. They warn us to be extra careful during our final tour, because that's when a soldier's guard is down and his head's somewhere else, maybe on the beaches of Koh Samoi. But soldiers think it's just dumb luck, that no matter how many tours you serve in Lebanon, it's always one tour too many.

Night after night I stare into the darkness, waiting for an enemy who never comes. Then, when he finally arrives, I discover the enemy is not my enemy, at least not the one I'm looking for.

I'm sitting in my tank, around eleven at night, staring into my yellow TV screen, looking for black—heat—Hezbollah—when suddenly, I see two figures, men, black and full of heat, walking upright, left to right, across my screen.

"Yaniv!" I shout, and kick him awake. Yaniv checks his screen. "How far?" he says.

I fire a laser at the first guy's feet. "Two kilometers, one hundred," I say.

"We should fire," says Tal, and he's right. We're in an Open Fire Zone in an area of known Hezbollah activity. Only Hezbollah or an idiot would walk upright through an Open Fire Zone at eleven at night. Yet something doesn't make sense.

"This makes no sense," I say to Yaniv. "They're walking so slowly. And upright. Why aren't they hiding?"

Yaniv stares into his screen. "Lock on and load up. I'll call it in."

I put the crosshairs on the first guy's chest and lock on. Tal shoves an antipersonnel missile into the cannon and hoists a second missile out of the cache. In Lebanon, standard operating procedure is to fire two antipersonnel missiles at any live target, followed by one antitank missile to finish him off.

"Loaded!" Tal shouts.

"Just hang on," says Yaniv.

"They're decoys!" says Tal. "They're walking because they want us to think they're not Hezbollah. But they are, and then they'll blow us up!"

"Not logical," says Yaniv, and he's right. But if there's one place in the world where this makes sense, it'd be here in this house of mirrors.

"We should blow 'em the hell away," says Tal.

Pasha, in the driver's hatch, says nothing.

Yaniv calls headquarters on the radio. He describes the situation: two men, two kilometers away, walking upright, west to east, through an Open Fire Zone. Headquarters asks Yaniv for details. Are they armed? Are they carrying anything on their backs? Do they appear to be speaking? I can't answer any of these questions because the men are half an inch tall on my television screen.

"We should kill the bastards," says Tal.

Headquarters puts us on hold, orders us to keep them in our sites, while they call a liaison officer who deals with the Lebanese. After fifteen minutes of this three-way back and forth, Yaniv clicks off the radio.

"They're U.N.," he says. "Two Dutch guys. Out for a walk. Made a wrong turn into an Open Fire Zone."

"Idiots," says Tal. "We should kill 'em."

"If we didn't call it in . . ." says Yaniv.

We let his comment hang there.

THE FARM

Around April 1, we deploy to a local mountaintop known simply as the Shamees.

The Shamees is the highest mountain in the region. Every week, a different tank takes command of the top. The mountain is a tapestry of boulders and twisted trees. On the peak, we camp on a patch of brown-green grass that's been shredded to bits by Israeli tank treads. From our camp, we have a panoramic view of every valley, hill, and Lebanese village within range.

I'm not happy to be up on this mountain. At Eshyeh, I feel safe, or I at least have the illusion of safety. Concrete walls topped by coils of barbed wire surround the compound, and there's a watchtower at each corner. Here on the Shamees, I am naked and exposed. There are no walls, no wire, no boundaries. At any moment, a Hezbollah guerrilla could pop out from behind a bush. If and when he does, I am meat.

Because we are out in the open, quite literally in no-man's-land, we have explicit rules that dictate how we operate. At all times, one of us stands watch on the turret with his hand on the MAG, continuously rotating 360 degrees to check the terrain. The rest of us must stay either on the tank, inside the tank, or within ten meters of it. The one exception is shitting: when we shit, we are permitted to wander up to twenty meters away, and then we bury it.

At night, we conduct our operations in normal commander-driver/gunner-loader two-hour shifts. During these ambushes, no one may leave the tank, not even to shit. Instead, we eliminate off the side, either standing or crouching on the hull, while the other crew members make mental notes to watch their steps in the morning. Our first night on the mountain, I watch Pasha defecate off the side of the tank. Through my heat-seeking goggles, his turd emerges black, full of heat—more alive than anything I've witnessed on my night-vision screen to date.

Since, up here on the Shamees, we are trapped within our four hundred-meter square, we busy ourselves any way we can to pass the time. My loader, Tal, smokes incessantly from an endless supply of cigarettes. Every Friday, Tal meets a weathered South Lebanese Army officer at the back gate of our base and purchases a dozen cartons of Marlboro Reds at Lebanese market value. While Tal smokes, Pasha holes up inside the driver's hatch and reads one Russian novel after another. I go hours without hearing his voice.

I wonder what Pasha's parents think about all this. When Pasha was sixteen, they emigrated from Russia because, I imagine, they wanted to escape the tyranny of Soviet rule and offer their children a better life. Now, less than two years later, their son is deployed to a war zone, a soldier in a conflict that began when Pasha was three. I wonder if they're proud at how quickly their son, and by extension, they, have become Israeli, or if they worry this is just the same tiger dressed in different stripes.

During the hottest hours of the afternoon, from noon until four, I hook up to the tank's air-conditioning system. One of the main features of the Merkava 3 Baz battle tank is that each crew member can connect directly to the tank's AC via a black hose that plugs into a plastic canister on the crotch of his tank suit. The only problem with the setup is that the cool air doesn't circulate. The rest of my body continues to sweat while my gonads turn to ice.

Our third afternoon on the Shamees, Colonel Avi, head of the 188th Armored, shows up in a jeep. He sits us in a circle and asks us questions about our deployment: Are we getting enough to eat? Are we in touch with our families? Do we realize how important our mission is to the state? He then briefs us on the plan he's hatched to teach Hezbollah, once and for all, that the Armored Corps is not to be messed with. He explains that tomorrow, at noon on the dot, three separate Israeli tanks on three separate hilltops in the Security Zone will fire a missile at the same target.

"And?" I say.

"That's it!" Colonel Avi exclaims. "Imagine it! Three separate missiles from three separate tanks—they'll know Armored is everywhere!"

I have many questions about Colonel Avi's plan—such as, unless Hezbollah actually sees the missiles flying, how will they know the missiles came from three separate tanks? And wouldn't it make more sense to fire the missiles a couple of minutes apart, so when Hezbollah inspects the site of the first missile landing, we can nail them with our second and third shots? And since each Israeli missile costs five thousand dollars then wouldn't that

But truly, how long can a man stare at a yellow television screen, look-
for black?

, our final morning on the Shamees, I'm asleep in the gunner's chair,
ming of beautiful things, when Yaniv shakes me awake. "Yoel! Up!" he
ts. "Hezbollah!"

throw on my helmet, my gloves, while Pasha starts the engine. "What's
ews?" I shout into the intercom.

Hezbollah," says Yaniv.

How many?"

bunch. Let's move!"

e chug along a dirt road, weave between trees. As we rumble along,
briefs us. A squad of infantry guys had been lying on their bellies for
ast thirty-six hours when they spotted what appeared to be a platoon
zbollah guerrillas transporting supplies. Given the numbers, it didn't
sense to engage in a firefight. Instead, better to obliterate them with a
e of shots from a tank.

niv directs Pasha left. We climb a hill by way of a winding path. When
ch the top, Yaniv orders Pasha to kill the engine.

here they are," says Yaniv.

heck my periscope. Below, in the valley, a column of men march
o left like ants. I see six men in my periscope, then eight, ten. I can't
out their faces, but I can see that they're armed. Many of them carry
ppear to be wooden crates. I swivel the turret left to see where they're
l. They walk through a green field toward a dilapidated gray barn.

l—how many you count?" says Yaniv.

venty-six," says Tal.

iv whistles. "How far?"

e a laser. "Eight hundred meters. Close."

epare to fire," Yaniv orders.

heart pounds. I feel exhilarated, dizzy. I don't want to kill, but this
ent. This is two dozen armed Hezbollah guerrillas carrying supplies
use to kill us.

aded!" shouts Tal.

t the crosshairs on the first guerrilla, dead center in his torso.
l."

fifteen grand be better spent as a payoff for information
of Hezbollah's supreme leader, Hassan Nasrallah? An
nel Avi, that you're doing this because Armored isn't s
as Infantry, and you want to feel important?

But I keep my questions to myself, because I've lost
would listen, much less answer.

The next day, at quarter to noon, we sit in our tan
in the cannon, crosshairs locked on to an abandone
Fire Zone. Twenty minutes later, Colonel Avi's voice
"Ten," he counts. "Nine. Eight." When he reaches O
ton on my joystick. There's an explosion, the tank
with the smell of sulfur, and Colonel Avi congratulat
tanks on our success. Then Yaniv fills out the requisi
I clean out the cannon, Tal stands watch, and Pasha
sandwiches.

By our fourth night on the mountain, I reach a po
is crippling. We know Hezbollah is out there, but t
hunting for black on my television screen, drives m
ten minutes of my shift staring at my television set.
gerous they are and how badly they want to kill m
vince myself that they'll show up on my yellow scre

So instead of hunting for Hezbollah, I sit on the
twenty questions, sip tea, and eat snacks. The nigh
ant, full of crickets, moonlight, and many stars. F
ing red light on a radio tower; below, in the valle
village of Eshyeh.

One night, after a long conversation with Tal
dozes off and I'm left in sole command of the enti
centrate on my television screen, but I can't. Inste
and when I reach the point that it becomes unbe
tank and sneak off to pleasure myself beneath th
mates sleep.

Even as I do this I think about how I'm a fa
dreamed I'd be. I realize, too, that this is exactly
that we be lulled into a boredom so deep that we

Yaniv calls headquarters to request formal permission to fire, which, given the circumstances, headquarters will of course grant.

A minute later, Yaniv clicks off the radio. "Hold fire," he says.

I swivel around in my seat. "You kidding?"

"No go," says Yaniv. "It's a farm."

"So?" I say.

"There's a rule," Yaniv says. "No firing at farms." He explains that U.N. Resolution Something or Other forbids enemy combatants from attacking farms.

"But wait," I say. "Isn't part of the deal that they're not allowed to hide out on farms, or stash their weapons on farms, or go anywhere near a god-damn farm?"

"Yes," says Yaniv.

"So?"

"Nothing we can do about it," he says.

I think about this for a second. It reminds me of how when I was a kid and played freeze tag, there'd always be "Base" where whoever was "It" couldn't get you. That's what Lebanon is—Israelis chasing around Hezbollah while Hezbollah shouts "Base!"

I call Yaniv over the intercom.

"What now?" he says.

"One more question, Yaniv. If Hezbollah knows we won't shoot them on farms, and we know that they're just going to keep on hiding on farms, then what in God's name are we doing here?"

That evening, ten hours after the farm fiasco, I'm back at Eshyeh, packing up for the nightly mission, when Pasha walks in the bunk and says, "The ambush is postponed."

I gasp. "Why?"

"Yaniv didn't say," he answers.

This is bad. Our operations are never postponed. The first rule of our nightly ambush is that we leave at dusk and return before dawn. Otherwise, Hezbollah could easily ambush us on the way there or back. If we're leaving late, that means we have intelligence that Hezbollah plans to attack our tank.

I lie back on my bed. I feel nauseous, cold. Tomorrow morning, we're scheduled to depart for a weeklong leave. Which means that tonight's the night we'll bite it—the legendary death just before a final tour. Suddenly I feel certain tonight's the night I'm going to die.

Just then, Tal bursts into the bunk and snatches down the big Israeli flag. "You coming?" he yelps.

"Where?" I say.

"The barbecue!" he shouts, and runs off with the flag.

Barbecue?

I walk outside and hear loud, pulsing techno music. Outside the dining hall, it's pandemonium. The Golani infantry guys dance wildly and smoke. One soldier rides around on his buddy, piggyback. A couple of others carry their friends on their shoulders. In the middle of it all, Tal and an infantry grunt dance with the Israeli flag, each holding an edge. Over in the corner, a sergeant cooks hot dogs and meatballs on a tiny aluminum grill.

"Yoel!" someone shouts. It's Yaniv. He's eating a meatball and has ketchup on his chin.

"Yaniv, what is this?" I say.

"Barbecue!" he cries. "You hungry?"

"No," I say, still in shock. "What the hell's going on?"

"It's a pre-Passover barbecue," says Yaniv. "The cook was cleaning out the kitchen, getting rid of everything that's not kosher for Passover. So the Golani guys took the stuff and made a barbecue!"

"Where'd they get the grill, the charcoal?" I ask.

"They brought it up for Independence Day. We'll do another barbecue then."

For a few seconds, I just stand there speechless. Then I turn to Yaniv. "So that's why you postponed the ambush? For a barbecue?"

"What's the big deal?" says Yaniv.

"We're giving Hezbollah a two-hour head start for a fucking barbecue!" I cry. "That's insane!"

"It's one night," says Yaniv. "Relax." He holds out a meatball on a stick. "Kabob?"

Twelve hours later, I'm on a military transport truck, headed out. After eighteen days in country, we've been granted a one-week R&R leave. It's not a moment too soon. I'm still seething from the incident at the farm and last night's life-threatening cookout. I want out of this crazy backward land.

We drive through the countryside, past Najaf's Café. At the Good Fence—the Israeli-Lebanese border—I hop out and walk through a gate marked "Soldiers Only." A couple of meters away, Lebanese day workers file into Israel through a second gate. I wonder if any are related to the guerrillas I saw on the farm.

HARD-CORE JEWS, PART II

My week of rest and relaxation contains almost no rest and even less relaxation. It's strange to be back in Tel Aviv. On Dizengoff Street, a man and woman make out next to a falafel stand. At an outdoor café, two women sit across from each other and talk on cell phones while a third puts on lipstick. All the while, a hundred miles north, eighteen-year-old boys stare into yellow television screens looking for black.

With five months until the wedding, Dorit and I are on a mad dash to tie up loose ends. We've booked a hall at the Hilton in Hertzeliyah for a price that includes an open bar, a handicap-accessible room for my mother, and a security guard to keep away suicide bombers. This morning, Tuesday, we're on the highway, driving south to Modi'in to meet a DJ named Rafi, when I get a call from Esther at the Rabbinical Council in Tel Aviv.

"You applied for a marriage license, yes?" she asks.

I confirm that I did.

"On your application, you wrote that your mother's Hebrew name is Leah, Daughter of Abraham our Forefather."

"That's right," I say.

"So your mother converted?"

"Yes."

"Was that in Israel or the United States?"

"The States," I say. "Her conversion was Orthodox."

"That's what I wanted to know. And you were raised Orthodox?"

"Hm?" I say.

"I asked if you were raised Orthodox," says Esther.

"Yes. Of course," I lie.

"Good. So I need you to fax over your mother's conversion certificate." I repeat the number out loud while Dorit jots it in her notebook. "And we need you to come in for an interview."

"Interview?" I say.

Esther explains that when someone, or someone's mother, converted outside of Israel, it's standard procedure to bring the person in for an interview. "How's next week?" she asks. I tell her I'm in the army and headed back to Lebanon.

"I could squeeze you in this Thursday morning, eight-fifteen."

"I'll be there," I say.

"Great," says Esther. "Bring two witnesses, both male and at least eighteen years old, who can verify that you're Jewish. They need to have known you at least three years. Will that be a problem?"

"Of course not," I say.

Shit.

I rack my brain for who I can ask to be my witnesses. I can't think of anyone I've known for more than three years. I consider old camp friends who might be living in Israel, classmates from college, exchange students . . .

Then I get an idea.

I dig out my phone book, find the number for my friend Mike. We met in Israel the summer I staffed the teen tour to Poland. He's Australian, chubby, and kind of a goof. When I met him, he was just about to join an artillery unit of the Israeli Army. He got out the month I went in and has been living at his grandmother's in Tel Aviv.

He answers on the second ring. "Mike?" I say.

"Mate!" he yelps.

Mike's happy to help out. We agree to meet at Rabin Square, outside City Hall, at seven-thirty Thursday morning. "And Mike," I say. "One last thing. Can you dress like you're Orthodox?"

Next, I call my second cousin Gary. He's from Houston. A year ago, after he graduated from the University of Texas, he moved to Jerusalem, joined a yeshiva, and changed his name to Gershon.

"Hello?" he answers in his Texas accent.

"Is this Gary? Er, Gershon?" I say. I'm still not used to the name change.

"Who is this?" he says.

"Your cousin, Joel."

He doesn't say a word.

"Daniel's grandson."

"Joel!" he shouts.

"Gary! I mean, Gershon! How are you?"

"Praise God!" he says. "You?"

"About the same. Listen. I need your help . . ."

Thursday morning, I dress like a Yeshiva Boy: navy pants, white shirt, knit yarmulke. Under my shirt, I wear tzitzit, a religious undergarment with strings hanging off the corners. Per my request, Dorit wears a long denim skirt and long-sleeved shirt, like a right-wing Jewish settler in Hebron.

By seven-fifteen, we're in Rabin Square. The plaza is a bustle of activity. Israelis stroll through holding coffee cups and the morning paper. A flock of pigeons bop their heads near the steps up to City Hall.

At quarter to eight, Mike gets out of a taxi. I barely recognize him. Gone are the ponytail and fifty pounds. Like me, he's dressed like a Yeshiva Boy.

"How do I look, mate?" he says and spins around.

"Like a Yid," I say.

A few minutes later, Gary-Gershon gets off a bus. I don't recognize him, either. The last time I saw him was six years ago at my grandparents' fiftieth wedding anniversary. Then, he wore a red Speedo to the swimming pool. Today Gary-Gershon wears black pants, black jacket, black suede yarmulke, and tzitzit strings that hang out of his white shirt—a look you might call Classic Ultra-Orthodox Jew.

"Look at you!" I shriek.

We hug. "This is Dorit," I introduce him. Dorit, wisely, doesn't offer her hand. Gary-Gershon, who won't touch a girl until he's married to her, simply nods. This reminds me that I shouldn't touch Dorit in front of the rabbi.

As we climb the front steps of City Hall, I brief my witnesses one last time. "Basically, just make it clear I'm Orthodox," I say.

"You know," says Gary-Gershon, "until you told me, I didn't even realize your mom converted."

"Good!" I cry. "Say that! It's perfect. We're so Jewish, my own cousin didn't even know."

We strut into City Hall like the Jewish Three Musketeers.

• • •

The rabbi's name is Yoblanski. He's short, about sixty years old, with gray hair and a gray beard. He shakes our hands, except for Dorit, to whom he nods. "Sit," he says.

We sit—Dorit and I in front of his desk, Mike and Gary-Gershon behind us.

The rabbi sets a folder before him on the table. "Your mother's certificate states that she converted in San Antonio, Texas, in June 1969, under the authority of Rabbi Tuckerman."

I nod.

"I got in touch with the Rabbinical Council of Central Texas and they confirmed that Rabbi Tuckerman was Orthodox."

"That's right," I say triumphantly.

"It also says that prior to her conversion, your mother studied Jewish law with Rabbi Posner. The Rabbinical Council didn't recognize his name. So they did some research. They found that Rabbi Posner was ordained at the Jewish Theological Seminary in New York as a Conservative rabbi. Not Orthodox."

"So?" I say.

"So," he says, "if your mother studied with a rabbi who's not Orthodox, then her conversion isn't Orthodox. Which means that according to the state of Israel . . ."

"What?" I say.

The rabbi looks me square in the eye. "You're not a Jew."

I sit frozen in shock. I heard his words. But I'm certain I've misunderstood. "Excuse me?" I say.

The rabbi leans forward on his elbows. "You're not a Jew," he says.

I look at Dorit. She's just as bewildered as I am.

"But her conversion was Orthodox!" I cry. "She dipped in the pool, she got a new name—"

"It's doesn't matter." The rabbi cuts me off. "The Judaism your mother studied is not a valid brand of Judaism."

I look at Gary-Gershon, then at Mike. They sit stupefied. I look back at the rabbi. I want to punch him in his big Jewish nose. I'm infuriated. Seething. It's as if my entire identity just got kicked in the nuts.

Then I remember something. "Hang on," I say, and hold up my hand. "A year ago, when I immigrated, I had to prove I was Jewish. I turned in my bar mitzvah certificate and they accepted it. So I'm already approved."

The rabbi shakes his head. "That's civil law," he says. "Marriage is religious law. It's the law of God."

I squirm in my seat. "This makes no sense. I went to Jewish school. I had a bar mitzvah."

"He's in the army!" Mike chimes in from the back. "He's in Lebanon. What could be more Jewish than that?"

"No connection," says the rabbi.

Dorit pounds her fist on the desk. "No connection?" she shouts. "A young man risks his life for the Jewish state, and you have the chutzpah to say there's no connection?"

"It's not chutzpah, it's religious law."

"Let me ask you something, Rabbi," Dorit says, and glares at him. "Did your sons serve in the army?"

"Dorit, don't," I mutter.

"Why not?" shrieks Dorit. "He thinks he's king of the Jews, I'm allowed to ask!" She turns to the rabbi. *"Nu?"*

"My sons went to yeshiva," he says.

"Oh, yeshiva!" Dorit howls. "So when the Katyushas fall, your sons recite Psalms?"

The room goes quiet. Then, in a voice just above a whisper, the rabbi says, "Look. I'm not saying he doesn't live a Jewish life. I'm saying that according to Jewish law, this young man is not a Jew."

I look down at the floor. I feel sick.

"So in other words," Dorit says, "you don't mind if he dies for your country, so long as he doesn't get married here."

"God forbid," the rabbi says.

The taxi ride home is grim. Dorit stares out her window, and I mine. The closest we come to a conversation is when Dorit says, "You said you checked."

"I did check!" I say.

Then we go back to our windows.

As we wind our way through the city, I see the same things I've seen on a hundred other taxi rides through Tel Aviv. We pass the Habima Theatre and Dizengoff Fountain. We drive past the bookstore where my dad bought me my first prayer book when I was nine.

On King Solomon Street, a man and his young son walk along the sidewalk holding hands. Both father and son wear yarmulkes.

Right then, it hits me:

As far as this country is concerned, I'm a Gentile.

THIRTY-NINE DAYS

I get out in thirty-nine days. In thirty-nine days, I'll turn in my rifle, strip off my boots, and walk away from this godforsaken army forever.

Ever since the meeting with the rabbi, I've been trapped in a catatonic funk. I tell myself it's just a technicality. But deep down, I can't shake the feeling that my whole life was a lie. My bar mitzvah, those nine years at Solomon Schechter, the Sabbath dinners—over a thousand of them—lies. And if those are lies, then who am I?

Yesterday afternoon, I called Tim at his apartment in Tel Aviv, where he was home on leave. I figured he of all people would understand. After all, he'd been there—except for him, it was the other way around.

I told Tim the whole story. "It's like finding out you were adopted," he said.

"Only worse!" I blurted out. "It's like finding out you were adopted, and then your adoptive parents tell you they've decided to give you back to your birth parents because they're sick of having you around."

I can't stop thinking about what Dorit said in the rabbi's office: "So you'll let him die for this country, but you won't let him marry here."

The thing is, if I do die during these next thirty-nine days, they won't even bury me in a goddamn Jewish cemetery.

On the Dorit front, we've decided to take a break. Ever since I got the news that I'm not a Jew, we've been fighting more, and harder, than ever. I canceled the wedding hall. The woman even gave me back my deposit. I had such a unique excuse—"It turns out I'm not a Jew"—that I suppose she felt bad keeping my money.

· · ·

This morning, I return to the bunk after the ambush and find an orange shoebox on my bed. Taped to the top is a piece of pink construction paper cut out in the shape of a heart. Written in Hebrew on the pink heart, in a child's handwriting, are the words "To A Brave Soldier in Lebanon!"

I open the shoebox. Inside are chocolate bars, hard candies, a bag of Bamba potato chips, a sticker that says "Mazel tov!" and a pack of gum. Taped to the underside of the lid is a piece of notebook paper, folded in half, with a note scrawled inside.

I pull out the paper and read the note:

Dear Soldier,

My name is Tamar. I am 8 years old. I live in Kiryat Shmoneh. I go to Ben Gurion Elementary School where I am in second grade. I have a brother named Ohad and a dog named Kova. Thank you for protecting me and my family.

Love,
Tamar

I don't know if I should laugh or cry. I don't feel like I'm saving anybody. I'm just trying not to die.

As I rummage through the shoebox for a chocolate I like, I think about little Tamar at her school in Kiryat Shmoneh. I worry that this war will one day be her war, and if not this one then some other conflict that's just another version of the same war Israel's been fighting since 1948. When I watch the television footage of Hezbollah's victory parades after they kill an Israeli soldier and I see the look of pure, unadulterated joy in the guerrillas' eyes, I know for certain that Israel's wars have nothing to do with land. Nor can Israel, stubborn country that she is, bear the thought of pulling out, lest we send a signal that Hezbollah's tactics worked. And so the story continues until one day Tamar inherits the story and the war becomes hers.

THE UNLUCKIEST DOG IN LEBANON

My final Friday night in Lebanon, I'm eating Sabbath dinner in the dining hall when Yaniv charges through the door. "Get your gear and meet at the tank," he orders. "Now."

We drive north for an hour. We climb a hill, clamber along the edge of a bone-dry riverbed, and drive through a forest of knobby, leafless trees that, on my night-vision screen, look like ashen-skinned old men. Outside, the pink sky dissolves to purple, and then black.

As we rattle through the countryside, Yaniv briefs us on our mission. At the northern lip of the Security Zone, an infantry soldier in a watchtower spotted a Hezbollah guerrilla crouched in the bushes, twenty meters from the base. The soldier fired a shot, but the guerrilla scampered away. Since the Merkava has the best night vision in the Security Zone, headquarters has ordered us to hunt him down.

When we reach our designated hilltop, I peer into my night-vision screen and scan the terrain. Ahead, two kilometers away, the Israeli base sits on a mountain. Below, between our position and the base, is a valley thick with trees.

"Find him, Yoel," Yaniv orders.

I rotate the turret clockwise over the valley. On my screen, I see nothing but shrubs, boulders, trees. Everything white.

"*Nu?*" Yaniv says.

"Nothing," I reply.

"We're not leaving without him," says Yaniv.

I take a deep breath. Inside my Nomex gloves, my hands sweat. I nudge the joystick forward, back, survey the slope of the adjacent mountain. I scan the valley a second time, and the edge of the forest, where mountain meets trees—

And then I see it. Black. A black blob darts out from the bushes, and then dashes back in. "I've got him!" I shout.

"Lock on!" says Yaniv.

I twist the joystick frantically, left and right. A second ago, I had him in my sights. Yaniv radios headquarters. They respond with a simple order: shoot to kill.

My heart begins to pound. My body floods with a mixture of excitement and fear. Excitement, that I might be a hero. Fear, that I might take a life. My problem is, I picture him in diapers. As I scrutinize the landscape, hunting my target, I suddenly imagine the Hezbollah guerrilla as a toddler crawling around on his hands and knees with a pacifier in his mouth. No matter how evil he is now, he used to wear diapers. If I kill him, I kill that, too.

In the background, Yaniv and headquarters prattle back and forth in bursts of coded Hebrew. As they babble, it occurs to me that I'm glad this is happening in Hebrew. The Hebrew makes it surreal, like an adventure. Maybe that's why I could never join the American army: I could never kill a man in my native tongue.

All of a sudden, the figure pops out from the trees. He stands perfectly still in the center of my screen—a mass of black, hot and alive.

"I'm on and locked!" I say.

"How far?"

I shoot the laser. "A kilometer four-fifty."

"Let's fire," says Yaniv.

I guide the crosshairs onto the exact center of the blob. But then the blob does something strange: he lies down in the grass and rolls over, like he's taking a nap.

I zoom in for a closer look. I twist a silver knob, bring the image into focus.

"Oh, my God," I say.

"What?" says Yaniv.

On my night-vision screen, the figure lifts his head, curls up, and licks himself.

"Hey, Yaniv," I say. "I think our target is a dog."

"What?"

"Check it out on close-up."

Yaniv peers into his screen. *"Koos emok!"* he curses.

Yaniv picks up the radio and delivers the bad news. I stare at my screen and watch as the creature, clearly a dog, flops playfully in the dirt. He looks happy. And why not? What could possibly be better than rolling around in the grass on a summer night, licking yourself?

Yaniv clicks off the radio. "We're firing," he says.

"But it's a dog," I say.

"They want to be sure."

"Loaded!" shouts Tal.

"But Yaniv, I'm positive it's—"

"Fire!" he roars.

I push the red button. The turret cracks with the deafening boom of a thunderclap. A thick, stinky cloud of yellow sulfur swirls into the gunner hatch.

"Loaded!" says Tal.

"Fire!" says Yaniv.

Another explosion, piercing, like a lightning bolt crashing into my skull.

"What do you see?" says Yaniv.

I check my screen. "A lump. Gray. He's losing heat."

"Let's do one more, antitank," Yaniv orders.

"Loaded!"

"Fire!"

A jolt, an ear-splitting boom, more sulfur. On my screen, the countryside erupts into a cloud. When the smoke clears and the dust settles, all that's left is a crater.

"He's gone," I say.

Yaniv picks up the handset, calls headquarters. Jubilant, he reports our success. While he chatters with the higher-ups, I stare at my screen, at the crater that used to be a dog.

A second later, Yaniv shuts off the radio. "It's gonna be a long night, boys," he says. "We're calling in artillery."

I turn around in my seat. "Why?"

"They want to be sure," says Yaniv.

"But it's a dog, Yaniv. And he's dead."

Yaniv shrugs. "Rules," he replies.

I slump forward and clunk my head against the controls. Finally, I have found the word that describes what happens when insanity becomes more insane:

Lebanon.

"Hey, Yoel," Yaniv says, and kicks me in the back. "You ever see artillery?"

I shake my head.

"Come," he says.

I unplug my helmet and hoist myself up onto the turret. Outside, the air is warm. The sky, brilliant and black, twinkles with stars.

"Sit," Yaniv says. He knocks the turret with his fist.

I lie back on the turret, hands clasped behind my head, and stare at the sky. In the quiet, I hear crickets and the soft, swishy sound of grass bending in the breeze.

"Quite a night, huh?" says Yaniv.

I chuckle. "I'm telling you, Yaniv—this army's so fucked-up it's a miracle Israel still exists."

Yaniv smiles. "Thank God the Arabs are more fucked-up than we are," he says.

Suddenly the sky lights up with a flash. A thunderous boom echoes off the hills. Then a second flash, and another, and soon the entire sky is a flurry of popping flashbulbs, one flash after the next, like paparazzi photographing God, while explosions echo through the mountains in layers.

"Showtime," says Yaniv.

Overhead, an orange missile streaks across the sky in a gentle yellow arc, like a comet with a glowing tail. I watch the missile sail through the night, past a half-moon and twinkling stars. And I laugh. I laugh because there is nothing left to do but laugh. Soon, I am laughing uncontrollably, tears in my eyes. I am shaking on the turret, laughing so hard I can barely breathe. That poor animal! All he wanted was a little fresh air. Instead, twenty-four tons of artillery rain down on the unluckiest dog in Lebanon. And all I can do is laugh.

DISCHARGE

SON OF DAVID

The rabbi is poking my balls.

It's awkward.

I've been trapped in this chilly room since ten o'clock. In five minutes it'll be ten-thirty, and I feel like a dope, what with my towel at my ankles and my dick in my hand so the rabbi can get a good view.

"May I?" he says.

I nod.

The rabbi scoots forward on his knees until his face is an inch from my penis. He is fifty years old and dressed completely in black, with a black beard, spectacles, and a yarmulke. Behind him, two rabbinical students stand patiently against the wall.

The rabbi clutches my penis between his forefinger and thumb. He stares at the tip. He brings it close to his eye like he's inspecting a diamond.

"Hmm."

It's September, and I'm in a mikveh—the Jewish ritual bath—in New York City. The mikveh is the size of a Jacuzzi and dimly lit. At ten o'clock this morning, I met the rabbi and his witnesses in his office and signed the conversion papers. Then we walked downstairs to the mikveh, and I undressed. In a matter of minutes, I will dip three times in the mikveh and officially become a Jew. But first the rabbi must verify that I was properly circumcised at my bris nearly twenty-five years ago.

The rabbi twists my penis left and right. "Is he kosher?" says one of the students.

"Come look," says the rabbi.

The students kneel on either side of the rabbi. The rabbi passes my penis to the student on the left.

"Kosher," says the student. The student passes my penis back to the rabbi, who then passes it to the student on his right, as if they're playing hot potato.

The student on the left nods. "Kosher," he says.

"Definitely kosher," says the rabbi. Then he looks up at me and smiles. "Ready?"

On July 30, one year to the day after I joined up, I took a bus to the Induction Center and turned in my gear. In the Discharge Office, I signed the papers officially releasing me from the 188th Armored Brigade. Then, in the Reserve Office, a heavyset woman soldier assigned me to Armored Reserve Company 136, where I will serve one week every three months and one month a year until I'm fifty.

"Can I please do something besides Armored?" I begged.

"What's wrong with Armored?" she asked.

"I hate tanks," I said.

The woman laughed. Then she stamped my paper, ARMORED.

That afternoon, I walked around Tel Aviv with my hands in my pockets. I had no idea what to do or who I was, or whether I belonged in this country in the first place. On Dizengoff Street, I passed a handwritten sign, taped to a phone booth, that said

LONDON
LAST-MINUTE FARES
CHEAP!
I.M.B. TRAVEL, 34 SHENKIN STREET, ASK FOR DAVE.

I walked to 34 Shenkin and asked for Dave.

"When do I leave?"

"Tonight."

I step down into the pool. The water is warm and covered with a greasy film. Pubic hairs float slowly in the congealed scum, suspended in the water like fruit in Jell-O.

I gag. I don't understand how I'm supposed to purify myself with all these pubic hairs floating past me in the water.

The rabbi crouches next to the pool. "The procedure is simple," he says.

"Dunk three times. Be sure to immerse yourself completely. When you finish, I'll place my hands on your head and recite the benediction."

"And then?" I say.

"That's it. You'll be a Jew."

London was a circus. I walked Chelsea Market, saw a show every night on
the West End, and blew half my spending money in three days. Best of all, I
lived like a Gentile. I ate Big Macs for dinner, sometimes with milkshakes.
Outside Buckingham Palace, I bought a hot dog from an Indian guy with
a cart.

"In a bun?" he asked.

"In a bun," I said. I didn't even ask to read the ingredients.

I went to London because I simply had to get out of Israel. When the rabbi
told me I wasn't Jewish, I was crushed. But as my army service came to a close,
I found myself not only distraught, but enraged at how Israel had stabbed me
in the back. I joined the army thinking the experience would strengthen and
reinforce who I was. Instead, all it did was lead to more questions.

I didn't tell my mother I'd been declared a non-Jew, because I was afraid
she'd be hurt or think I was blaming her. But I told my dad. Over the
phone, my father tried to convince me to forget about it, that it was just a
glitch. But no matter how hard I tried, I couldn't get it out of my head that
this country that I'd fought for had rejected me.

I also knew I couldn't go back to the States, because that would only
confuse me more. So the trip to Europe, a nowhere land somewhere in the
middle, seemed perfect. As I traveled, I thought more about how, my entire
life, I'd ignored half of my story—the story of my mother's side. I decided I
had to sort it out.

My fifth night in London, I sat in a bar and made eyes with a blond
woman who told me her name was Marie. I decided I would put a move on
Marie, because that is what Gentiles do—they meet blond women in bars
and kiss them. But before I knew it, I was too buzzed to walk. I stumbled
back to the youth hostel, suddenly depressed. Then I passed a red phone
booth and was struck with a brilliant idea. I stepped inside and drunk-
dialed the one woman in the world who could solve the riddle of my
identity.

"Gramma Ruth?" I spluttered.

"Joel—is that you?"

I told Gramma Ruth about Reserve Company 136 and Dave the one-way-ticket-to-London guy. Then I said, "Hey, Gramma, tell me something. Great-Grandpa Dever—where's he from again?"

"Ireland," she said. "County Donegal. Why?"

I took a boat to Dublin, hitchhiked to Donegal, and made it my quest to explore my missing half. Then I'd know, once and for all, who I was.

At the public library, I met with a genealogist named Ian. He was bald, with crooked yellow teeth. Together, Ian and I researched the name Dever and determined they were an offshoot of the McDevitts, who themselves were derived from Devitsons, also known as the Davidson Clan. "Looks like you're a Davidson," said Ian.

Davidson. Son of David. I liked that.

Today, Ian told me, the Davidsons are McDades.

I rented a three-speed bicycle and set off in search of McDades. I had no idea who or what exactly I was looking for, only that I'd know them when I found them. And find them I did—right next to the highway a mile out of town was a warehouse with a giant block-letter sign on top that said

McDADE'S
HARDWARE AND BUILDING SUPPLIES

I steered into the gravel parking lot, hit the brakes, and skidded into a parked car, gashing my forehead. I hobbled into the store, blood trickling down my temple, and told the first cashier I saw that I was looking for a McDade. I limped behind her to an office in the back, where she introduced me to the owner, Sean McDade. He was tall, about sixty years old, and wore a red and white checkered shirt. "We're related!" I cried.

"Aye?" he said.

I explained about Davidsons and McDevitts. I told him about my great-uncle William Dever, mayor of Chicago, where I'm from—

"Michael Jordan," Sean said.

"Aye," I said.

—and how I rode my bike through County Donegal in search of McDades and how thrilled I was to finally find one.

Sean put his arm around me and smiled. He stuck his head in the office and called out his sister, Sharon, and son, Sean, Jr.

"Ye bloodied yer forehead," Sharon said.

"Aye," I said.

"Ye didn't wear a helmet?" she asked.

I shook my head.

"Next time, wear yer helmet," she advised. Clearly, she was related to my Gramma Ruth.

That night, I lay awake in the hostel and tried to piece together the puzzle of my identity. I'd gotten a kick out of meeting the McDades. It was fun to imagine I'd finally found my roots and knew exactly who I was and where I belonged.

But deep down, I knew that wasn't the real me. The real me was the little rabbi who wore his yarmulke every chance he got. I was the kid who dressed up like Bible characters on Halloween and scrutinized food labels to make sure he didn't accidentally sin. I was a Jew, through and through. I couldn't reinvent myself if I tried.

Once I decided that my Jewish soul was here to stay, I quickly reached a second conclusion:

I'm not the one with the identity crisis. Israel is.

After twenty-five years of living as a Jew, I know exactly who I am. But after two generations in which Israel defined itself as a post-Holocaust haven from anti-Semitism—in other words, the past—Israel now faces a much greater challenge: defining its future. In the meantime, the country has no idea who it is. It's a democracy with no separation between church and state. It's a sovereign nation with only one rigidly defined border: the Mediterranean Sea. It's a Jewish state where observant Jewish soldiers have to choose between breakfast and prayers, where the most religious Jews don't even have to serve in the army, and where the criteria for getting drafted aren't enough to get you buried in the military graveyard.

The country is confused.

Meanwhile, at the top of the pyramid is this tiny group of rabbis who think they're Kings of the Jews and therefore get to decide who's in and who's out. But the Kings of the Jews are out of touch, because they fail to realize that Israel's future, if it has one, depends on all the reject-Jews they've been pushing away from the table: the half-Jews and intermarried Jews, the queer and bi Jews, the women rabbis and young, freethinking Israelis who crave spirituality, not just restrictions, and the children of supposedly illegitimate converts, like me.

Because Israel has no idea who it is, the rabbis in charge saw me as a threat. They then proceeded to do the only thing they could: steal my identity.

This left me with one option:

Steal it back.

I hold my nose and dunk. Bubbles surge past my head in a muffled rush.

I pop up and take a breath.

Dunk.

Underwater, it occurs to me that what I should be thinking about is Torah, redemption, and the oneness of God. Instead, I think about the pubic hairs floating past my head and how disgusted I'll be if one lands on my mouth.

I flew back to Israel and immediately called Rabbi Jonathan at Penn. He'd been a mentor and friend all through college. I trusted that, provided I spun the story correctly, he'd help.

Rabbi Jonathan referred me to a rabbi in Brooklyn who specialized in legal complexities like disputed conversions. The rabbi in Brooklyn referred me to a famous rabbi in Israel, Rabbi R, who he believed could help me out.

I called Rabbi R and explained my quandary. When necessary, I embellished.

"So you were raised Orthodox?" he asked.

"Yes," I said.

"And you're Orthodox now?"

"Absolutely," I lied.

I didn't feel the least bit guilty lying to this famous rabbi because as far as I was concerned, Israel's policy toward my mother's conversion—a policy Rabbi R subscribed to—is unjust. In fact, in my eyes, I wasn't even lying. I was simply saying what needed to be said to counter their shortsightedness and fix their egregious error.

Rabbi R invited me to his compound in the West Bank. The next morning, I awoke and dressed like a Yeshiva Boy. Then I rode the bus to Jerusalem and caught a second bus, this one armored and with windows of bulletproof glass, to Rabbi R's enclave deep in the Occupied Territories.

Rabbi R and I sat outside his trailer in the desert. We talked about the Bible and the challenges facing observant Jews. He asked if I found it difficult to be Orthodox in the army.

"Yes. Very," I said. "I had to skip breakfast to pray. Sometimes my buddies forgot to make me sandwiches."

I told him about the nine years I studied in Yeshiva and my stint on the basketball team. All of it lies.

Rabbi R explained that, ordinarily, a conversion required three years of intensive study. But, seeing how I was raised in an Orthodox home, was Orthodox now, and had attended Orthodox Yeshiva since kindergarten, he'd waive the study period, perform the ceremony, and fix the glitch. For paperwork reasons, it would be simplest if we did the ceremony outside Israel.

I told Rabbi R I'd be in Chicago for Rosh Hashanah. He said he'd be spending Yom Kippur in New York. We agreed to meet on a Monday morning in late September at the mikveh on the Upper West Side.

After I dunk a third time, I wipe my face with my hand and waddle to the edge of the pool. The rabbi crouches down. His students kneel beside him.

The rabbi places his hands on my soaking wet hair.

"May the Lord bless you and keep you," he says.

"Amen," the students say.

"May the Lord shine his countenance upon you and be gracious unto you."

"Amen."

"May the Lord turn his countenance to you and grant you peace."

"Amen."

"With this blessing, I accord you membership in the People of Moses and bestow upon you your new Hebrew name, Yoel Ben Avraham Avinu—Joel, Son of Abraham our Forefather."

He lifts his hands from my head.

"Mazel tov."

Upstairs, in the lobby, the rabbi hands me the certificate. I shake hands with the rabbi and his students and walk to the door.

"Joel," the rabbi calls.

I turn.

"May you lead a meaningful and fulfilling Jewish life."

I nod.

I push open the door and step outside into the sun. There, beneath a gnarled tree, Dorit is waiting for me.

"Is it over?" she asks.

I nod. Dorit buries her face in my chest. I hold her close.

"I'm sorry," she says, and hugs me tight.

"It's not your fault," I mumble. Then I pull away. "And anyway—since when do you apologize?"

Dorit smiles, and I hug her again. Our wedding is in six weeks. We will be married outdoors, at a hotel in Ramat Gan, a suburb of Tel Aviv. We have a caterer. Dorit has a dress. We still haven't decided on a DJ or a band. After the wedding, we will travel—like a good recently discharged Israeli soldier, I booked tickets to Thailand. From there, we'll move to Chicago and build a life in the States. Perhaps one day we'll end up in Israel. But not yet.

I hold out my hand, and Dorit takes it. *"Nu?"* she says.

Our flight to Israel leaves at midnight. Since we have nothing to do, I suggest we walk.

We walk in big circles through the Upper West Side, past delicatessens and dry cleaners, a flower shop. The sky is blue and cloudless, a lake. Sunshine floods our faces. The air is warm.

I can't figure out what I feel. On the one hand, I'm elated that it's finally over. No more questions. No more doubts. I know I made the right choice, because if I didn't convert, I'd spend the rest of my life wondering if I was legitimate. Every time I'd put on a yarmulke or step into a synagogue, I'd question whether or not I truly belonged.

But if all I feel is elated, then there wouldn't be tears. But there are, quite suddenly. Big, fat tears well up in my eyes and stream down my cheeks. I wipe the tears away with my hand but they won't stop. Before I know it, I'm sobbing. Dorit is bewildered but I can't explain just now. I am bawling because something is over. The stage in my life where I could innocently take for granted that I belonged to the Jewish people simply by virtue of being me—when I dunked in the water, that part of my life ended and a piece of me died. Even though I chose to convert, I'm furious at Israel for forcing me to choose, for humiliating me, for making me stand naked before three rabbis. I'm also furious at myself for going through with it, because by dunking in that pool, I accepted their claim that it is they, not I, who get to determine who I am.

I hope that one day I will forgive myself. Maybe, soon after, I'll forgive Israel. But for now, all I can do is walk. I have a wedding to plan. A life to begin. A flight to catch.

I tell Dorit we will walk until there are no more tears. We will walk as long as it takes, her hand in mine, past bakeries and bodegas, then to Central Park West, and maybe all the way to Times Square.

EPILOGUE

I married Dorit in December, two weeks after my twenty-fifth birthday, at the Maccabiah Hotel in Ramat Gan.

Of the 350 guests in attendance, I knew twenty. My best friend, Dan, flew in from Cairo. Tim Bailey did not attend, as he was already back in the States, debating whether to join the U.S. Park Service or the U.S. Army Rangers ("I want a job where I carry a gun," he described his employment search). Tomer, Doni, Ganz, and Ronen Peretz all attended the wedding with their new officer, Second Lieutenant Dror Boy Genius. Eldad, the runaway, showed up uninvited and pulled me aside to read me a poem he'd composed in Dorit's and my honor.

The wedding itself was a blur, though one moment in particular stands out. At the end of the ceremony, when I attempted to break the glass, I raised my right foot and held it, dramatically, and then stomped on the glass as hard as I could—only the glass would not break. I stomped again, but this time the glass only scooted away. To the cheers of the assembled guests, I removed my jacket, mimed a few karate moves, and stomped again. But no matter how hard I tried, I could not break the glass. Only after upwards of a dozen attempts did the glass finally shatter.

A month after the wedding, Dorit's father, Menashe, submitted our wedding video to the television show *Israel's Funniest Home Videos*. The producers found my inability to break the glass hilarious and invited Menashe onto the show. Our video took second prize, right behind a home video of a cat sniffing a dog's ass.

What Menashe didn't realize was that by submitting our video, we'd forfeited the rights to the producers of the show. Without our knowledge, but not illegally, the Israeli production company sold our wedding video to a slew of funniest home video shows around the globe. The result is that I've had friends from as nearby as New Jersey and as far away as Australia tell me they were up late, watching some or other funniest wedding video show when, suddenly, I showed up on their television screens stomping a glass in vain.

Should you find yourself awake one night, in the wee hours of darkness, unable to sleep, and you switch on the TV, and there, before your eyes, is a baby-faced groom, in a shirt and tie with his jacket off, stomping over and over on a glass that refuses to break, while the voices off camera alternately cheer and laugh at his futility, but despite it all the young man continues to stomp, because he knows he's come too far and been through too much to stop now, and upon this young man's face is a look of at once glee and outright terror while, inside, he wonders if this is some kind of existential prank, the result of lying to a rabbi, or, perhaps, a cleverly masked sign from God, that's me.

APPENDIX A:
SOUTH LEBANON
SECURITY ZONE RECIPES

THE LITTLE MEAT LOAF THAT COULD

INGREDIENTS

> 1 can Luf Israeli Army-issue kosher canned meat

DIRECTIONS

1. With tank ignition in OFF position, open hood and place Luf directly on engine.

   CAUTION: Do not open hood if tank ignition was in ON position in the last hour. Otherwise, fire and/or bodily burns may occur.

2. Turn tank ignition to ON.

3. Drive 20–30 minutes to ambush site.

4. Turn off tank. Wait one hour.

5. Open hood and remove warm Luf.

Serve: directly on tank turret, sliced or in cubes.

SECURITY ZONE SWEET TEA

INGREDIENTS

> 8 cups of water
> 4 tea bags
> 30 teaspoons sugar

DIRECTIONS

1. Bring water to a boil.
2. Pour water into an Israeli Army-approved stainless-steel thermos. Toss in tea bags and sugar.
3. Shake.
4. En route to ambush, store thermos under gunner's chair, adjacent to right tread. Tread friction will keep tea warm. Titanium-enforced armored plates will keep tea safe in the event of a surprise confrontation with Hezbollah.

Yields: 8 cups of tea that tastes like hot Coca-Cola, only sweeter.

SEARCHLIGHT GRILLED CHEESE

INGREDIENTS

> 2 slices of white bread
> 2 slices of mozzarella cheese

DIRECTIONS

1. Prepare one cheese sandwich, ensuring that cheese does not extend beyond crusts.

   CAUTION: Excess cheese can lead to cheese-drip and possible fire.

2. Remove 200-watt antiterrorist searchlight from commander hatch.

3. Unfasten searchlight cover.

4. Plug antiterrorist searchlight into external AC jack on right side of turret, beneath tank commander MAG.

   CAUTION: Failure to remove searchlight cover before plugging in searchlight can result in fire and/or explosion of ordnance.

5. Heat searchlight for ten minutes. Unplug.

6. Place cheese sandwich on hot spotlight. Fasten plastic cover and hold spotlight shut for two minutes or until sandwich is brown.

   CAUTION: Failure to unplug spotlight before inserting sandwich can lead to fire and/or explosion of ordnance.

Yields: one grilled-cheese sandwich

WARNING: If smoke emerges from spotlight and/or electrical cord, or if spotlight and/or electrical cord burst into flames, or if searchlight cover melts into a thick, foul-smelling black syrup, or if chef erupts into flames, discontinue cooking IMMEDIATELY and use foam-based fire extinguisher from the commander hatch to put out the blaze.

APPENDIX B:
GLOSSARY OF ISRAELI MILITARY SLANG

abal (n.): Moron.

achi (n.): My brother (term of endearment).

ahlah (adj.): Awesome.

beezayone (n.): Disgrace.

ch'noon (n.): Nerd.

cham-shoosh (n.): A Thursday-through-Sunday Sabbath leave. ETYMOLOGY: a combination of the words *hamishi* (fifth) and *shishi* (sixth).

chapash (n.): Literally, "simple soldier," i.e., a regular enlisted guy who's not an officer or commander. ETYMOLOGY: a combination of the words *chayal* (soldier) and *pashut* (simple).

chips (n., pl.): Old, outdated, pre-Merkava tanks, including the Magach and Centurion. Based on the idea that when these antique tanks are hit by missiles, they erupt in flames like a pan of sizzling French fries.

choopar (n.): A treat, including anything from a piece of chocolate to a surprise Sabbath leave.

dibeelee (n.): Nincompoop.

emok (n.): (1) Literally, "your mother" or "your mother's." (2) Shortened form of *koos-emok* (your mother's cunt). ETYMOLOGY: Arabic.

eser (adj.): Literally, "ten"; awesome, most often as a reply when asked about a situation or how one is feeling.

fahdeecha (n.): Mistake, usually a social one that leads to embarrassment (e.g., asking a soldier if his heavyset sister is pregnant). ETYMOLOGY: Arabic.

fashlah (n.): Mistake, usually a procedural one that leads to undesirable consequences (e.g., falling asleep during guard duty and losing one's Sabbath leave because of it). ETYMOLOGY: Arabic.

fuckim (n., pl.): Technical mistakes, for which soldiers are punished (e.g., showing up late, forgetting one's rifle in the latrine). ETYMOLOGY: based on the English word *fuck*.

galchatz (adj.): Shaved and with polished boots. ETYMOLOGY: a combination of the words *gilu'ach* (shaved) and *tzich'tzuach* (scrubbed).

hutznik (n.): One who was born in a country other than Israel. ETYMOLOGY: derived from the word *hutz* (outside).

jeefah (n.): Dirt; slime; sludge.

jobnik (n.): A noncombat soldier who works a desk job. ETYMOLOGY: based on the English word *job*.

kader (n.): The act of running back and forth between two stationary objects, over and over, as punishment, while a sergeant or officer keeps time on his watch. ETYMOLOGY: based on the word *kadoor* (ball).

klee (n.): Literally, "tool"; hero; champion; badass.

koos (n.): Vagina. ETYMOLOGY: Arabic.

koos-emok (n.): Your mother's vagina. ETYMOLOGY: Arabic.

koosit (n.): Good-looking woman; babe. ETYMOLOGY: derived from the Arabic word *koos* (vagina).

laf-laf (n.): Goofball.

l'nylen (v.): To seal an object in plastic, making it watertight. ETYMOLOGY: based on the English word *nylon*.

mizron b'sisi (n.): Literally, "base mattress"; the whore of the base, upon whom any soldier can lie simply by signing up.

moor'al (adj.): Literally, "poisoned"; a soldier who loves the army with overwhelming (and at times annoying) zeal.

pazam (n.): The amount of army service a soldier has already completed; a soldier with lots of *pazam* is close to his discharge date. ETYMOLOGY: an acronym of the three words making up the phrase *perek z'man moogbal* (Period of Obligated Service)

pazamnik (n.): A soldier with lots of *pazam* and, therefore, very close to his discharge date.

p'tornik (n.): A soldier who relies on medical excuses to get out of guard duty, kitchen work, hikes, and other physical activity. ETYMOLOGY: based on the Hebrew word *p'tor* (excuse).

rejectim (n., pl.): Oversights and errors that lead to an inspection not being passed (e.g., unmade beds and dirty rifles). ETYMOLOGY: based on the English word *reject*.

rosh gadol (n.): Literally, "big head"; a soldier who does above and beyond what's asked.

rosh katan (n.): Literally, "small head"; a soldier who does the absolute minimum required.

sababa (adj.): Awesome; cool. ETYMOLOGY: Arabic.

sharmootah (n.): Whore. ETYMOLOGY: Arabic.

shavuz (adj.): Depressed; emotionally beaten.

she'elat kit bag (n.): Literally, "a kit bag question"; an idiotic question that leads to more work than there would have been had the question not been asked; based on the scenario where a sergeant says, "In three minutes, be outside the bunk with boots polished and rifles cleaned," and one soldier asks, "And should we bring our kit bag?"

shok (n.): State of shock. ETYMOLOGY: based on the English word *shock*.

shoko'ist (n.): A soldier who behaves like he's in shock.

teepoos (n.): A soldier who's unsophisticated and therefore understands everything literally.

teezuz (n.): Punishment involving grueling physical activity.

yoram (n.): Nerd.

zayin (n.): Penis.

z'rikat zayin (adj.): Literally, "throwing a penis"; the state of not giving a damn.

ACKNOWLEDGMENTS

One of the best parts about writing this book is the opportunity I got to work with such incredible people.

I am grateful to Wylie O'Sullivan for editing my manuscript with precision and care. Blessed with an impeccable eye for detail, she didn't let me get away with anything. Also at Free Press—Martha Levin, Dominick Anfuso, Eric Fuentecilla, Heidi Metcalfe, Edith Lewis, and Sydney Tanigawa.

My agent at Writers House, Dan Lazar, believed in this book from the start. Dan once told me that ninety-five percent of his job was to fight for me and five percent was to fight with me. I look back on that five percent as the most important conversation we had. When you're old enough, Dan, please allow me to buy you a drink. Also at Writers House—the incredible Stephen Barr, for critiquing my last-minute changes in the moments before the manuscript went to press.

Dan Lefkovitz, Grant Rosenberg, Michelle Levy, Andrea Hoffman, Erika Meitner, Dave Bressler, Chanan Tigay, Rachel Gurshman, Brian Chasnoff, and Molly Antopol read the manuscript at its various stages and offered the feedback, both positive and scathing, that I needed to take it forward.

I thank my parents, Carol and Ira Chasnoff, and brothers, Ari and Gabe, for allowing themselves to appear in the book. Though, come to think of it, I never bothered to ask. (Are we still speaking?)

I am indebted to the boys of Platoon Two, Company B for providing me with an experience worth writing about. Particularly: Bailey, Barebby, Brooks, Lavert, Ori, Oren, and Shafir.

And, finally, I thank wonderful Dorit—for her love, for sticking by me, and for making sure life continued like something resembling normal during the time it took me to write this book. I know you can't wait for the next one.

ABOUT THE AUTHOR

Joel Chasnoff is a stand-up comedian and writer with stage and screen credits in eight countries, including a U.S.O. Comedy Tour of Japan and Korea entertaining American Marines, stand-up spots on Israeli late-night TV, and voice work for cartoons. He lives in New York.

A portion of all proceeds from Joel's stand-up comedy performances and this book is donated to Joel's foundation, Project Elijah, which distributes money to organizations promoting humanitarian causes. Most recently, Project Elijah sent 100 low-income New York City school-children to the circus.

To meet the characters from *The 188th Crybaby Brigade*, view photographs and video clips from Joel's military service, and learn more about Project Elijah, visit www.joelchasnoff.com.